I0814120

Alexander O. Brodie

Alexander Oswald Brodie, Governor of Arizona Territory, 1902-1905.
Arizona State Library, Archives and Public Records, History and Archives Division, Phoenix, 97-8064.

Alexander O. Brodie: Frontiersman, Rough Rider, Governor

Charles H. Herner

Fort Worth, Texas

Library of Congress Cataloging-in-Publication Data

Herner, Charles.
Major Alexander Oswald Brodie : Frontiersman, rough rider, governor / Charles H. Herner.
p. cm.
Includes bibliographical references and index.
ISBN 978-0-87565-532-1 (cloth: alk. paper)
ISBN 978-0-87565-425-6 (paper : alk. paper)
1. Brodie, Alexander O. (Alexander Oswald), 1849-1918. 2. Brodie, Alexander O. (Alexander Oswald), 1849-1918--Military leadership. 3. Governors--Arizona--Biography. 4. Soldiers--Arizona--Biography. 5. United States. Army. Volunteer Cavalry, 1st--Officers--Biography. 6. Soldiers--United States--Biography. 7. Arizona--History--To 1912. 8. Arizona--History, Military. 9. Indians of North America--Wars--Arizona. 10. Frontier and pioneer life--Arizona. I. Title.
F811.B87H47 2012
979.1'04092--dc22
[B]

2011015104

TCU Press
P. O. Box 298300
Fort Worth, Texas 76129
817.257.7822
http://www.prs.tcu.edu

To order books: 800.826.8911

Designed by Bill Brammer, fusion29.com

Contents

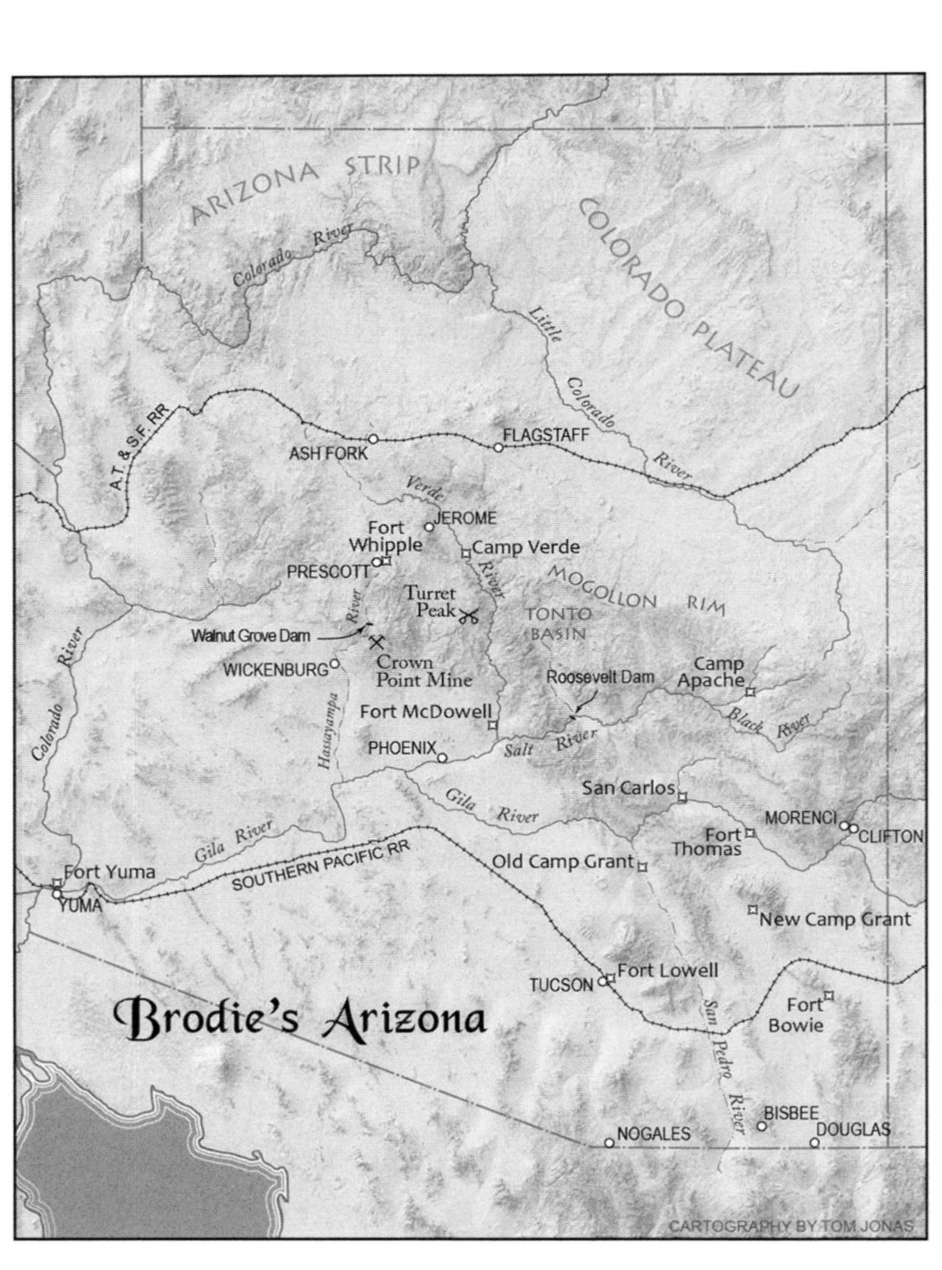

Brodie's Arizona
ARIZONA STRIP
COLORADO PLATEAU
Colorado River
Little Colorado River
A.T. & S.F. RR
ASH FORK
FLAGSTAFF
Verde River
JEROME
Fort Whipple
Camp Verde
PRESCOTT
MOGOLLON RIM
Turret Peak
TONTO BASIN
Walnut Grove Dam
Crown Point Mine
WICKENBURG
Roosevelt Dam
Camp Apache
Black River
Hassayampa River
Fort McDowell
PHOENIX
Salt River
San Carlos
Gila River
MORENCI
CLIFTON
Fort Thomas
Fort Yuma
YUMA
SOUTHERN PACIFIC RR
Old Camp Grant
New Camp Grant
TUCSON
Fort Lowell
Fort Bowie
San Pedro River
BISBEE
DOUGLAS
NOGALES
CARTOGRAPHY BY TOM JONAS

Preface

I first became interested in Alexander Oswald Brodie in the early 1960s while researching the history of the Arizona Rough Riders in the Spanish-American War. At the time, I knew little about Brodie other than his service in the Rough Riders and later appointment as governor of Arizona Territory by his friend President Theodore Roosevelt. But, as the story of the Arizona Rough Riders began to unfold in detail, I realized that Brodie had never received proper credit for his role in originating and publicizing the concept of cowboy cavalry, which ultimately led to the passing of legislation making possible the organization of the First United States Volunteer Cavalry Regiment, or "Rough Riders." It also became clear that Brodie was an outstanding officer, whose leadership abilities and military skills played a key, but largely unheralded, role in molding the cowboy regiment into an effective fighting force. Moreover, tantalizing bits of evidence began to surface suggesting that Brodie had been equally effective as governor. Intrigued by these brief glimpses into the life and character of the West Point graduate, I began to suspect that he had been too long overlooked.

Following my retirement in 1990, I began examining Brodie's career in detail, and my expectations proved well-founded. Indeed, the New York native had been involved in many important events; but his main contribution, at least to Arizona, was overcoming powerful political opposition in both Washington and Arizona to establish an administration noted for integrity and commitment to Progressive ideas popularized by President Roosevelt, Brodie's friend and mentor.

Brodie's personal life proved only slightly less intriguing. The untimely death of his first wife and infant daughter hit him hard, apparently causing him to resign from his beloved army and seek solace in liquor to the extent that in today's vernacular he would be characterized as an alcoholic. However, by sheer force of his own personality, he brought his drinking habit under control and turned his life around. Other than a ten- to fifteen-year period of alcohol-induced instability, Brodie governed his personal life with unwavering loyalty to his friends, unquestioned integrity, love of his country, and total commitment to what he believed was right. No hint of scandal or impropriety ever darkened his public or personal life.

Unfortunately, Brodie did not leave a large collection of personal papers, causing me to ferret out Brodie material in a large number of related collections held in both private and public hands. However, this proved to be a blessing in disguise, for my research brought me into contact with many wonderful individuals I otherwise would never have encountered. I wish to acknowledge them all, but the completion of such a list raises the possibility that I could overlook some contributors. In that event, I extend my heartfelt apologies.

It was my good fortune to locate two of the three then surviving Brodie grandchildren: David Bonsal Brodie and Mary Brodie De Lanie. Both cheerfully provided family papers and personal recollections of the stories told to them by their grandmother, Mary Hanlon Brodie. Tragically, neither lived to see this work completed, but Mary De Lanie's two daughters, Michelle and Pat De Lanie, and David's widow, Penny Brodie, continued the tradition of providing assistance and encouragement. I extend my heartfelt thanks to them.

Special recognition should be made of Joseph Wittmann, great grandson of Henry S. Van Beuren. Joe and his charming wife, Barbara, entertained me in their New York home for three days, enabling me to copy those portions of the Van Beuren personal papers dealing with the Walnut Grove Water Storage Company and the Crown Point mine. Truly, the Wittmanns are an engaging couple, whose friendship I greatly cherish.

No list of those who provided assistance would be complete without including William J. Kilcullen and Art Seaman, two friends of many years standing. Now deceased, Bill Kilcullen offered valuable comments from an engineer's perspective regarding the design and collapse of the Walnut Grove dam, and also pointed out some important interpretations of Colonel Crook's Tonto Basin campaign. Art Seaman twice climbed formidable Turret Mountain with me in search of the camp where twenty-three Tonto Apaches died on the morning of March 23, 1873, and, like me, experienced an eerie sensation of death while surveying that isolated battle site. A good field companion, Art also accompanied me to the Walnut Grove dam site and Crown Point mine.

I also am indebted to the following institutions and individuals across the nation for providing documents and information: Michael Pilgrim and Ann Cummings of the National Archives; Doug McChristian, National Park Service; Ceil Gallagher, Washington, DC; Ruth Evans, Clinton County Historical Society (Iowa); Bill Welge, Oklahoma Historical Society; Harry Wassmann, Benicia Historical Museum; Lolita A. Clayton, Walla Walla Genealogical Society; Lawrence L. Dodd, Whitman College; Jeff Hohanson, Greenwood County Historical Society (Kansas); Jocelyne Rubinetti, Drew University; Steve L. Nure, Golden Gate National Cemetery; LaVerne Freeman, Edwards, New York; and Korin L. Rosenkrans, Morristown, New Jersey.

In Arizona I would like to extend my appreciation to Lori Davisson, Dr. Sam Palmer, Pat Atchinson, James Liggett, Marty Fees, Jan Cleere, and Dave Tackenberg. All graciously shared information on a specific event or individual. I also extend special thanks to the offices of Senator Jon Kyl and Representative James Kolbe for locating important material in the National Archives. The professional staffs of the Arizona Historical Society in Tucson, the Arizona Historical Foundation in the Hayden Library at Arizona State University in Tempe, the Sharlot Hall Museum in Prescott, Special Collections at the University of Arizona Library in Tucson, and the Arizona State Department of Library and Archives never failed to assist in every way possible.

Not to be overlooked are the friends who provided welcome support—if only with a few words of encouragement or show of interest. A number of individuals fit into that category, but I wish to specifically acknowledge Samuel Truett, Larry Ball, James Christiansen, Peter and Doris Weber, Boyd and Polly Finch, Andrew Wallace, David Goodman (who read and critiqued some of the earlier chapters), Jim Turner, Tom and Doris Summer, and New York friend Bob Pearlman. Included in this group are also those members of the infamous Wednesday "Lunch Bunch" as well as those of the Adobe Corral of the Westerners who followed Brodie's progress. They know who they are.

Finally, I wish to thank Bruce Dinges, the Arizona Historical Society's superb director of publications, who never failed to take time from his busy schedule to read portions of the manuscript and offer constructive criticism. Kudos also go to Victor Beer, who provided technical support in preparing the illustrations, and to Dawn Santiago, who undertook the challenge of transforming my wretched handwriting into a readable tome. Of course, any errors found in this study are my own. Needless to say, my wife, Joan, deserves unending credit for tolerating my obsession with bringing the story of Major Brodie to a final conclusion.

CHAPTER 1

"Our First Major Is a Dandy"

Sunday, May 25, 1898, proved to be another hot and humid day in San Antonio, Texas. Seated uncomfortably in his tent on the Fair Grounds, with the side flaps rolled up to admit any passing breeze, Lt. Col. Theodore Roosevelt took advantage of the Sunday stand-down from military activities to catch up on his personal correspondence. Only ten days earlier he had arrived at San Antonio to join his regiment, the First United States Volunteer Cavalry. In a long letter to his friend and political ally Henry Cabot Lodge, Roosevelt shared his initial reaction to the regiment. One member in particular, medium-sized, blue-eyed Maj. Alexander Oswald Brodie, had made a deep impression. "Our First Major is a dandy," Roosevelt wrote, "Major Brodie of Arizona—a grizzled old frontier soldier."[1]

Beginning with that initial meeting at San Antonio, a mutually beneficial friendship developed between Roosevelt and Brodie, which would last as long as they both lived. Significantly different in many respects, but remarkably similar in others, both dedicated themselves to a life of public service. One, a full-time politician turned part-time soldier, and the other, a career soldier and part-time politician, they both shared a deep respect for their nation and a common devotion to duty. Many of Brodie's characteristics, which Roosevelt so obviously admired, may be credited to the major's rich Scottish heritage.

Extremely proud of his family origins, Alexander Oswald Brodie traced his roots to the Lethen branch of Clan Brodie of Brodie, one of the oldest names in the Scottish Highlands. Descendants of the ancient Picts, according to some accounts, the Brodies by 1100 had established themselves on the south bank of Moray Firth just east of Inverness. Official title to the land first had been issued to the Brodie clan in 1160 by Malcolm IX, King of Scots, and confirmed 150 years later by Robert the Bruce. In contrast with many Scot clans, which traditionally relied on broadswords and claymores to maintain their position, the Brodies reputedly turned to diplomacy and intermarriage. They also established a reputation for being shrewd businessmen, willing to take up station anywhere in the British Empire—and even beyond.[2]

As one would expect, the search for economic opportunity eventually brought some of the Brodies, along with their Pitcairn and McCormick relatives, to British colonial America. The marriage of Alexander O. Brodie's great-grandfather, the Reverend Alexander Brodie (1734-1804), laid the foundation for that move.

While serving as minister at Carnbee, a small village north of Edinburgh, the Reverend Brodie married Helen Pitcairn, a woman reputedly of royal descent. Gregarious and family oriented, Helen continued after her marriage to maintain a close family relationship with an uncle, Daniel McCormick (1743-1834) and with a favorite brother, Joseph Pitcairn (1763-1844). Both men shared a particular fondness for Helen and helped establish the Brodie Family in colonial America. Daniel McCormick led the way.[3]

An Orangeman born in Dublin in 1743, the polished, talented Daniel McCormick arrived in New York City in 1766, quickly establishing himself as a highly successful public auctioneer. Within a few years he became one of the wealthiest men in the city, owning a mercantile firm and residing in an elaborate and luxurious home on Wall Street. After the American Revolution he became a silent partner in frontier land speculation with the legendary Alexander Macomb, a fellow Orangeman.[4]

One of the most ambitious and freewheeling land speculators in America, Alexander Macomb at an early age settled in Detroit, where he engaged in the fur trade and also served as a fiscal agent of the British government. After the American Revolution he moved to New York City and became involved in land speculation. In 1791, after enlisting Daniel McCormick and several other wealthy entrepreneurs to serve as silent partners, Macomb purchased 3,693,755 acres from the state of New York for eight cents an acre. Known as the "Great Purchase," Macomb's acquisition included all unclaimed land in New York between the St. Lawrence River and the Adirondack Mountains. The project overextended Macomb financially, however, and the following year pressing debts forced him to call on McCormick to help bail him out. The arrangement is not clear, but in exchange for badly needed cash, Macomb transferred a substantial parcel of land in northwest New York to McCormick.[5]

Determined to turn a profit from his investment, McCormick,

Alexander Oswald Brodie (1787-1856). A wealthy merchant living in New York, this A. O. Brodie helped establish the Brodie Family in the United States from Scotland. Brodie family collection.

who had no intention of abandoning the comforts of New York City to personally administer his western land, engaged several reliable agents to attract settlers. One was his nephew, Joseph Pitcairn, then residing in Hamburg, Germany.

Born in Carnbee in 1763, Pitcairn as a young man had joined McCormick and other relatives in New York. Becoming a United States citizen after the Revolution, he soon made friends with many Federalist politicians, including future president John Adams. In 1795, he secured an appointment to Paris as vice-consul and, three years later, was promoted to United States consul at Hamburg. Once established at his new post, Pitcairn convinced Joseph Brodie, second-born son of his favorite sister, Helen Pitcairn Brodie, and future grandfather of Alexander Oswald Brodie, to relocate to Hamburg from Scotland and help Pitcairn establish a mercantile firm.[6]

Removed from his consul's position by President Thomas Jefferson following the 1800 election, Pitcairn continued to conduct business in Hamburg. Unfortunately, economic conditions in Europe during the Napoleonic Wars proved unstable. Pitcairn's American citizenship and earlier consulship service in Paris, however, saved the Pitcairn-Brodie firm from confiscation after the French occupied Hamburg. Following Napoleon's defeat in 1815, the United States once again appeared

Margaret Brown Brodie.
Photograph taken slightly before her death in 1878 at the age of forty-nine. Brodie family collection.

attractive to the former consul. He quickly accepted McCormick's offer to help settle the land acquired from Macomb and sailed for New York, leaving Joseph Brodie, his nephew and business partner, to handle affairs in Hamburg.[7]

Although the complex financial arrangements between McCormick and Pitcairn never have been unraveled, McCormick in 1816 transferred at least one township of the original Macomb tract to Pitcairn. Located in what now is St. Lawrence County, the parcel included the fledging community of Edwards, named after McCormick's brother. Pitcairn immediately launched an ambitious plan to recruit settlers.[8]

In 1819, Pitcairn gathered a group of Scots in Edinburgh and contracted for their passage to New York. According to agreement, the former consul paid for the immigrants' sea passage and gave the head of each household forty pounds sterling, annual wages and other benefits. In return, the settlers promised to work Pitcairn's land for three years. They then would be eligible to purchase land from the owner at a favorable rate. The group sailed on three ships up the St. Lawrence River as far as Montreal and then followed an old military road to Edwards. One of the immigrants, Robert Brown, a farmer from Edinburgh, eventually would impact the Brodie family significantly.[9]

Pitcairn's recruiting in Edinburgh solved a knotty problem for Rob-

Joseph Brodie Jr.
Brodie family collection.

ert Brown. His wife had died recently, leaving him with three small children. The farmer wanted to marry Agnes Gowen, his sister-in-law, but Scottish law prohibited such a union. In order to marry the woman of his choice, Brown joined Pitcairn's group, sailing for New York with his bride-to-be and three children. Once clear of Scotland's territorial waters, Brown married Agnes on the ship, and the family continued on to settle in Edwards.[10]

Meanwhile, Joseph Brodie died in Hamburg at age forty-two. His widow, Maria, an attractive and artistically talented woman, immediately took her brood to Edinburgh, but she died soon after, orphaning her nine-year-old son, Joseph Jr., and five other children. Upon Joseph's death, one of his brothers who already had migrated to New York, Alexander Oswald Brodie (1787-1856), assumed guardianship of Joseph Jr. and another nephew, James. Alexander agreed to bring his two wards to New York after they completed their education in Scotland.[11]

Unfortunately, this particular Alexander Oswald Brodie, great-uncle of Roosevelt's Major Brodie, remains a mystery. Obviously a shrewd businessman, but sometimes stern and inflexible in his personal life, he apparently shunned publicity. Born in Scotland in 1787, probably in Carnbee, he established himself at an early age as a merchant in New York City, where he became involved in land speculation with Daniel McCormick and Joseph Pitcairn. Like them, he became wealthy.

Joseph and Margaret Brodie's family.
Left to right: Alexander Oswald, Elizabeth, Robert Brown, and Harriet Louisa. Brodie family collection.

In 1842, Alexander brought his two wards, nineteen-year-old Joseph Jr. and James, from Scotland to live with him. His severe treatment of the two young men, however, reveals a harsh side of his character.[12]

One evening, Joseph and James, as young men are prone to do, decided to sample the local nightlife. Inveigling a sympathetic servant to give them a latchkey, the two spent a night on the town. Somehow, their uncle learned of the escapade. Enraged at what now seems to have been a rather innocuous indiscretion, the merchant banished James back to Scotland and sent Joseph up the Hudson River to live with a Quaker family and learn to be a farmer. Apparently, Alexander decided to develop his holdings in St. Lawrence County as farmland and felt that with proper training, Joseph would be able to achieve that goal.[13] Joseph, however, did not remain long with the Quaker family. By 1844, he was farming in the vicinity of Edwards. That same year Pitcairn died, leaving the bulk of his land in St. Lawrence County to Alexander Brodie. Joseph, who always resented his uncle's decision to banish him from New York City, made the best of what he considered to be a bad situation. In 1847, he married Margaret Brown, the nineteen-year-old daughter of Robert and Agnes Brown. Since their arrival in Edwards in 1819 from Edinburgh, the prolific couple had raised a total of thirteen children and prospered as farmers. A good match, the Brodie-Brown marriage would last thirty-one years.[14]

Margaret and Joseph, who apparently retained the old country pronunciation of "Broad-ie," moved into a comfortable home they built near Edwards and started a family. In 1848, their first child, Harriet Louisa, was born, followed in quick succession by two boys and another girl. For unknown reasons, the young couple named their first son, born November 13, 1849, Alexander Oswald Brodie in honor of the uncle who had forced Joseph to leave New York City. That they were living on land owned by the uncle possibly influenced their decision. At any rate, Joseph and Margaret had no way of knowing that their first son, born on the banks of the Oswegatchie River in the obscure hamlet of Edwards, would one day be described by a future president of the United States as a "grizzled old frontier soldier." They would have been pleased. [15]

CHAPTER 2

"The Life of a Country Gentleman"

Although Joseph Brodie did not settle in Edwards by choice, the small community did turn out to be a pleasant place to raise his family. Nestled in rolling hills rising above the Oswegatchie River, the community and surrounding countryside boasted the legendary benefits associated with rural America in the mid-nineteenth century. A homogenous population, consisting largely of descendants of hardworking Scottish immigrants—some of whom had been recruited by Joseph Pitcairn—and transplanted down-east Yankees from New England, gave the area a certain degree of stability, a sense of community pride and a traditional work ethic. In 1849, the year of Alexander's birth, Edwards sported a population of one thousand residents.[1]

In spite of Edwards's rural environment, the children of Joseph and Margaret enjoyed all the comforts and amenities that their parents could provide. The family home, or "Brodie Mansion," as it became known locally, stood on the Brodie farm approximately half a mile south of town. Built by the newlyweds in 1847, the three-story frame structure contained twenty-two rooms.

Determined to provide a quality education for his family, Joseph moved a governess from New York City into a vacant bedroom, engaging her to school not only his own children but a few from neighboring farms, as well. Whoever the woman (or women) was, she obviously earned her keep. Alexander first would hold his own in the academic environment at St. Lawrence University and later at West Point.[2]

From his father, Alexander acquired a sense of community pride and service. Joseph, at various times, served as supervisor of the town of Edwards, eschewing, however, involvement in politics above the local level. "My father," Alexander once pointed out, "constantly refused public office, preferring always the life of a country gentleman without many ties in a business way."[3]

Yet, Joseph did have one significant and long-lasting political legacy to pass on to his first-born son. Most residents of St. Lawrence County abhorred slavery and strongly opposed dissolution of the Union. Consequently, as the question of states' rights and the spread of slavery into the territories in the 1850s became the dominant political issue, many New Yorkers turned to the fledging Republican Party. Joseph quickly embraced the Republican platform, often representing Edwards at the party's county conventions. As he grew older, Alexander shared his father's political philosophy and, emulating his father, became a lifelong Republican.

The comfortable environment that Joseph provided for his family could easily have fostered in his children a sense of elitism or superiority. Fortunately, at least in Alexander's case, that character flaw did not develop. The small size of Edwards may well have been the reason. Based on the ease with which Alexander later accepted the physical inconveniences of the more primitive conditions in the Far West, it is safe to assume that, as a young boy, he spent many hours hunting and exploring the nearby woods and streams. Naturally, any existing social stratification, either natural or artificial, would have disappeared as young Brodie cultivated boyhood chums who shared his interest in outdoor activities. Arthur L. Tuttle, a precocious eighteen-year-old cowboy from Safford, Arizona, who enlisted many years later in Brodie's command during the Spanish-American War, drove that point home by recalling that Brodie "never looked down on anyone."[4]

The outbreak of the Civil War in 1861 immediately impacted the Brodie household. Eleven-year-old Alexander, caught up in the exciting pageantry of flag-waving and unfettered patriotism, decided that he, too, wanted to join the army and help save the Union. He realized that he was too young to enlist, but thought he could find a place as a drummer boy. Joseph and Margaret, as expected, stood firmly in opposition. Joseph, physically disqualified for military service because of the effects of scarlet fever contracted as a child, tried his best to explain why he would not permit his son to enlist. He made little headway. Finally, exasperated with Alexander's constant badgering, Joseph worked out a compromise. In return for Alexander's commitment to prepare himself academically by diligently pursuing a formal education, Joseph promised to use his influence in the Republican Party to secure for Alexander an appointment to the United States Military Academy.[5]

In order to prepare Alexander to cope with the demanding engineering curriculum at the academy, which eliminated many prospective

Cadet Alexander O. Brodie.
This may be Brodie's 1870 graduation photograph from West Point. Brodie family collection.

cadets, Joseph enrolled his son (and daughter Harriet) in St. Lawrence University, a highly regarded boarding school in Ogdensburg, fifty miles north of Edwards. Alexander remained a student at that institution until June 1866, when his appointment to the academy took effect.[6]

At the academy, Brodie earned a respectable, although not outstanding, record as a cadet . Upon graduation in 1870, he ranked twenty-seven out of fifty-eight graduates. But the official class ranking may not tell the whole story.[7]

Final class standing of each cadet was determined by a composite score based on numerical evaluations in fourteen academic and military subjects, plus a separate category of discipline. The complicated formula, however, permitted a cadet's academic score in any subject to be revised downward for disciplinary reasons. Brodie claimed to have been a victim of such adjustments. Many years later, he confessed to a cousin in Scotland that, based on a strictly academic evaluation, he actually stood eleventh in his class, but had been lowered sixteen positions for disciplinary reasons. This claim, of course, is now impossible to verify, but a review of Brodie's academic and disciplinary record does suggest that might well have been the case. In the separate category of discipline, which would have been the tally of infractions committed outside the classroom, Brodie ranked a dismal forty-six. Even the class "goat" beat him by fifty points in that category, suggesting that Brodie, who had entered the academy at age sixteen, still harbored a youthful tendency to rebel against authority.[8]

Brodie earned his highest marks in mineralogy (geology) and chemistry, ranking fourteenth and fifteenth respectively. He performed less well in mathematics, English, and French. In military subjects he stood ninth in artillery tactics, twelfth in ordnance and gunnery, seventeenth in infantry tactics, and twenty-first in cavalry.[9]

Other than his academic record, little is known of Brodie's activities at the academy. Obviously, he avoided any major breach of discipline, although he certainly committed his share of minor infractions, such as throwing bread in the mess hall and talking in ranks. Drinking by cadets was strictly forbidden, but Brodie undoubtedly embraced a long-standing tradition of slipping away with a few friends for a clandestine visit to a popular tavern in nearby Highland Park named "Benny Havens," after the proprietor. Possibly the highlight of Brodie's four years at the academy was marching with his fellow cadets in the inaugural parade of President Ulysses S. Grant on a cold and windy March 4, 1869.[10]

Graduation took place on June 25, 1870. As Brodie stepped forward to receive his commission and appointment to M Troop, First Cavalry, he had every reason to expect a rewarding military career. In addition to a satisfactory class ranking, he appeared to be in good health and eager to join his regiment. Physically, the new second lieutenant of cavalry stood five feet and eleven inches in his boots and weighed approximately 140 pounds, although his erect bearing and well-proportioned frame made him appear larger. He had blue eyes and thick brown hair trimmed, at least by modern military standards, stylishly long. Smooth shaven, Brodie had not yet affected the large, drooping mustache which later would become a trademark.

Following the customary graduation leave, Brodie and five classmates entrained for Sacramento, California. Second Lt. Otto L. Hein, a twenty-three-year-old native of Washington, DC, recalled that the novice young officers headed west with a "bountiful supply of smoking and liquid requisites"—not a good omen. In Wyoming, the group had the unique experience of witnessing one of the great, short-lived romantic spectacles of the American West. More than once the train screeched to an unscheduled halt to permit a seemingly endless herd of American bison or buffalo to cross the tracks before it. Although all six lieutenants on board had been assigned to the First Cavalry Regiment, they would serve at installations scattered all the way from Oregon to Arizona.[11]

Command structure of the army in 1870 reflected a hybrid combination of unit and geographic entities. The War Department had divided the West into two divisions, each commanded by a general officer with subordinate commands called departments. The Division of the Pacific, with the exception of Utah, included all units and installations west of the Continental Divide. Within that division, the Department of Columbia had responsibility for Oregon, Washington, and Idaho territories. The Department of California controlled most of California and all of Nevada. The new Department of Arizona, created in April 1870, included all of the future copper state and that part of California south of Point Concepción, northwest of Los Angeles.[12]

Total army combat units consisted of ten cavalry regiments, twenty-five infantry, and five of artillery. Cavalry regiments, headed by a colonel with a lieutenant colonel as second in command, included twelve troops (companies) divided into three squadrons, each commanded by a major. Infantry regiments contained ten companies, but only one major. Troop or company officers in both branches included a captain, a first lieutenant, and a second lieutenant.[13]

Division commanders attempted to staff each frontier post with at least one troop of cavalry and one company of infantry. Unless a regimental major happened to be assigned, the senior captain at each remote installation served as post commander. This decentralized system afforded local commanders ample opportunity to develop their leadership and management skills. As Brodie soon would learn, some became thoroughly capable officers, commanding aggressively with common sense, initiative, and good judgment. Others, unable to cope with isolation and lack of supervision, appeared tentative or complacent. A few, possibly a little arrogant by nature, became abusive. Some simply turned to alcohol.

All twelve troops of the First Cavalry were far removed from regimental headquarters located at Benicia Barracks, a small post and supply depot thirty-five miles east of San Francisco. One troop in northern California and one in Nevada functioned under operational control of the Department of California, but three troops in Oregon and one in Idaho served in the Department of Columbia. The Department of Arizona contained six troops, including Brodie's M Troop. Col. Alvin C. Gillem, commander of the First Cavalry, did not like the arrangement, complaining that such a wide dispersion completely negated regimental headquarters as a functional tactical command, relegating it to a purely administrative entity.[14]

Brodie and his traveling companions did not even have an opportunity to meet Colonel Gillem. Reaching Winnemucca, a remote village on the Central Pacific rail line in northern Nevada, the group found military escorts waiting there to convey three officers to their respective duty stations in Nevada and Oregon. Brodie and his two remaining classmates destined for Arizona continued over the Sierra Nevada

Mountains to Sacramento, where a riverboat waited to take them down the Sacramento River directly to Angel Island, a recruiting and replacement depot in San Francisco Bay.[15]

At Angel Island, Brodie and his comrades joined one officer and fifty-one enlisted men already there waiting for transportation. On October 9, 1870, the entire group sailed for San Diego—gateway to Arizona.[16]

Reaching San Diego five days later, Brodie found a bustling community of 2,500 residents overlooking a fine natural harbor. The city's strategic location in Southern California provided a convenient conduit to funnel men and supplies into and out of Arizona. In fact, the tiny post of San Diego Barracks in reality had no other purpose than to provide logistical support to units in Arizona.[17]

Brodie and his Arizona-bound companions remained at San Diego for a week. During that period, while the commander of San Diego Barracks arranged for wagons, tents, ambulances, rations, and water barrels required for the 190 mile march across the Mojave Desert to Fort Yuma, 201 more soldiers and three officers en route to Arizona from New York by way of Panama arrived by steamer. By a strange twist of circumstances, one of the newly arrived officers, thirty-seven-year-old 1st Lt. Royal Emerson Whitman, inadvertently later would provide Brodie with his first taste of combat.[18]

On the morning of October 29, accompanied by seven officers riding in wagons and 252 enlisted men marching on foot, Brodie departed San Diego on the final leg of his long journey to Arizona. Two lieutenants, classmates John G. Kyle and Peter S. Bomus, still traveled with him. Kyle, a native of Ohio ranked forty-second in the class at the academy, had been assigned to G Troop, First Cavalry, at Fort Bowie, 100 miles east of Tucson. Bomus and Brodie would report to Camp Thomas in the mountains of eastern Arizona. Bomus, a fellow New Yorker, two years older than Brodie, had been slotted in L Troop, First Cavalry.[19]

During the uncomfortable twenty-day march to Fort Yuma, Brodie had ample opportunity to ponder his situation. Less than a month short of his twenty-first birthday, the young lieutenant had invested four years in preparation for this moment. Now, as he studied the barren, desolate bluffs in Arizona across the slow-moving, chocolate-colored Colorado River, he realized the long-anticipated opportunity to test his knowledge, training, and ability finally had been thrust upon him. Somewhere, deep in Apachería, the three-company post of Camp Thomas awaited his arrival.

CHAPTER 3

"One of the Most Beautiful Sites in the US"

Upon crossing the Colorado River into Arizona, Brodie took up duty in a department plagued by almost overwhelming command and logistical problems. Approximately 400 miles long and 350 miles wide, Arizona Territory sported a non-Indian population of 9,627 residents living in widely scattered communities. Telegraph communication had not been established, and only a few primitive roads connected the twelve existing and understaffed military installations. Indian depredations, a constant and ongoing problem, had residents literally up in arms. Under such challenging conditions, the army needed a strong commander capable of making tough decisions and then enforcing them. Unfortunately, the newly appointed commander of the Department of Arizona, Col. George Stoneman, in spite of an impressive Civil War record, lacked those sorely needed characteristics.[1]

In Stoneman's defense, the colonel clearly did not have sufficient personnel under his command to adequately cover an area as large as Arizona. But size was not the only problem. Arizona's three distinct terrain features rendered troop deployment, transportation, and communication extremely difficult. The barren desert region in the southwest quadrant and an intermittent chain of mountains angling generally southeast to northwest across the center of the territory effectively restricted east-west movement. Conversely, the windswept Colorado Plateau, which covers the northeastern quarter of the territory, blocked easy access to the north. The southern edge of the Colorado Plateau, a sheer escarpment or cliff known as the Mogollon Rim, rises abruptly as much as 2,000 feet above the lower land to the south. Easily recognized on the ground, this imposing barrier sweeps in a gentle arc from the vicinity of present-day Flagstaff southeast to merge with the towering White Mountains along the border of New Mexico.

Nearly all of Arizona lies within the Colorado River drainage basin. The Colorado River, which forms the boundary of Arizona with California, flows into Arizona from Utah and continues south to the Gulf of California. In Arizona, the major tributary of the Colorado is the Gila River, a westward-flowing stream originating in New Mexico and crossing Arizona to merge with the Colorado near Yuma. The Salt River, an important tributary to the Gila, rises in the White Mountains and flows southwest to merge with the Gila near present-day Phoenix. The Salt River is fed by the Verde River and several smaller, fast-moving streams tumbling from the north, such as Tonto and Canyon creeks. Two intermittent "rivers," the San Pedro and Santa Cruz, rise near the Mexican border and flow north into the Gila.

In 1870, most Arizona residents lived in or near three major communities: Tucson in the south, Yuma in the west, and Prescott in the north. A lack of transportation facilities, economic opportunity, and availability of water made it difficult to locate elsewhere. Moreover, the Apaches and occasionally the Mojave and Yavapai Indians, who inhabited the mountains near Prescott as far west as the Colorado River, still posed a constant and very real threat to travelers and would-be settlers. Even the ranchers and farmers located close to a military installation habitually kept their rifles loaded and ready.

The Apaches in Arizona consisted of two separate divisions, each containing several groups or subdivisions. The universally feared Chiricahua Division occupied the southeastern corner of the territory. Led by the famous Cochise, the Chiricahua received blame for practically every Indian depredation committed in southern Arizona in the decades immediately before and after the Civil War. The Western Apache Division, including the Pinal, Aravaipa, White Mountain, and Tonto subdivisions, roamed the mountains and valleys north of the Chiricahuas and south of the Mogollon Rim.[2]

The aggressive Tontos occupied a convoluted, remote depression known as the Tonto Basin. Sandwiched between the Mogollon Rim to the north, the White Mountains to the east, and the Mazatzal Mountains rising above the Verde River to the west, the Tonto Basin is scored by a series of broken, heavily forested hills separated by deep canyons. Several fast-moving streams flow south out of the basin into the Salt River.

Sometimes called Coyoteros, the large White Mountain band controlled the well-watered valleys of the White Mountains east of the Tonto Basin. Unlike their Tonto neighbors, the White Mountain group enjoyed a reputation for being friendly and peaceful. Consequently, no military presence existed in their homeland until May 1870, when a column led by Maj. John Green, First Cavalry, arrived to establish a reservation and lay out a post initially named Camp Mogollon, but quickly rechristened Camp Thomas.[3]

These were the conditions Brodie found when he first entered the territory. It was a far different environment, perhaps, from what he envisioned as he donned the shoulder straps of a second lieutenant on the parade ground at West Point; but frontier Arizona would provide a good training ground where an officer fresh out of the military academy could learn to be a soldier.

On November 10, after spending two uneventful days at Fort Yuma, Brodie's group ferried across the Colorado River into Arizona. Passing through the Yuma Quartermaster Depot and the squalid village of Yuma, which Brodie's classmate Lt. Otto L. Hein later described as a "sink of inequity," the detachment followed the well-used Gila Trail up the Gila River to Sacaton, a Pima Indian village south of present-day Phoenix. There, military escorts waited to accompany the newly arrived personnel to their respective duty stations. Lts. Brodie, Royal E. Whitman, Peter S. Bomus, and John G. Kyle, with thirty-seven recruits, continued south to Tucson, arriving November 27. Whitman left immediately with six soldiers headed for Camp Grant north of Tucson, and Kyle departed shortly thereafter to join his troop 100 miles to the east at Fort Bowie. Brodie and Bomus reported to the commanding officer at Camp Lowell for additional instructions.[4]

Expecting to leave immediately for Camp Thomas, Brodie and his traveling companion found themselves cooling their heels for unknown reasons at Camp Lowell, on the outskirts of Tucson, for over a month. The two officers considered Tucson, the largest city in Arizona with a population of 3,200 residents, to be a disappointment. Consisting of a hodgepodge of unattractive, flat-topped adobe buildings overlooking narrow, filthy streets, the territorial capital boasted a number of smoke-filled saloons and gambling dens where local residents rubbed shoulders with miners, ranchers, soldiers, Mexican traders from Sonora, and immigrants on their way to California. Topics of conversation covered the gamut from Indian attacks to national affairs and the relative merits of girls currently working the "Sporting District."[5]

Although disappointed that he would not immediately join his troop, Brodie later admitted that he thoroughly enjoyed his unexpected stay in Tucson, where he attended several 1870 Christmas *fiestas* at the old San Xavier Mission a few miles south of town. An accomplished horseman in his own right, he particularly appreciated the skills displayed by Mexican *vaqueros* as they competed in a popular sport called *Sacar del Gallo*, or "rooster pulling." Riding at a full gallop, participants, without losing their balance, swung down from the saddle and attempted to grab roosters which had been buried in sand, leaving only their heads and necks exposed. Successful riders usually threw their hard-won prizes into the crowd of spectators. According to Brodie, however, participants sometimes got into fights, using the battered fowls to pummel each other.[6]

Always interested in politics—a trait inherited from his father—Brodie undoubtedly visited the locally popular Shoo-Fly Restaurant in Tucson on a regular basis. Army officers, private citizens, and government officials routinely gathered there to discuss current events and general conditions throughout the territory. Even Anson P. K. Safford, the diminutive and feisty territorial governor, made a frequent appearance. Based on these conversations, Brodie realized that Arizona residents considered Indian depredations to be the most critical problem facing the territory, and the reputation of any army officer assigned to units in Arizona depended almost exclusively upon his success in running down hostile Indians. During late November and December, while Brodie waited at Camp Lowell, four white men in southern Arizona died at the hands of Apaches.[7]

On January 3, 1871, Brodie finally reported for duty at Camp Thomas. Lieutenant Bomus remained in Tucson sick in quarters and did not reach the post until five weeks later. Brodie's first view of the camp, as he descended Seven Mile Hill, drove home the realization that duty at this isolated outpost would not be easy. Established on the southwestern slopes of the heavily forested White Mountains, the rustic post occupied a small mesa overlooking the confluence of the East and North Forks of the White River, two cold, fast-moving mountain streams. The elevation of 5,000 feet afforded not only pleasant summers, but protection from brutal winter storms which occasionally paralyzed the higher elevations to the northeast. One officer considered the location to be "one of the most beautiful sites in the US." But the scenic location, as Brodie soon learned, scarcely compensated for the numerous drawbacks.[8]

A three-company post consisting of L and M Troops, First Cavalry, and B Company, Twenty-first Infantry, Camp Thomas had been located the previous May. Maj. John Green, the post commander, intended to have the garrison quartered in log barracks before the first heavy snowfall, but Brodie found the troopers still facing the January chill in tents. The only completed wooden structures consisted of the quartermaster's structure, the post trader's store, and a corral. Green explained that a shortage of personnel and other military requirements had caused construction to proceed at a snail's pace.

In addition to maintaining two supply lines, one to Fort Wingate in

New Mexico and the other to Tucson by way of Camp Goodwin, Green had the responsibility of providing escorts to military travelers and supply trains, dispatching occasional scouting parties and ensuring a strong military presence on post to supervise the issue of rations to 1,000 or more Apaches living nearby. Green was expected to accomplish all this with a significantly understrength garrison.[9]

Authorized ten officers and approximately 250 enlisted men, Green's command fell significantly short. Upon arrival, Brodie found three officers and 168 enlisted men available for duty. Only 104 enlisted men actually could be immediately deployed, however. The remaining sixty-four had been assigned special duty, reported sick, or placed under arrest. Although short in numbers, the garrison appeared long on experience, at least in the higher ranks.[10]

All three officers on post, Major Green, Capt. James C. Hunt, and 1st Lt. Moses Harris, had seen extensive combat in the Civil War. Dark-haired, short-tempered John Green led the way. Born in Germany in 1825, Green enlisted in the First United States Mounted Rifles in 1846, accepting a commission nine years later in the Second Regiment of Dragoons. Shortly after the outbreak of the Civil War, he accepted a promotion to captain in the First Cavalry, serving in that capacity until the end of the war. He also received two brevet promotions. Capt. James C. Hunt, a forty-four-year-old native of New Jersey, commanded M Troop, Brodie's unit of assignment. Hunt had soldiered in the First Cavalry since 1862, subsequently winning a captaincy and two brevets. First Lt. Moses Harris, also assigned to M Troop, had won the Medal of Honor as a lieutenant in the First Cavalry at the battle of Smithfield, West Virginia. An excellent marksman and reportedly widely read, Harris was born in 1839 in New Hampshire. Neither L Troop nor B Company had an assigned officer present for duty at Camp Thomas when Brodie arrived, but several were en route.[11]

Eager to begin his military career, Brodie expected that he and his troop soon would be skirmishing with hostile Indians. Major Green, however, immediately threw cold water on that expectation.

The shortage of officers, Green explained to his novice lieutenant, had forced him to organize the post along functional instead of normal command lines. He had placed all direct command authority in the hands of Captain Hunt, the assigned commander of M Troop, by appointing him temporary commander of both L Troop and B Company. All post administrative and logistical functions had been entrusted to Lieutenant Harris, who served as post adjutant, acting assistant quartermaster (AAQM), and acting commissary of subsistence (ACS). After evaluating Brodie for a few days and aware that Harris would soon be reassigned elsewhere, Green directed Brodie to relieve Harris of his duties as AAQM and ACS. Three weeks later, as expected, Harris left Camp Apache—as the post had been renamed on February 2—for recruiting duty in the East, and Brodie assumed the position of post adjutant as well. To Brodie's chagrin, Lieutenant Bomus, who arrived in February, would be relied upon to handle most field operations until other officers reported for duty.[12]

Contrary to what he had learned in Tucson, Brodie found the Indian situation at Camp Apache to be much more complicated and less threatening than he had been led to believe. The White Mountain Apaches actually consisted of five separate subdivisions. One band, led by a respected although sometimes erratic chief named Esh-kel-dah-silah, lived along the White River near the post. Members of this group routinely visited the camp, sometimes even bringing in firewood and hay to sell to the post quartermaster.

Four other bands lived nearby. One group, headed by one-eyed Chief Miguel, usually could be found near Cibique Creek, thirty miles to the west. Two other subdivisions lived in that same general area. Chief Pedro's band normally camped along White River, fifteen miles to the north. When Miguel's and Pedro's followers were not actually planting or harvesting corn, the two chiefs often moved their villages closer to Camp Apache to facilitate being counted and issued rations.[13]

Although military authorities considered the White Mountain Apaches to be peaceful, Brodie found that many civilians and soldiers did not share that assessment. The post had no stockade, and warriors routinely visited the cantonment area, often carrying relatively modern weapons, which they probably secured in trade with the Zuñi Indians. Some post personnel openly expressed concern about such unrestricted visits, particularly on ration-issuing days, when large groups of Apaches appeared to be counted and draw rations of beef, corn, flour, and sugar. As a routine precaution, garrison members assigned to work details in and around the camp habitually kept their weapons loaded and close at hand. Frequently, however, as a sign of friendship, military personnel received invitations to attend ceremonies and dances in the Apache villages. Many accepted.[14]

On a different note, Brodie or another junior officer often drew the unpleasant duty of destroying freshly brewed *tiswin*, a native drink concocted from fermented corn. Not particularly intoxicating when consumed in small quantities, the brew induced a powerful, long-term reaction when taken in large amounts. The fermentation process required a week and usually culminated in a group binge the whites called a "*tiswin* drunk," which lasted for several days. Participants frequently became violent. Fights broke out and inebriated husbands often beat their equally drunken wives, causing post commanders and Indian agents to ban the liquor from all reservations in Arizona. Enforcing the *tiswin* ban remained an unwanted, tension-filled operation. Usually alerted by informers or by the smoke of distilling fires, Green would send Brodie or another officer with a small detachment into the designated village. Sometimes, as many as 200 half-drunken Apaches, some armed, watched sullenly as the nervous troopers poured their brew on the ground in front of them. At such times trouble was only a heartbeat away.[15]

For a variety of reasons, maintaining good morale at all frontier posts was extremely difficult, and Brodie found Camp Apache to be no exception. Other than hunting and drinking, few recreational opportunities existed. No towns or settlements, other than an occasional ranch, could be found within miles, and, with very few exceptions, Apache women showed no interest in white men. Brodie and many other members of the garrison enjoyed scouring the surrounding mountains in search of turkey, deer, bear, elk, and antelope, which provided welcome additions to army rations. But even that activity could be dangerous. One of Brodie's favorite enlisted men, Cpl. Henry J. Hyde, and a companion on a routine patrol to the Zuñi villages were badly mauled by a large grizzly bear they attempted to kill with their underpowered Spencer carbines. Both men recovered, and Hyde later would see hard service under Brodie's command against hostile Indians in the Tonto Basin.[16]

One of the most important lessons Brodie learned early in his career at Camp Apache hinged on the necessity of maintaining good public relations. Colonel Stoneman's ineptitude in that regard provided Brodie a classic example of how not to deal with civilians. Even before Brodie arrived in Arizona, Stoneman unwisely had involved himself in a bitter political vendetta with local residents regarding the wisdom of his plan to control Arizona Indians. The resulting furor would be Brodie's first harsh lesson in frontier politics. It would not be his last.

Shortly after arriving in Prescott on July 3, 1870, and establishing headquarters at nearby Fort Whipple, Stoneman conducted an extensive tour of all Arizona military installations. Such an inspection, of course, reflected normal military procedure, but Stoneman unwisely permitted the editor of the Prescott *Arizona Miner* to accompany him. Not only did that decision apparently irritate the editor of the rival Tucson *Arizona Citizen*, but it also enabled the journalistic community to gain premature insight into Stoneman's conclusions and intentions. In the fall, when the colonel forwarded his first annual report to the commander of the Division of the Pacific, his recommendations had been anticipated, and opposition surfaced with a vengeance.[17]

In his report, Stoneman stated that seven military installations in Arizona had become superfluous and recommended that they be closed.

Significantly, the hit list included three posts located in or near the two largest communities in the territory: Camp Lowell and the quartermaster depot, both at Tucson, and Fort Whipple near Prescott. These posts were no longer necessary, Stoneman assured his division commander, because all the Indian groups in Arizona except the Tonto and Pinal Apaches desired peace.[18]

Stoneman further justified his recommendations by pointing out that the cost of maintaining unnecessary posts had become prohibitive because Arizona merchants and contractors routinely charged the military exorbitant prices for inferior merchandise. Moreover, Stoneman went on to state that a shortage of tents and permanent buildings at Fort Whipple had forced him to "temporarily" relocate headquarters of the Department of Arizona from Fort Whipple to Drum Barracks at Wilmington, just south of Los Angeles, California. Thus, with a stroke of a pen, Stoneman signed a document that alienated almost every significant political and economic faction in Arizona. The colonel had committed a serious blunder, which would have far-reaching consequences.[19]

Both Arizona newspapers viciously attacked Stoneman's report, arguing that the colonel had greatly underestimated the Indian threat. The *Miner* stated unequivocally that the military required twice as many troops to maintain peace as Stoneman had recommended. The *Citizen* claimed that the colonel's plan, if implemented, would result in the "virtual abandonment of the country." Moreover, many residents considered Stoneman's remarks about contractors and merchants to be a personal insult. Finally, his decision to move department headquarters to California invoked universal contempt.[20]

Sensing that he had gone too far and that an uncontrollable storm was about to break about him, Stoneman belatedly made a futile effort to appease his critics. On December 30, he ordered a winter campaign against the Pinal and Tonto Apaches, the two groups he had identified in his report as still hostile. He directed the post commanders at camps Thomas, Grant, and McDowell, the latter an important, strategically-located post near the confluence of the Verde and Salt rivers, to dispatch scouting expeditions as soon as possible. Pleased with even this token effort, the *Miner* printed the entire order.[21]

Brodie hoped to accompany the Camp Thomas column, but Green chose Lieutenant Bomus instead. An experienced combat soldier, Green liked to test newly assigned officers in the field, and Bomus had been under his command for only six days. On February 1, 1871, with the mountains above camp glistening with fresh snow, Brodie joined Capt. James Hunt, acting post commander during Green's absence, on the parade ground to watch Green and Bomus lead thirty warmly dressed cavalrymen, Spencer carbines slung, out of camp en route to the Tonto Basin and Pinal Mountains.[22]

Returning on March 19, Green reported two brushes with hostiles in the Pinal Mountains. His troopers had killed one Apache, captured four horses, and destroyed a small quantity of supplies. Obviously, such meager success would not silence Stoneman's critics. Within a month, powerful voices in Arizona would call for Stoneman's head. Meanwhile, during Stoneman's halfhearted winter campaign in central Arizona, incidents involving Indians farther south actually escalated. During March and April, hostiles committed a number of depredations in the vicinity of Tucson and Camp Grant. The residents of Tucson decided they had had enough.[23]

On April 30, 1871, a group of six Anglo Americans, ninety-two Papagoes (Tohono O'odham), and forty-two Mexicans from Tucson vented their frustrations. Just before dawn, they attacked a sleeping village of perhaps 500 Aravaipa Apaches, who were living under the protection of the garrison at Camp Grant commanded by 1st Lt. Royal E. Whitman, one of Brodie's former traveling companions from California. The raiders killed over 100 Apaches, and the Papagos took twenty-seven Aravaipa children to sell as slaves. This tragic affair, known as the Camp Grant Massacre, triggered an immediate reaction in Washington, and repercussions thundered back with a vengeance. Conditions in Arizona involving Indians would never again be the same.[24]

CHAPTER 4

"I Do Not Believe They Can Again Be Trusted"

Few events in Arizona have had an impact equal to that of the Camp Grant Massacre. President Grant, understandably embarrassed by having over one hundred Indians living under military protection murdered by civilians and goaded by an outraged Eastern press, concluded that a change in policy had become necessary. Within a few weeks, embattled Colonel Stoneman relinquished his command to Lt. Col. George Crook. The new commander brought to Arizona a locally popular determination to settle the Indian question with military force. Ultimately, Crook proved successful, but not until two peace commissioners sent from Washington first attempted to resolve the issue through negotiation. In the meantime, Brodie experienced his first taste of combat.[1]

It took time for Eastern reaction to the Camp Grant Massacre to filter back to Arizona, but local consequences surfaced immediately. As news of what had transpired at Camp Grant spread to the various Indian tribes, many, including some who had a long tradition of living in peace, suddenly became suspicious and resentful. At Camp Apache, a group uncharacteristically even retaliated.

Early in the morning of May 13, 1871, members of Esh-kel-dah-silah's band, waving blankets and whooping shrilly, erupted unexpectedly from concealed positions in the brush to stampede the Camp Apache horse herd, which had been turned out to graze on the lush native grass growing along White River. Catching the three-man guard completely by surprise, the marauders fatally wounded one herder, Pvt. Frank Walton of L Troop, with a well-placed arrow and disappeared into the mountains to the southeast, driving ten government horses and twelve mules. The frightened corporal in charge of the detachment, meanwhile, galloped into camp to spread the alarm.[2]

Major Green immediately directed Brodie, the only cavalry officer available, to take charge of the post guard detail and recover the herd. Brodie was ecstatic. For over four months he had been waiting for an opportunity to lead a combat patrol, or "scout" as it was called, and he intended to make the most of it. Selecting his favorite horse, a magnificent dapple-gray, Brodie trotted out of camp at the head of a relief force as quickly as he could get one organized. Unfortunately, a shortage of horses forced the novice Indian fighter to mount some of his men on mules—sure-footed, but relatively slow animals, poorly suited for fast-moving cavalry operations. Meanwhile, Capt. William D. Fuller, who had joined the garrison two months earlier to take command of B Company, assembled a handful of his infantrymen to follow on foot in support.[3]

Pushing hard his ten-man detachment, Brodie overtook the hostiles on a tree-studded mesa twelve miles from the post. He quickly engaged the horse thieves in a running fight, but it turned into an uneven contest. Even before making contact, Brodie had outdistanced his infantry support, and his own force was beginning to unravel. Most of the mules had begun to lag, and some of the weaker horses could not keep up the pace. The Apache rear guard, meanwhile, skillfully placed themselves between the stolen herd and the pursuing soldiers. Nevertheless, Brodie's troopers doggedly continued the chase for most of the afternoon, occasionally exchanging shots with the shadowy figures flitting through the trees ahead of them and on their flanks. Finally, realizing that his strung-out command was becoming progressively weaker while the number of Indians opposing him seemed to be increasing, Brodie broke off the engagement and returned to camp. He reported two Indians killed with no loss to his detachment except for one sergeant, who had his horse shot from under him. The sergeant was not injured.

Although disappointed at Brodie's failure to recover the horse herd, Green had more important matters to consider. At this point, the major did not know the extent of the uprising. Obviously, every soldier and civilian in the vicinity had to be warned, but Green's primary concern was the safety of eleven members of his command guarding a large quantity of government property still stored at abandoned Camp Goodwin, approximately 100 miles to the south. That evening, after giving Brodie an opportunity to resupply and reorganize, Green sent him with fifteen men mounted on mules trotting down the Tucson-Camp Goodwin road to spread the alarm.[4]

Encountering no evidence of hostile activity, Brodie briefed the noncommissioned officer in charge of the detachment at Camp Goodwin, warning him to take every precaution against a surprise attack.

He then hurried back to Camp Apache, finding conditions there still unstable. During his absence, the Apaches had launched a second raid, successfully driving away five head of the post cattle herd. Major Green, pleased to have Brodie and his fifteen men safely back on post, explained that until he could learn the intentions of Miguel, Pedro, and other Apache chiefs, he had to consider the possibility that he faced a general uprising. In that event, he would have his hands full. Even with Brodie back on post, Green could muster only himself, two other officers, and approximately 100 enlisted men for duty. Moreover, he had only twenty-six horses available, which explains why he had mounted Brodie's second scouting expedition on mules.[5]

Reporting the two incidents to his superiors, a disappointed Green revealed that he had lost confidence in the White Mountain Apaches. "I know of no course," he confided, "to pursue now towards them but extermination for after the kind treatment received here, I do not believe they can again be trusted." Within a few days, however, Chief Miguel and another prominent Indian leader, Capitán Chiquito (Little Captain), contacted Green denying any involvement in the two raids and pledging continued friendship. Pleased with this response and lack of additional hostile action, Green concluded that the crisis had passed. The hostiles, he suspected, had fled south to join the Aravaipa band near Camp Grant. Slowly, the situation returned to normal—but not without one final incident.[6]

Early the following month, June, Brodie led a small detachment on a routine mission to Camp Grant. What took place on that patrol is still not clear. According to one account, a group of Apaches, including a few from the White Mountains, came across Brodie's troopers watering their horses at Aravaipa Creek. Some of the Indians, allegedly recognizing Brodie as the officer who had responded to the May 15 attack, began pelting the cavalrymen with stones. Brodie's men reacted by driving their assailants away with pistol fire.[7]

The Aravaipa Apaches, of course, saw it differently, later accusing Brodie's men of having opened fire on them without warning or provocation. In retrospect, it is entirely possible that the Indians involved in this obscure incident did include some from the White Mountains who, as Green suspected, had participated in the May raids and then, to avoid punishment, fled south to join the Aravaipa group. At any rate, Brodie's little-known altercation near Camp Grant may have helped cause the Aravaipa Apaches, still grieving the Camp Grant Massacre, to decide to place more distance between themselves and the ever-encroaching whites by relocating on the San Carlos Reservation to the northeast.[8]

Although Major Green's reports detail reasonably well the May 15 and May 17 raids at Camp Apache, there are several perplexing aspects of those two incidents. Years later, badly garbled accounts of Brodie's skirmish made the rounds in Arizona. Most made no mention of stolen livestock, relating only that Brodie, while in command of a small detachment on a routine mission in June, was attacked by a large number of Apaches. Rallying his demoralized force, Brodie skillfully led a charge under heavy fire through the enemy and back to camp. One such story, surprisingly enough, was written by Brodie's private secretary after Brodie became governor. Surely, Brodie knew prior to publication that his secretary's version contained errors, but apparently he made no effort to correct the account. The secretary even wrongly recorded the date, although that may not have been his fault. Brodie himself, on more than one occasion, stated that the fight took place in June, not in May. It is difficult to understand how Brodie could forget the date of his first combat patrol, but that is exactly what seems to have occurred.[9]

The May attacks also brought to a head a long-simmering feud between Major Green and John Wasson, the hard-boiled editor of the Tucson *Arizona Citizen*. Copies of Wasson's newspaper were widely read at Camp Apache, of course, enabling Brodie to easily follow Wasson's accusations concerning the situation at Camp Apache. The resulting Green-Wasson controversy would prove to be another valuable lesson in frontier politics for Lieutenant Brodie.[10]

Beginning in March 1871, Wasson published a series of anonymous letters purportedly describing conditions at Camp Apache. The first, supposedly written by Pvt. John Thompson of Brodie's M Troop—post records reveal no man by that name assigned to the camp—criticized both Major Green and Captain Hunt for their failure to punish a member of Esh-kel-dah-silah's band for lancing to death Perry Redmond, an employee of the post trader. Details of the incident are not clear, but apparently Redmond and an unidentified Apache became involved in some kind of an altercation in the post trader's store, which resulted in Redmond's death. Upon learning of the incident, Brodie and the post surgeon recovered Redmond's body, but the Indian involved had already made his escape. According to Thompson, Captain Hunt, acting post commander in Green's absence, refused to arrest the murderer, even after he had been positively identified.

Instead of demanding that the culprit be turned over to the military for trial, Captain Hunt, Thompson complained, made a special distribution of corn and beef to the Indians in exchange for their promise that Redmond's killer would be punished. Incensed over this perceived lack of firmness, Thompson made a dire prediction that, as events unfolded, proved to be surprisingly accurate. "Some more hair will be raised [a slang term for killing] before long," Thompson wrote, "as punishment [here] is corn and meat." Wasson, concluding that the unpopular Green had lost control of his Indian charges, swung into action. As a proverbial Indian-hater, the uncompromising editor could not abide any officer who appeared to be soft on Apaches. He went after Green with a vengeance surpassed only by the spirited and personal attacks he later directed at Col. Stoneman and Lt. Royal Whitman because they, too, in Wasson's view, did not effectively control Indians under their supervision.[11]

Wasson quickly followed Thompson's letter with several others accusing Green of failure to supervise Indians, excessive drinking, and even fraternization with Apache women. On April 1, however, Wasson leveled a charge of his own, stating that the military at Camp Apache routinely issued arms and ammunition to the Apaches. These weapons, Wasson asserted, were used to commit depredations against white settlers. He closed his article with an invitation for Green to respond.

Not sensing the trap that had been set for him, Green, who should have known better, foolishly rose to the bait. In a long letter to the *Citizen*, the major vigorously denied issuing weapons to Indians, referring to his unnamed critics as "blackguards" who "not only do not stick to the truth but fabricate and invent lies." The people of Arizona, Green concluded, "are either liars or d_____ scoundrals [*sic*] and fools." By such a petty and intemperate response, of course, Green had joined a battle he could not win. Three weeks later he would send Brodie with ten poorly mounted troopers on a futile mission to recover his stolen horse herd, thereby giving Wasson a golden opportunity to gloat over the major's misfortune.[12]

A triumphant Wasson could not even wait for accurate details about Brodie's fight before commenting. Invoking an inappropriate parody on Mother Goose rhymes, the editor, in a long front-page article, scored both Colonel Stoneman and Brevet Lieutenant Colonel Green:

> "THE HUMOR OF IT"
> Full History of the Arizona Indian Wars Desireable—
>   A Tale of Two Colonels
> Ding, ding dell—the cat's in the Well!
> Who put her in? little Johnny Green
> Mother Goose

Wasson went on to relate a garbled account of the raid, which, he assured his readers, had been "long expected."[13]

Clearly, the Green-Wasson feud illustrated the futility of army officers being drawn into such no-win confrontations with civilians. Throughout the remainder of his military and later political careers, Brodie carefully maintained cordial relations with the press. John

Wasson and Major Green had taught him well.

As conditions at Camp Apache gradually returned to normal following the Camp Grant Massacre, Brodie and the remainder of the garrison waited to see what the new department commander had in store for them. Even then, Bvt. Maj. Gen. George Crook (Lt. Col.) was putting the finishing touches on his plan of attack.

At Tucson, which he reached on June 19, Crook, accurately sensing the attitude of Arizona residents regarding Indians, made it clear that he intended to solve the problem with military force. After conferring with selected army officers and prominent citizens including Governor Safford, the department commander decided to personally organize independent columns of cavalry at selected posts to strike simultaneously into the heartland of Apachería and eliminate all remaining hostile bands. Each command would be led by an experienced, hard-driving officer with an attending pack train and a company of Indian or Mexican scouts.

On July 11, ready to test his concept in the field, Crook left Tucson with five troops of the Third Cavalry, a large pack train, and fifty Mexican scouts, recruited locally at Governor Safford's request. A month later he rode into Camp Apache.[14]

Crook made an impressive entrance. Standing over six feet with a muscular build and imposing side-whiskers, the colonel demonstrated why he was known as a man of action. Quickly dispensing with the usual amenities of military protocol, he directed Major Green to assemble the leading White Mountain Apache chiefs for a conference. Miguel, Pedro, and Capitán Chiquito immediately responded, but Esh-kel-dah-silah did not.

Firmly and confidently, Crook assured the 500 assembled Apaches that they would be treated fairly and not harmed as long as they remained at peace on a reservation. He emphasized, however, that it was his duty to ensure that all Apache groups either relocated to a reservation or "died in the mountains." He also requested that the bands present assist the military by providing a company of scouts to help run down any Indians who rejected his terms. The colonel then departed for Camp Verde, a three-company post on the west bank of the Verde River approximately sixty miles north of Camp McDowell. He instructed Capt. Guy V. Henry, D Troop, Third Cavalry, to remain at Camp Apache and enlist the company of scouts, which the White Mountain chiefs had promised to provide.[15]

Selecting forty-four of the seventy-five young Apaches who volunteered, Henry organized them into two equal groups. He then departed on a scouting mission with one group, leaving the second in reserve at Camp Apache. Meanwhile, Brodie left the post on August 14 to sit on a court-martial board at Camp Grant. Returning twelve days later, expecting to find Crook's campaign well under way, he found to his surprise that the situation had changed dramatically. All military operations had been suspended, and a new player bearing impressive credentials directly from Washington had entered the game.

Major Green introduced Brodie to Vincent Colyer, Secretary of the Permanent Board of Peace Commissioners, explaining that Colyer had been empowered personally by President Grant to negotiate peace with all Indian tribes in New Mexico and Arizona still considered to be hostile. Colyer's sudden arrival had caught the military by surprise. Even Crook had received no prior notification of Colyer's mission. Nevertheless, he canceled all pending military operations until Colyer's exact role and authority could be clarified.[16]

Colyer spent three days at Camp Apache conferring with the leading Apache chiefs, dispensing gifts, and assuring the Indians that the president desired peace. In contrast with Green, who considered Pedro and Miguel to be the most reliable Apache leaders, Colyer clearly sided with Esh-kel-dah-silah, who convinced the commissioner that Green had created much of the tension at Camp Apache by unjustly accusing his band of instigating the May attacks on the post. On September 18, 1871, having concluded his negotiations with the White Mountain Apaches, Colyer headed south to confer with the Aravaipa Apaches, leaving unclear the status of the scouts initially selected by Captain Henry.

Henry actually enlisted only twenty-two Apaches, but he identified an equal number to be enrolled later by Brodie, who assumed command of the entire detachment upon returning from Camp Grant. The military authorities believed that the White Mountain scouts had volunteered eagerly, but Colyer took an opposing view, reporting that the scouts had been enrolled "much against their will." Colyer also claimed that he raised the issue with Crook, who immediately suspended further enlistments. Colyer's statement, however, clearly conflicts with the actual situation. There is no doubt that Brodie commanded the entire forty-four man White Mountain Scout Detachment from August 1871 until February 23, 1872, when the six-month term of enlistment expired and the unit disbanded. Other than Captain Henry's brief swing toward Camp McDowell, Brodie's scouts saw no meaningful field duty during that period.[17]

As commander of the scouts, Brodie quickly came to appreciate their dedication to duty, good humor, and overall natural ability. The assignment also gave him the opportunity to work closely with Corydon E. Cooley, his guide, interpreter, and one of the most unforgettable characters in northern Arizona.

In the spring of 1870, the Virginia-born Cooley with three companions entered the White Mountains in search of the legendary lost "Doc Thorne" gold mine. The group found no gold, but Cooley remained in the area to establish a ranch and farm eight miles north of Camp Apache, where he later married Mollie, a sister of Chief Pedro. Brodie and other officers stopped frequently at Cooley's ranch to enjoy Mollie's culinary skills. Fluent in Apache and trusted by the Indians, the Virginian proved to be a reliable guide and chief scout. Brodie and Cooley became good friends.[18]

As many civilian and military personnel in Arizona predicted, the brief period of peace following Colyer's visit ended abruptly. On November 15, 1871, a group of Indians attacked a stagecoach near Wickenburg, killing seven passengers. With Colyer already back in Washington rendering his report, Crook assumed the incident would give him a green light to launch his long-delayed offensive. But President Grant again intervened, placing Crook's plans on hold and dispatching a second peace envoy, Brig. Gen. Oliver O. Howard, a devout one-armed veteran of the Civil War sometimes called "the Christian General."[19]

Reaching Camp Apache on May 29, 1872, Howard found the Apaches there unhappy with a pending change in the beef contract. Previously, the contractor had delivered all beef purchased for the Indians alive to the reservation, thus enabling the Apaches to use the hides for leather. Under the terms of a new contract, scheduled to take effect July 1, the contractor now would provide dressed beef, retaining the valuable hides for himself. The Apaches strongly protested the change to Howard, who agreed with them. Until the matter could be resolved by contract negotiation, Howard directed Major Green to ignore the existing agreement and purchase all steers on the open market and issue them on the hoof. Howard's decision, of course, later caused problems for the post commander, who was accused of contract violation and even fraud. Post Adjutant Brodie, watching the beef controversy with interest, had learned another valuable lesson: deviation from established procedure should not be done without good cause. Howard, meanwhile, had returned to Washington, taking several White Mountain Apache chiefs with him.[20]

President Grant, convinced that peace in Arizona would never be a reality until the Chiricahua agreed, directed Howard to return and contact Cochise, whom the general had failed to meet on his first trip. Arriving at Camp Apache en route to southern Arizona, Howard found the Apaches at odds with their new post commander, Maj. Alexander J. Dallas. After listening to the Indians' complaints, which hinged largely on the question of adequate rations, Howard again sided with the Apaches, replacing Dallas as Indian Agent with the post surgeon. He then headed south to seek out Cochise.[21]

The assignment of Major Dallas, Twenty-third Infantry, marked the first of several important personnel changes Brodie experienced in the spring and summer of 1872. The previous December, beleaguered Major Green had been transferred to northern California, leaving Captain Hunt acting post commander until Dallas arrived in April. A forty-two-year-old Civil War veteran, Dallas appears to have been detail-oriented and of high moral character. He successfully pressured Corydon Cooley, for example, to marry Mollie. Unfortunately, the reports written by Dallas indicate he was inflexible and tentative. Possibly, he may have been a better garrison soldier than field commander. He retained Brodie as post adjutant.[22]

Brodie quickly briefed Major Dallas on an existing personnel problem, which required immediate attention. Shortly before Dallas arrived, Captain Hunt had arrested Captain Fuller. Details are unclear, but apparently Fuller, who had a reputation as hair-triggered, became involved in an altercation with Lt. Frank K. Upham of L Troop, who had returned from leave with a vivacious bride the previous year. Upham called Fuller "an insane man," whereupon Fuller drew his revolver and threatened to shoot Upham.[23]

Dallas investigated, approved Hunt's actions, and sent Fuller to Fort Whipple to be court-martialed. Three weeks later, while Brodie was absent with a fifteen-man detachment escorting military prisoners to Fort Yuma, Dallas for unknown reasons arrested Captain Hunt and sent him to Fort Whipple, as well. Returning on June 16, Brodie assumed temporary command of M Troop, serving in that capacity until August 14, when he again reported to Camp Grant on court-martial duty.[24]

In September, another significant personnel change took place at Camp Apache, enabling Brodie to serve with one of the most capable officers ever assigned to that post. Capt. George Morton Randall, commonly known as "Jake," arrived with I Company, Twenty-third Infantry, to replace B Company, which had been rotated out of Arizona. Physically imposing with a large distinctive mustache, the forty-one-year-old native of Ohio had an outstanding Civil War record, rising to rank of lieutenant colonel in the Union Army and earning four brevets. Unlike many Civil War veterans who after the war seem to have lost their stomach for close combat, Randall retained an aggressive, fighting spirit. Under the big captain's firm hand, Brodie would learn a hard and valuable lesson regarding field operations.[25]

That fall, as he watched the aspen groves on the higher slopes of the White Mountains break into their annual display of fall colors, Brodie realized that conditions in Arizona were changing. For two years he had been largely occupied with routine military functions as he watched both Colyer's and Howard's efforts to establish peace through negotiation fail. That period of indecision now had ended. Lt. Colonel Crook finally had secured authorization to use force, if necessary, to place all Indians in Arizona on a reservation.

Initially, Crook planned to "iron the wrinkles out of Cochise's band," but in October General Howard forestalled that operation by negotiating peace with the Chiricahua. The department commander quickly shifted his attention to the hostile groups in the Tonto Basin and mountains of north-central Arizona. Twice before, his plans had been thwarted by peace commissioners sent from Washington, but not this time. For his part, Brodie stood ready for his next lesson in military operations—an actual field campaign.[26]

CHAPTER 5

"He Could Not Fight the White and Indian Soldiers"

Lt. Col. George Crook's long delayed campaign into the Tonto Basin and nearby Apache strongholds proved to be short, violent, and highly successful. Beginning November 15, 1872, and ending April 7, 1873, this bloody, two-phased operation, with few isolated exceptions, effectively shattered Indian resistance in north-central Arizona. Troops from seven installations took part. Brodie, whose tour of duty in Arizona would soon come to an end, participated only in the second phase.

Utilizing the organizational concept he had tested back in the summer of 1871, Crook planned his 1872-73 campaign carefully. During the first phase, he would send fast-moving columns from seven designated posts first to locate and then crowd into the Tonto Basin all existing hostile bands not destroyed. That accomplished, Crook would halt the operation only long enough to resupply his troopers and then unleash the second phase by sending his men back into the Tonto Basin for the final kill. Each column, consisting of a small cavalry detachment, a well-organized pack train, and, where available, a group of Indian scouts, would be led by an aggressive officer personally selected by Crook. All columns would operate independently, although in strict conformity with the overall concept. Leaving nothing to chance, Crook or one of his capable aides visited each post to supervise preparation and impart clearly to the officer in charge the desires and expectations of the department commander. Women, children, and men who surrendered, Crook emphasized, would not be mistreated.[1]

In November, the initial impact of Crook's preparation hit Camp Apache. The colonel suddenly, for unclear reasons, transferred Major Dallas to Fort Lowell, directing Capt. George Randall to take charge of Camp Apache, retaining at the same time command of I Company. Prior to Randall's arrival, Brodie had not had the opportunity to observe a truly outstanding company commander. That would change. The big captain proved to be an excellent field soldier and a capable administrator. Brodie would learn much from Captain Randall.[2]

Lt. Colonel Crook launched the first phase of his offense as scheduled. In November, he personally sent three separate columns out of Camp Hualpai, a short-lived post forty miles northwest of Prescott, followed by two more out of Camp Date Creek. He then headed for camps Apache and Grant to personally organize the troops there, detailing one of his aides to assist in getting columns from Camp Verde, Fort Whipple, and Camp McDowell into the field.[3]

Crook rode into Camp Apache with his entourage as scheduled, but Brodie was not on hand to greet him. Three days earlier, Captain Randall had sent him with a small escort to track down and arrest several deserters. Returning from that unsuccessful mission a few days later, Brodie found Camp Apache virtually deserted. The only officer on post, 1st Lt. Frank K. Upham, explained the situation. Upon Crook's arrival, Upham related, the colonel had convinced the local Apache chiefs to provide forty-seven young men to form a detachment of Indian scouts. He then directed Randall to immediately clear all hostile Indians from the southern reaches of the Tonto Basin utilizing forty-two enlisted men and three officers from the post garrison, a pack train, and the recently enlisted Indian scouts led by Chief Scout Corydon Cooley. During Randall's absence, Upham would assume command of the post and L Troop. Brodie, upon his return, would take charge of M Troop and I Company. He would also serve as the designated commander of the scouts. Arrangements completed, Crook had then departed for New Camp Grant.[4]

Officially designated "2nd Lt. Alex O. Brodie's Detachment of Indian Scouts," the company members had been partially enlisted by Crook's aide, Lieutenant Bourke, who then departed Camp Apache with Crook, leaving much of the necessary enrollment paperwork to be completed by Brodie later. Two members of the scout detachment, José de Leon and Mickey Free, were Mexicans who had been captured as young boys and raised by Apaches.[5]

Mickey Free, known to his family as Felix Telles, had a storied career. Born in 1847 to a Mexican woman named Jesus María Martinez and her consort, Santiago Telles, Free later moved with his mother onto a ranch near Fort Buchanan owned by John Ward. In 1861, a group of Apaches raided Ward's ranch and took the boy captive. In an effort to recover the lad and some stolen cattle, 1st Lt. George N. Bascom, Seventh Infantry, led a detachment from Fort Buchanan to Apache Pass in the Chiricahua Mountains, contacted Cochise, and demanded that the boy and cattle be returned. Cochise refused, and a fight broke out. This controversial incident, later known as the Bascom Affair, is usually cited as the reason Cochise turned hostile toward Americans. Free subsequently spent much of his life with the White Mountain Apaches, frequently serving the military as a scout or interpreter. His first enlistment with Brodie started that career. The one-eyed Free must have demonstrated ability from the very beginning, for Brodie promoted him to corporal on April 2, 1873.[6]

By ordering Randall to sweep the southern end of the Tonto Basin, Crook hoped that the captain would run down the notorious Tonto Chief Delchay. A heavy-shouldered, lumbering individual in his thirties, Delchay normally maintained a ranchería for his band of 125 men with their families in the Four Peaks area east of Camp McDowell. Often referring to Delchay as "The Liar," Crook considered him to be one of the most untrustworthy Apache leaders in Arizona. He wanted Delchay's head badly.[7]

During Randall's expedition into the Tonto Basin, an obscure incident revealed that Brodie had already grasped one important facet of military leadership. In order to be truly effective, loyalty in a military organization must start at the top and filter down. Some officers never learn this basic concept, but the good ones do, and Brodie realized it early as evidenced by the Stratford incident.

In mid-December, as Randall's command bivouacked at Camp McDowell prior to returning to Camp Apache, an altercation broke out involving Sgt. William Stratford, Cpl. James W. Branagan, and Pvt. Carleton E. Hunt, all of M Troop. Stratford, a Civil War veteran with twelve years service, killed Hunt with the private's own knife as he attempted to disarm the soldier. Stratford claimed that he acted in self-defense. Brodie, upon learning of Stratford's arrest and confinement at Camp McDowell, wrote a letter of recommendation for the sergeant, stating that he had always found Stratford to be "a trustworthy and reliable man." Brodie's support did not save Stratford from being reduced to private, but it does demonstrate that Brodie would be loyal to those he considered to be reliable.[8]

Randall's return to Camp Apache in January marked the end of the first phase of Crook's campaign. The Camp Apache contingent had performed well. All three lieutenants with Randall had led attacks on elements of Delchay's band, killing a total of twenty-four warriors. But they failed to capture Delchay. Nevertheless, Crook recommended brevet promotions for Randall's three subordinates. Then, eager to launch the second phase of his operation, Crook directed Randall to reorganize his force and report as soon as possible to Crook at the rendezvous site at New Camp Grant.[9]

Randall wasted no time. Selecting Brodie to be his second-in-command, the captain ordered all forty-seven Apache scouts, a pack train, four men from I Company led by 1st Sgt. William Allen, one sergeant with twenty-four men from L Troop, and twenty-two men from M Troop, commanded by Sgt. Henry J. Hyde, to accompany him on the second phase of the campaign. For unknown reasons, Corydon Cooley did not participate. Possibly, Mickey Free served as interpreter.[10]

At New Camp Grant, Randall and Brodie joined nine other cavalry troops gathering there with Lt. Colonel Crook to make the final push into Apachería. To make maximum use of Brodie's scouts, Crook placed thirteen of them, along with the twenty-two men from Randall's L Troop, under the operational control of Lieutenant Bourke, who would reinforce M Troop, Fifth Cavalry, commanded by 1st Lt. Jacob Almy. Crook then assigned each of his columns a specific area to reconnoiter, directing them to the next rendezvous at Camp McDowell. Arrangements completed, the colonel departed for Fort Whipple, instructing his aides to provide any further coordinating details. On February 15, Randall and Brodie marched out of New Camp Grant headed north. Other commands departed about the same time.[11]

Eighteen days later, Randall and Brodie reached Camp McDowell, having swept the southern end of the Sierra Ancha Mountains and across the lower Tonto Basin. Disappointed in their march, they encountered no hostiles. A week later, March 4, Almy and Bourke also marched into McDowell. Their route roughly paralleled that of Randall, but they had scouted farther east and north along the San Carlos River. Like Randall, they located no sign of hostile activity.[12]

At Camp McDowell, probably on the advice of one of Crook's aides, Randall again reorganized his shrinking command. He attached nineteen of Brodie's remaining thirty-four scouts to Maj. William H. Brown, who had joined the expedition at New Camp Grant with five troops of the Fifth Cavalry. In compensation, Randall received the services of Mason McCoy, an experienced civilian guide. As the troops prepared to again take the field, a serious epidemic of epizootic, or influenza, broke out among the horses and mules. The disease did not stop the operation, however. It merely forced the cavalrymen, in some cases, to operate on foot, carrying their blankets, rations, and ammunition on their own backs—infantry style.[13]

Under a clear sky and warm temperatures on March 11, Randall and Brodie led their small command out of Camp McDowell. Crossing the Verde River they moved slowly north along the western slope of the Mazatzal Mountains, scouting continuously. After a few days they turned west, re-crossed the Verde and began working the brush-choked hills and ravines on the west bank; but the weather had changed, and a cold rain was beginning to hinder troop movement. Other columns were sweeping the same general area. Major Brown was reconnoitering the Mazatzals to the east, and 1st Lt. Albert E. Woodson with A Troop, Fifth Cavalry, was moving north along the Verde.[14]

Meanwhile, in an effort to intercept a band of Tonto Apaches who had killed three men near Wickenburg the week before, Almy and Bourke led their command into the mountains above New River. Finding no sign of their quarry, the two lieutenants turned east toward the Tonto Basin. The targeted band of Tontos, meanwhile, after shaking Almy's pursuit and eluding at least one other column of soldiers, sought refuge in a favorite camping site on the steep slopes of Turret Mountain. There, on a rock ledge high above the Verde River, Randall found them.[15]

Randall's trail to Turret Mountain and exactly what transpired on the rocky face of that precipice is difficult to unravel. After splashing across the Verde River headed west, undoubtedly on March 21, Randall and Brodie encountered Lieutenant Woodson with A Troop, Fifth Cavalry, camped along the river. Woodson, who had no Indian scouts in his command, was awaiting the return of 1st Sgt. James M. Hill, Sgt. Daniel Bishop, and fourteen men he had sent on foot to scout the hills to the west. Randall and Brodie were present when Hill returned. The sergeant stated that he had jumped a ranchería "near Turret Mountain" on March 22. He reported killing thirteen Tontos and he brought two captured women back with him. One of the women, undoubtedly under considerable pressure from Brodie's scouts, agreed to lead the soldiers to the Apache camp.[16]

Seizing the opportunity to strike a possibly decisive blow at this particular group of hostiles, Randall took charge. Early the following morning, March 23, he set out on foot to locate the Tonto camp. His force included Mason McCoy, five infantrymen from I Company, fifteen Apache scouts, and at least one of the two Tonto women First Sergeant Hill had captured to serve as guide. He also arranged with Lieutenant Woodson to assume operational control of Sergeant Bishop and the twelve men from A Troop that Hill had left near the site of his fight the day before. That group would accompany Randall to the Apache camp. Brodie, much to his disappointment, remained behind with the detachment from M Troop to secure the horses and mules. Lieutenant Woodson, with the bulk of A Troop, bivouacked nearby.[17]

The ensuing battle of Turret Mountain truly is an enigma. Unfortunately, the only contemporary descriptions of the fight are those provided by Bourke and Crook—neither of whom was present. All subsequent accounts have relied almost exclusively on those two sources. Recently,

Turret Mountain Battle site.
Photograph taken from the approximate center of the soldiers' attack position. The Apaches were camped on top of and just below the flat basalt outcropping. Note the ease with which the rock ledge may be scaled in several places. Author's files.

however, additional evidence has come to light revealing serious discrepancies in Bourke's and Crook's long-accepted versions. To understand more accurately what actually took place on Turret Mountain, one must begin with the standard descriptions.

Located nine-and-a-half miles west of the Verde River, oblong-shaped Turret Mountain presents a formidable obstacle, difficult even to approach. Approximately 400 yards in length on the crest and 5,840 feet high, the mountain angles northeast to southwest with a promontory, or turret, on the southwest end. The sides are extremely steep and covered with loose rocks and thick brush. Nearby Bishop Creek provides a reliable water supply.

According to Bourke and Crook, who agreed in substance with only minor variations, the battle took place on the summit. Randall, they reported, using the captured woman as a guide, marched his command partly at night from the Verde River up the steep sides of Turret Mountain. As he approached the sleeping Tonto camp above a rock cliff, or palisade, near the summit, the captain ordered his men to wrap their feet in gunnysacks to deaden any sound of their approach. Just before dawn, the soldiers crawled on their stomachs, single file, through the only break in the protecting rock formation and deployed silently in front of the Indian camp. At first light they charged, killing many Apaches, capturing a few, and throwing the remainder into such panic that some warriors actually leaped to their deaths over a rock ledge. This makes a dramatic tale that certainly inspires the imagination, and it has been told in that fashion many times. A visit to the battlefield, however, reveals clearly that it did not—could not—have happened in that manner.[18]

Historian Dan Thrapp, after failing to reconcile Bourke's and Crook's descriptions with the topography of Turret Mountain, concluded that the battle actually had been fought on Skeleton Ridge, seven miles to the northeast. Thrapp probably was correct in concluding that a skirmish took place on Skeleton Ridge but, if so, undoubtedly it was fought by 1st Sgt. James M. Hill and not by Randall at all. Thrapp failed to locate Randall's battle site on Turret Mountain because he looked in the wrong place. Accepting the standard accounts, Thrapp searched the crest of the mountain, but Randall actually had found the Tontos camped on a low, flat, crescent-shaped rock ledge overlooking a small saddle approximately halfway up the northeast face.[19]

An analysis of all available evidence indicates that Randall left camp on the Verde River on the morning of March 23. By hard marching on foot, probably in part along Bishop Creek, Randall, assuming command of Sergeant Bishop's detachment of A Troop en route, reached the base of Turret Mountain late that same day. After dark, the troopers stealthily climbed out of the creek bed and up the ridge above them. By dawn, Randall had his thirty-four men deployed along the edge of a small, open saddle approximately 300 yards from the unsuspecting Indian camp. As the men lay shivering in the cold mountain air, they easily could see flames from cooking fires flickering against the rocks, clearly marking the Apache position. Randall's skirmish line extended no more than 400 yards in length, with the left flank anchored on top of a ridge overlooking a sheer, rock-strewn, and brush-covered canyon wall dropping off dramatically to the southeast. There would be no escape for the Tontos in that direction.[20]

Behind the ranchería a similar slope leading up the mountain blocked any withdrawal in that direction. The only possible—albeit extremely difficult—escape route would have been across a brush-choked ravine and around the mountain to the northwest. Randall tried to seal that route by extending his right flank into the ravine, probably employing his scouts for that purpose. In short, Randall had his quarry trapped.[21]

At daybreak, Randall ordered his men forward. The troopers withheld their fire until a howl of warning revealed that the Tontos had spotted them. At that point, with their rifles and carbines flashing in the morning gloom, the soldiers swept across the intervening saddle. All used weapons chambered for the standard-issue .50-70 cartridge. The cavalrymen brandished Sharps carbines; the infantrymen and scouts carried modified breech-loading Springfield rifles. The Tontos, realizing that all escape routes had been sealed, recovered quickly from their surprise and fought desperately, but the struggle lasted only two hours. After destroying the Indian camp, Randall's force withdrew, taking captive eight women and leaving twenty-three bodies sprawled in the rocks. A few Apaches, of course, may have slipped away, but it could not have been many. Randall reported no casualties of his own.[22]

Many of the confusing aspects of the Turret Mountain fight may be credited to Bourke's and Crook's obviously incorrect descriptions and the long overlooked role of A Troop's First Sergeant Hill. Although he did not accompany Captain Randall to Turret Mountain, Hill, more than any other person, made Randall's victory possible.

After attacking the Tonto camp "near Turret Mountain" with fifteen men on March 22, Hill would have been eager to locate the main band of Apaches before they slipped away. To do that effectively, however, he needed reinforcements and his commander's approval. Leaving Sergeant Bishop with twelve men near the battle site, Hill with two troopers escorted the two captive women as quickly as possible back to the Verde River, where Woodson and Randall waited. At that point, Randall swung into action.

Early the following morning, March 23, Randall led his composite force toward Turret Mountain. Hill, possibly tired from the previous day's strenuous activity, remained with Woodson. This scenario certainly reveals how and where Randall located the Tonto camp, but it does not explain Crook's and Bourke's garbled accounts. Again, a review of First Sergeant Hill's activities may provide an explanation.[23]

Sergeant Hill's skirmish long has been ignored by writers and historians. We know only that he surprised a ranchería near Turret Mountain on March 22, killing thirteen hostiles and capturing two women. Hill's commander, Lieutenant Woodson, would not have rendered a report of the sergeant's action until both he and Randall reported to Lt. Colonel Crook several days later at Camp Verde. Both officers would have submitted their reports—possibly only verbal—to Crook at about the same time. This raises the distinct possibility that Crook and Bourke, both of whom recorded their accounts several years later, somehow confused the two engagements. It seems probable that it was Sergeant Hill and not Randall at all who, ordering his men to crawl on their bellies up a steep mountain slope at night, surprised a ranchería so completely that some warriors panicked and jumped to their death. It appears that this might well have been the case, unless Bourke and Crook fabricated the entire story, which seems unlikely. Someday, perhaps, an account of Hill's fight will surface and end all speculation.[24]

One aspect of the Turret Mountain affair, however, is clear. Much to his regret, Brodie did not participate, remaining instead in camp along the Verde River until Randall returned. On March 26, probably late in the afternoon, Randall's now reunited command with ten captive women marched into Crook's designated rendezvous site at Camp Verde, where the department commander, who had come down from Fort Whipple, waited to greet his soldiers. Woodson arrived the next day.[25]

For the next several days, Brodie watched other trail-worn troopers with their scouts and captives, if any, straggle into the post. Obviously, the rigorous field duty had taken a toll. Lieutenant Bourke recalled "that a dirtier, greasier, more uncouth-looking set of officers and men it would be hard to encounter anywhere."[26]

The scouts obviously had shared the same discomforts as the soldiers, but the hostiles had suffered even more. They had been ground down by a war of attrition. Outgunned, usually outnumbered, and encumbered by women and children, the fugitives had searched in vain for a safe refuge. For almost four months, often enduring freezing temperatures and floundering through deep snow, they had been hounded from their most remote and secure strongholds by a blue-clad enemy guided by their own people. Many obscure skirmishes high in the mountains were not even recorded. The soldiers left precious few written accounts to tell their side of the story. The Indians left none.

On Sunday, April 6, the formerly hostile Indians officially surrendered. That morning, Brodie and his fellow officers gathered on the parade ground before the commander's quarters to witness the ceremony. Negotiations had scarcely begun when 150 Tontos under Chief Chalipum (or Charlie Pan, as the soldiers called him) unexpectedly crossed the river to surrender. As customary in such situations, there followed a great deal of handshaking, cigarette smoking, and speech making. In the afternoon, after Indian spokesmen had pledged their bands to live at peace, rations were distributed and Brodie's scouts organized a hard-earned victory dance.[27]

Following the ceremony, Crook declared the campaign ended and released his columns to return to their duty stations. But, the fighting was not yet over. Not quite. The elusive Delchay still was loose in the Mazatzals—or Sierra Anchas—or possibly in the Tonto Basin. Randall and Brodie would try and smoke him out.

Randall's route to Camp Apache took him through the heart of the Tonto Basin. Now that he had his entire force of forty-eight soldiers and forty-seven Apache scouts back under his own personal control, the big captain wanted one more crack at the well-known war leader, Delchay. While camped along Tonto Creek on April 22, Randall ordered Brodie to have his scouts make a reconnaissance east toward Canyon Creek. Near Diamond Butte, approximately four miles east of Randall's bivouac, the scouts stumbled across a small ranchería, which they quickly surrounded and placed under fire. Twenty-five Tonto men with an undisclosed number of women and children immediately surrendered. Delchay, however, who up to this point seemed to have had a charmed life, was not present. Apparently, at least one Tonto made his escape to warn Delchay that Crook's troopers again had penetrated his stronghold.[28]

Three days later, as Randall's troopers worked their way along Canyon Creek, five members of Delchay's band carrying a white flag suddenly appeared. Randall and Brodie listened intently as the Tonto delegation requested that their group be permitted to remain unmolested in the Tonto Basin and not be required to settle on a reservation. Such an emotional appeal might well have been successful with a Vincent Colyer or a General Howard, but not with Brodie's crusty commander. Randall simply informed the delegation to make it clear to Delchay that he must have his entire band in Randall's camp by sundown or face extermination. Determined to secure compliance, Randall directed Brodie to have his scouts follow the Indian group back to their camp and monitor their reaction to his ultimatum.[29]

That evening, seeing the handwriting on the wall, Delchay brought his entire band into Randall's camp and surrendered. Randall recalled that Delchay "approached me terribly frightened," stating "that he could not fight the White and Indian soldiers, that he had lost a great many of his people during the past few months and that he had given himself up to save what he had left." Randall, considering the chief's well-known reputation for duplicity, remained convinced that Delchay would continue to pose a problem. Accordingly, he advised the Tonto leader that he "regretted exceedingly that he had surrendered." Nevertheless, Randall pledged to protect the chief as long as he complied with the conditions of surrender.[30]

Delchay's submission ended Lt. Colonel Crook's 1872-73 Tonto Basin campaign. The last major hostile band had capitulated and was on its way to the White Mountain Reservation. The department commander, obviously pleased, recommended a brevet for both Randall and Brodie for the skirmish at Diamond Butte. Randall received the award, but Brodie, for unknown reasons, did not.

No sooner had Brodie returned to Camp Apache than both L and M Troops again were on the move. On April 11, a group of Modocs, after treacherously murdering Brig. Gen. Edward R. S. Canby, commander of the Department of Columbia, at a peace conference in northern California, withdrew into an immense, convoluted lava bed south of Tule Lake. Maj. Gen. John M. Schofield, commander of the Division of the

Pacific, sent a force to dig them out. Seeking reinforcements, Schofield ordered the four battle-tested troops of the First Cavalry still in Arizona to take station in California. L and M Troops, under command of Capt. Moses Harris, who had returned to Camp Apache to assume command of M Troop, rode out of the post on May 18 headed east through Santa Fe toward the railhead at Pueblo, Colorado.[31]

Although Brodie always would be honored in Arizona for participating in Crook's highly successful and popular 1872-73 campaign, his relationship with Captain Randall in the Tonto Basin is disturbing. During the first phase of the operation, Randall had ordered all three officers accompanying him to lead attacks on hostile camps, later recommending that each receive a brevet. In Brodie's case, however, during the second phase, Randall reversed his policy. By personally leading the troopers up Turret Mountain while Brodie remained in camp along the Verde River, Randall denied his lieutenant the opportunity to participate in one of the most important battles of the campaign. To be sure, Sergeant Hyde easily could have handled Brodie's assignment, particularly with Lieutenant Woodson and A Troop bivouacked nearby. Possibly, Randall considered destruction of the enemy force to be so important that he did not want to entrust the mission to a second lieutenant. But, in that event, why did he not take Brodie with him?

Even more puzzling is the manner in which Randall reported the capture of Delchay. Initially, Randall submitted a very brief and casual report of Delchay's capture. Two weeks later, however, responding to a specific request from Crook for additional information regarding the role played by Brodie's scouts, Randall penned a much more detailed account describing the skirmish at Diamond Butte and subsequent surrender of Delchay. Yet, even then, he made no mention of Brodie. Nevertheless, Crook recommended that Brodie be brevetted a first lieutenant for the affair at Diamond Butte. That Brodie never received the award suggests that Randall, Brodie's superior officer, failed to provide sufficient supporting evidence. Again, the situation is not clear, and there may well have been extenuating circumstances, but apparently Randall harbored reservations concerning Brodie's ability as a field soldier.[32]

At any rate, the 2d Lt. Alexander O. Brodie who left Arizona with his troop in the spring of 1873 bore little resemblance to the green young officer who had entered the territory in the fall of 1870. Twenty-eight months of continuous service had left its mark. Brodie had experienced all the normal duties of a subaltern on the frontier. Unfortunately, compared with some of his contemporaries, he had experienced less field duty. Conversely, during his extensive service as post adjutant, he had acquired a superior working knowledge of administration and logistics as related to stationary posts. That would bode well for the future. Junior officers armed with proven administrative ability always would be in demand.

Of course, participation in Crook's expedition into the Tonto Basin would be the highlight of Brodie's tour of duty in Arizona. That operation had provided invaluable training and experience involving small-unit tactics, but something was missing. Because of the small number of troops involved and the very nature of the campaign, Brodie and his contemporaries gained little insight into the command and logistical skills required to control and support large units operating in the field. Brodie had yet to learn there was much more to campaigning against a large, well-armed adversary, such as the Nez Perce Indians, for example, than individual, unsupported, and uncoordinated company-sized operations—no matter how well executed.

CHAPTER 6

"A Constant Throng of the Elite and Fashion"

After nearly three years in Arizona, Brodie spent the next four assigned to duty stations in California and Washington Territory. In contrast to the untamed frontier conditions endemic to sparsely settled Arizona, duty on the Pacific Coast largely consisted of relatively uneventful garrison life near established communities. Initially, Brodie found great personal satisfaction with his assignments, but eventually a devastating personal loss forced him into a painful reassessment of his future in the army.

Anticipating quick deployment against the Modocs, at last report still holding out in the convoluted lava beds near Tule Lake in northern California, Captain Harris, Brodie, and other veterans of Crook's Tonto Basin campaign wasted little time departing Arizona. On May 18, 1873, Harris led 4 officers and 116 enlisted men assigned to L and M Troops, their provisions secured in improvised farm wagons, out of Camp Apache. Following the military road east through Fort Wingate and Santa Fe, the troopers crossed Raton Pass and dropped down to Pueblo, Colorado, where they boarded a train bound for Sacramento. In Wyoming, however, Harris received dispatches informing him that the Modoc War had ended and his services were no longer needed in California. Instead, amended orders directed him to detrain at Cheyenne, march overland to Washington Territory, and report for duty at Fort Walla Walla, a post which once had been abandoned, but now was being reactivated.[1]

Following the end of the Modoc War, which raised fresh concerns for frontier safety in the Pacific Northwest, the War Department decided to rebuild and garrison old Fort Walla Walla. First laid out in 1857 in the rich farmland of southeastern Washington, the fort had been abandoned ten years later and allowed to deteriorate. Local residents, however, now expecting to reap significant economic benefits from a revived military presence in their valley, enthusiastically welcomed Maj. John Green, Brodie's former commander at Camp Apache, who arrived in July with B, F, H, and I Troops, First Cavalry, and Companies B and I, Twenty-first Infantry. All six units had seen action against the Modocs. Harris's arrival with L and M troops raised the assigned strength to fourteen officers and 344 enlisted men, although B, H, and I Troops would be reassigned two months later.[2]

Notwithstanding the deplorable physical conditions the troopers found at old Fort Walla Walla, Brodie and the Arizona veterans appreciated many aspects of their new assignment. They found the Indian situation, for example, to be much more stable than they had experienced previously. All five local tribes were living quietly on reservations. The Umatilla, Walla Walla, and Cayuse occupied an area twenty miles to the south in Oregon. The Yakima lived approximately 100 miles to the northwest, and the Nez Perce, with some exceptions, resided primarily in western Idaho.

Even more important to Crook's veterans was the availability of social amenities not easily found in Arizona. Inhabited by 2,500 civic-minded residents, the village of Walla Walla presented an attractive appearance, with permanent brick commercial buildings arranged along clean, tree-lined streets. Moreover, the friendly residents welcomed garrison personnel into the hotels, restaurants, and saloons. Brodie and other bachelors even found unmarried women receptive to their advances. Recognizing the opportunity, Brodie immediately moved into the local social life.[3]

After seven months of comparative inactivity, Brodie seized what appeared to be a significant career-enhancing opportunity by accepting the position of regimental adjutant. The previous adjutant, Brodie's friend and classmate at the Academy, Lt. James Rockwell, had resigned the position to accept an assignment with the Ordnance Department back East. By September 1, 1874, a paddle wheel riverboat had landed Brodie at Benicia Barracks, California, his new duty station.[4]

Brodie's first view of the impressive red sandstone post buildings confirmed Benicia Barrack's reputation as one of the most coveted duty stations on the West Coast. Located adjacent to the village of Benicia, a community of 1,600 residents on the north bank of Carquinez Strait, where the Sacramento River empties into San Francisco Bay, the military reservation consisted of Benicia Barracks and Benicia Arsenal, two separate but adjacent installations. The First Cavalry Regimental Headquarters, along with A and D Troops and the unit band, occupied the Barracks. Three officers and thirty-five enlisted men garrisoned the Arsenal.[5]

As a line officer, Brodie had always been at the bottom of the pecking order, looking up the chain of command and complaining about a lack of support. Now, as he began viewing the situation through the eyes of a staff officer, he learned to appreciate the complex command and logistical problems which, from the viewpoint of a junior officer stationed at some remote frontier post, did not appear particularly complicated. Brodie had been at Benicia only four months when the regimental commander, Col. Alvin C. Gillem, applied for immediate sick leave. Obviously not in good health, Gillem departed in January and died the following December. Lt. Col. Washington L. Elliott, an 1844 graduate of the Academy with an outstanding Civil War record, assumed temporary command until a colonel could be appointed. Elliott retained Brodie as adjutant.[6]

Social opportunities at Benicia exceeded anything Brodie yet had experienced in his military career. The presence of approximately eighty female students at the exclusive Benicia Young Ladies' Seminary, a forerunner of Mills College, provided one welcome diversion. Booming San Francisco, only thirty miles distant across the bay and easily reached by steamboat, offered its own wide variety of entertainment. Brodie certainly made the trip frequently—often on official business to other military installations—but sometimes for pleasure.[7]

On one of his trips to the city by the Golden Gate, Brodie posed for a formal portrait in his dress uniform, apparently his first since the Academy. The photograph reveals that he had matured in the past four years. His face was fuller, and he now sported a neatly trimmed mustache. Was the portrait intended for a young woman? Subsequent events reveal that a lass in Walla Walla had caught his eye, prevailing over the belles of the Benicia Seminary.

Up to this point, Brodie's career had progressed as expected. He had made all the correct moves normally associated with an officer of his rank. Suddenly, however, he made the first of several decisions which are difficult to understand. Early in 1875, Brodie resigned as adjutant and applied for two months' leave with permission to extend it for an additional ten months—an option he quickly exercised. The former adjutant left Benicia on March 12, headed back to Edwards.

The exact reason Brodie decided to take extended leave still is not clear. Family tradition holds that he went home to help care for his ailing mother. Brodie, himself, later suggested that was the case. There is one puzzling aspect to this explanation, however. Upon departing Benicia, Brodie told Lieutenant Colonel Elliott that he intended to resign his commission upon expiration of his leave. Possibly, Brodie felt that should his mother still be alive at the end of the year, it would be necessary for him to leave the army to care for her.[8]

First Cavalry Regimental Adjutant 2nd Lt. Alexander O. Brodie.
Photograph taken in San Francisco in 1874. Brodie family collection.

Brodie stayed with his family in Edwards for almost the full twelve months. Virtually nothing is known about his activities during that period, but one conclusion is certain. The Brodie household was not the same happy place that he had enjoyed as a boy. In 1873, Alexander's younger brother, Robert, had died in Florida at age twenty-two, probably of tuberculosis. His body had been returned to Edwards for burial in the family plot in the local cemetery. A year later, Brodie's older sister, Harriet Louisa, born in 1848 and married to a Dr. George Reno of Pennsylvania, died in Edwards. Brodie had not returned home for either event. Perhaps he felt guilty about not having been on hand to console his parents on either of those two tragic occasions.[9]

Brodie had been reassigned to M Troop upon resigning as adjutant, but only two months into his leave he received welcome news that he had been promoted to first lieutenant in C Troop. Under existing regulations, all company grade officers received promotions according to seniority, but only to fill existing vacancies within their own regiment. By accepting the promotion, Brodie automatically transferred to C Troop, then posted at Camp McDermit in northern Nevada. That same month, his former unit, M Troop, moved from Fort Walla Walla to Fort Colville in northern Washington.[10]

Early the following year, 1876, Brodie rejoined his regiment. Obviously, he had decided not to resign as he had once indicated. Possibly, the health of his mother had improved to the extent he felt comfortable returning to duty. He did not join C Troop upon arrival in California, however. Instead, on March 1, he relinquished ten days of leave to report on detached status to the Headquarters of the Military Division of the Pacific at San Francisco. Within a week he took charge of sixteen enlisted men and several laundresses, escorting them by ship to Fort Vancouver, Washington. Remaining on detached status, he then conveyed ten recruits up the Columbia River to Fort Walla Walla. Clearly, Brodie was pulling all available strings in order to stay close to Walla Walla. He knew how to work the system.[11]

A month later, Brodie and his hard-drinking, Irish-born friend from Camp Apache, 1st lt. Thomas A. Garvey, agreed to exchange assignments. Garvey, assigned to Fort Colville with M Troop, requested transfer to C Troop to replace Brodie, who would in turn transfer to M Troop. In May, having been granted three weeks' leave, Brodie revealed why he had been so determined to remain near Walla Walla.[12]

On May 27, 1876, in the comfortable Walla Walla home of Resselas (also spelled Rasscellas) P. Reynolds, a local merchant, Brodie married Resselas's nineteen-year-old sister, Kate M. Reynolds. Unfortunately, very little information is available on the ill-fated young woman. A daughter of Almon B. and Harriett Reynolds, Kate was born May 10, 1857, probably in Sterling, Illinois. But her middle name, if any, and the date of her arrival in Walla Walla are not known.

At the time of her marriage, Kate was living with her brother Resselas and his wife Nellie. Kate's brother, a Union veteran of the Civil War, was born in Fort Wayne, Indiana, in 1843. An early settler in the Walla Walla Valley, he arrived in 1866. Kate reached the area later, probably in 1873 or early 1874.[13]

Specific details of the wedding are not a matter of record. It would be expected, of course, that Brodie's friends from the fort formed the traditional arch of crossed sabers for the couple to pass under, but even that honor is not known to have taken place. A local newspaper reported only that "a constant throng of the elite and fashion" attended the reception. At any rate, the newlyweds did not enjoy a traditional honeymoon, instead leaving the next day for Fort Colville. Probably traveling by riverboat, Brodie and his bride reached their destination on June 4. Capt. Moses Harris, Brodie's former comrade in Arizona and now commanding Fort Colville, greeted the couple enthusiastically.[14]

Located thirty-five miles south of the Canadian border, Fort Colville had been established in 1859 in a well-watered valley fourteen miles west of the Columbia River. The area was well known for its rich soil, but the long, cold winters and short growing season so far had deterred rapid growth by settlers. The Columbia River provided easy access from the south by riverboat, and a good wagon road connected the fort with Walla Walla.[15]

The Brodies found garrison life at the fort pleasantly uneventful. The Colville Indians, along with several smaller tribes, lived quietly on their reservation and required no policing by the military. For nine months, Brodie enjoyed the luxury of not even being called upon for court-martial duty or sent in pursuit of deserters. The newlyweds appreciated this period of inactivity, for it enabled them to spend a great deal of time together. It was well they did. A terrible tragedy suddenly befell the Brodie family, leaving the husband deeply scarred for years.[16]

On March 24, 1877, Kate gave birth to a daughter, but the next day died of attending complications in the post hospital. Completely devastated, Brodie could not even take time to grieve. The necessity of caring for his daughter, named Kate M. Louisa, initially kept him occupied. There was much to be done. A wet nurse had to be engaged, a proper coffin had to be ordered from Portland, and the distraught father had to bury his wife temporarily until the casket arrived. Above all, arrangements had to be made to care for the baby. Fortunately, the Reynolds family in Walla Walla stepped forward to assume that responsibility—at least temporarily.[17]

Details are not clear, but in April, Nellie Reynolds graciously traveled to Colville and took charge of Kate. Brodie, meanwhile, after pondering his situation for several weeks, made his decision. On June 9, 1877, he tendered his resignation from the army effective July 31. In the interim, he and Nellie made plans to take the baby to Walla Walla. Captain Harris cooperated fully, assigning Brodie the mission of escorting four prisoners to Fort Canby by way of Walla Walla.

Exactly what Brodie intended to do with his life after discharge is a mystery. He may have intended to stay in Washington and raise his daughter with help from the Reynolds family, or perhaps he planned to return to Edwards, where he could be with his own relatives. In any event, fast-moving conditions soon took that decision out of his hands. Even before Brodie reached Walla Walla, the delicate, on-going negotiations between the army and the Nez Perce Indians exploded. Brodie would put his discharge on hold to once again take the field against hostile Indians.

CHAPTER 7

"A Gallant Soldier and Courteous Gentleman"

On June 19, escorted by five cavalrymen, Brodie rode out of Fort Colville with his daughter, sister-in-law, and four prisoners who had been sentenced to three years of hard labor at Fort Canby for desertion.[1]

Brodie had selected an escort of five reliable men from M Troop, one being the durable bear-killer Pvt. Henry J. Hyde, who had served with Brodie in the Tonto Basin campaign as the ranking sergeant in the M Troop detachment. Hyde subsequently had been discharged at Walla Walla, but later reenlisted as a private. He held Brodie in high regard.[2]

Setting a leisurely pace for his small group moving south on the Walla Walla road in mid-June, Brodie soon picked up disquieting rumors that the situation with the Nez Perce had turned ugly. This probably came as no surprise, for Brodie knew that relations with that tribe had been deteriorating since 1874. Basically, the problem originated with an arbitrary change in the Nez Perce Reservation boundaries.

Upon arriving in the Columbia River Basin in 1805, Anglo-Americans found the Nez Perce to be the locally dominant Indian force. Fifty years later, as settlers began moving into eastern Oregon, the Nez Perce agreed to accept a large reservation encompassing parts of what is now northeast Oregon, southeast Washington, and western Idaho. Later, the government reduced the allocation and limited the reservation to western Idaho. In 1873, by executive order, President Grant returned the Wallowa Valley and surrounding hills in northeast Oregon to the Nez Perce, but two years later rescinded the order.

Several bands of the Nez Perce refused to accept this later modification and continued to live in the disputed valley. Known as the "nontreaty Nez Perce," these groups carefully avoided any confrontation with the ever-encroaching whites. The most influential leader of these dissidents, known as Chief Joseph to the military and settlers, made it clear that he strongly opposed relocating his followers on the reservation.[3]

Realizing that other non-treaty leaders were standing firmly with Joseph on the relocation issue, Gen. Oliver O. Howard, commanding general of the Department of Columbia, moved to break the deadlock. Still basking in the accolades he had acquired for establishing peace with the Chiricahua Apaches in Arizona several years before and confident that he would be equally successful with the Nez Perce, Howard personally held a series of conferences with Joseph and other Indian leaders at Fort Lapwai, approximtely 110 miles east of Walla Walla near the Snake River. This time Howard failed. During the final meeting, the frustrated general finally lost his patience, bluntly informing the Indians that they had only thirty days to relocate to the reservation.[4]

Brodie knew of General Howard's negotiations and final ultimatum long before leaving Fort Colville on June 19. What he did not know at this point was that the situation had gotten completely out of hand. Only two days before, peaceful negotiations with the Nez Perce had gone up in a cloud of rifle smoke along the Salmon River in Idaho.

Upon arrival at Walla Walla, Brodie escorted Nellie and his daughter to the Reynolds's home and then continued to the fort, which he found almost deserted. Only the First Cavalry Headquarters and Band, which recently had been transferred from Benicia Barracks, remained on post. The three assigned cavalry troops and two infantry companies already had joined General Howard in the field. After turning his four prisoners over to the post guard detail, Brodie reported to his regimental commander, Col. Cuvier Grover, who had replaced Lt. Colonel Elliott. Grover and another officer on post, 1st Lt. Frank K. Upham, Brodie's friend from his days at Camp Apache, explained the situation. It was not good.[5]

The non-treaty Nez Perce at first, Grover related, had showed signs of complying with General Howard's ultimatum, but as the deadline for the Indians to be on the reservation approached, members of White Bird's band killed several settlers along the Salmon River. Fighting quickly spread and white farmers in the area appealed to the army for protection. Howard sent F and H Troops, First Cavalry, led by Capt. David Perry, a veteran of the Modoc uprising, to determine the extent of the trouble and reestablish control. Whatever happened, Howard cautioned Perry: "You must not get whipped."[6]

At daybreak on June 17, Perry, having located a Nez Perce village at the mouth of White Bird Canyon on the Salmon River, formed F and H Troops on line to attack. But the non-treaties struck first. Swarming unexpectedly out of concealed positions in ravines along Perry's route of march, the Nez Perce warriors unleashed rifle blasts of devastatingly accurate fire into the flanks of the advancing cavalrymen. Perry's troopers quickly fell back in disorder. Realizing he was about to be overrun, Perry skillfully rallied his demoralized force and fought a series of delaying actions back toward Fort Lapwai. He lost one officer and thirty-three men.[7]

As one would expect, Perry's defeat badly rattled the command structure of the Department of Columbia. Deliberate and cautious Brigadier General Howard, known to the Indians as "Cut Arm" because of his missing right arm, initially failed to support Perry with additional troops until he first could assemble a strong force at Fort Lapwai. Later, after considering Perry's battle report and undoubtedly remembering George A. Custer's debacle with the Seventh Cavalry on the Little Bighorn the year before, Howard sent for more reinforcements, even requesting that units be sent to him from stations beyond his own department.[8]

A field soldier by preference, Brodie could not resist putting his personal problems behind him and making the necessary arrangements to join Howard's campaign, but first he had to deliver his prisoners to Fort Canby. Returning to Walla Walla in mid-July, he found that additional fighting had taken place. Again, events had not gone well for Howard, particularly at the battle of the Clearwater, where the Nez Perce had fought him to a standstill. Nevertheless, Howard doggedly established a temporary camp 150 miles southwest of Lewiston and laid plans to resume the offensive.[9]

At Brodie's request, Colonel Grover placed a hold on his pending resignation and directed him to report on detached duty to General Howard. After saying goodbye to his daughter, then almost four months old, Brodie headed for Howard's bivouac. Four days later, July 18, he reached the general's field headquarters.

Pleased to have another experienced troop officer join him, Howard, who possibly remembered meeting Brodie at Camp Apache in 1872, attached his newly arrived lieutenant to Captain Perry's badly decimated F Troop, which had one officer, Perry, and fewer than thirty men present for duty. The troop suffered from low morale. In addition to the mauling taken at White Bird Canyon, Perry's troopers had performed poorly at the battle of Clearwater. Clearly, the troop needed all the help it could get.[10]

Meanwhile, Howard received information revealing that the Nez Perce were withdrawing east across the Bitterroot Mountains toward

Missoula, Montana. Technically, once the Indians crossed the Continental Divide, they would be outside the Department of Columbia and no longer Howard's problem. Nevertheless, Gen. William Tecumseh Sherman, Commanding General of the Army, directed Howard to continue in pursuit. But Howard did not move immediately. Instead, he waited for additional reinforcements, at the same time organizing his force into three columns.[11]

The right (or south) column, commanded by Howard personally, would follow Chief Joseph over the Lolo Trail into Montana. The left column, headed by Col. Frank Wheaton with the Second Infantry Regiment, which had been sent all the way from Georgia in response to Howard's appeal for reinforcements, would assemble at Fort Lapwai, march north toward Spokane, turn east, cross the Bitterroots, and swing south toward Missoula. Hopefully, these two commands would trap the Nez Perce between them. A third force of cavalry led by Maj. John Green would remain in reserve and patrol the Clearwater-Salmon-Snake River complex. Howard assigned F Troop, with Brodie attached, to Wheaton's command.[12]

Pleased to be back on duty with F Troop in the field, Brodie did not have much time to become acquainted with his comrades. On the same day that Brodie reported to Perry for duty, F Troop broke camp and made a forced march to join Colonel Wheaton's column, then gathering at Fort Lapwai and at Lewiston. Perry's force went into bivouac near Fort Lapwai at 3:00 a.m. on July 20. The troop had made good time, marching seventy miles through hostile territory in less than forty-eight hours.[13]

Within a week, Brodie's personal life abruptly took another downward turn. On July 25, his little daughter died suddenly of unknown causes. Because no telegraph service connected Forts Walla Walla and Lapwai, news of the infant's death did not reach the father until July 27 at the earliest. As far as Brodie's military career was concerned, the death of little Kate seems to have been the proverbial straw that broke the camel's back. On July 28, he rode into the military compound at Lewiston to discuss his situation with Colonel Wheaton, who agreed to detach Brodie from F Troop and assign him temporary duty at Lewiston until August 28. On that date, unless he changed his mind during the preceding thirty day cooling off period, Brodie would be granted a month's leave and his pending resignation would be reactivated effective September 30, 1877. Officials in the War Department, however, questioned Wheaton's authority to make these arrangements.[14]

The Adjutant General of the Army, considering it irregular for the commander of the Second Infantry to endorse the resignation of an officer assigned to the First Cavalry, requested clarification. Wheaton replied that he considered Brodie to be under his jurisdiction because the lieutenant, by competent authority, had been attached to F Troop, which was assigned to Fort Lapwai. As senior officer present, Wheaton had been placed in command of that post and all units in the vicinity. No further objections emanated from Washington, DC, but Captain Harris at Fort Colville harbored his own thoughts on the matter.[15]

Harris pointed out that Brodie had departed Fort Colville owing Mrs. Mary Kiesulo, the hospital matron, $160 for laundry services and the post quartermaster $80 for subsistence stores and quartermaster clothing, significant sums for a lieutenant whose monthly salary amounted to $146.76. In view of these obligations, Harris recommended that "action on Lieutenant Brodie's resignation should be delayed until he has made some arrangement for the payment of these debts." A lack of follow-up from Harris suggests that Brodie, who always seemed to have had money available, obviously from his parents, resolved the matter to his captain's satisfaction.[16]

The closing days of Brodie's military career proved uneventful. Waiting for his discharge on detached duty at Lewiston, he performed whatever assignments came his way, including commanding routine patrols and delivering dispatches. Finally, on August 27, approval arrived for his resignation to be effective September 30, following a thirty-day leave. Although technically still on duty for three more days, Brodie immediately departed for his home in New York. Regrettably, in his haste to leave the Pacific Northwest, he did not linger even long enough to ensure proper burial of his wife.[17]

Following Kate's death in March, Brodie had arranged to have shipped from Portland a metal coffin inscribed with his wife's name and age. Pending arrival of the casket, he had buried his spouse temporarily in the post cemetery. When the coffin arrived, however, Brodie already had departed for Walla Walla. Obviously, he intended to return to Colville and attend to the burial, but the Nez Perce War intervened, and he never returned to the place of Kate's death. Seven years later, the casket remained forgotten and still unused in a post warehouse. Meanwhile, the temporary marker identifying Kate's grave disappeared, and her burial site reportedly no longer could be identified.[18]

Surely, Kate M. Reynolds Brodie deserved better treatment from her husband than to have been committed in a temporary coffin to an inadequately marked grave. Brodie's callous handling of his wife's remains was not his finest hour.

The exact reason Brodie resigned never has been determined, but years later he offered his most complete extant explanation to his cousin in Scotland. "I resigned from the service," Brodie wrote, "at my father's request and in order to keep a promise I had made to my mother to come to her when she needed me." Clearly, this explanation does not tell the complete story. Brodie's reluctance to even acknowledge to his cousin the impact of his wife and daughter's deaths certainly clouds the issue. With the passage of time, the facts and legends surrounding his resignation have become inextricably woven together. It is clear, however, that more than one issue affected the decision.[19]

There is little doubt that the 1874 illness of Margaret Brodie caused her son to take an extended leave to visit her. At the time, Brodie may have seriously considered resigning, but his return to duty a year later and subsequent marriage indicates that he had decided to remain in the army. Following the untimely death of his wife, however, Brodie submitted a resignation, which he withdrew to participate in the Nez Perce War. Then, shortly after learning of his daughter's death, he even lost interest in that still unfinished campaign and did, in fact, resign. This sequence of events suggests that grief became Brodie's primary motivating factor in deciding to leave the army. The loss of his family would haunt him for many years to come.

Brodie's resignation did not pass unnoticed in Walla Walla. As the former officer left Washington Territory, a local newsman, pointing out that Brodie had once withdrawn his resignation to take the field against the Nez Perce, commented that the army "lost a gallant soldier and courteous gentleman when Lieut. Brodie resigned."[20]

The long journey by rail back to Edwards afforded Brodie ample opportunity to reflect upon his seven years in the First Cavalry. Except for the past few stressful months, it had been a rewarding experience. His three years in Arizona, by any criteria an exciting and challenging period, had provided more than one opportunity to trade shots with hostile Apaches. In contrast with Arizona, however, duty in the Pacific Northwest, except for the Nez Perce troubles, had been largely routine, almost mundane. To be sure, he had experienced the joy of taking a young bride with intentions of starting a family, but the untimely death of his wife and daughter shattered that dream. Deeply wounded by the twin tragedies and evidently striving to put them behind him, Brodie chose to abandon his once-promising army career—a decision he would soon regret.

CHAPTER 8

"Moving About"

For nearly ten years following his resignation from the army, Brodie encountered much difficulty adjusting to civilian life. In his own words, he spent much of that decade "moving about."[1]

Although Brodie returned to Edwards following his resignation ostensibly to help care for his ailing mother, he did not remain long in the place of his birth. Conditions in the Brodie household had changed dramatically. The exact sequence of events still is unclear, but Alexander's father was in the process of selling his holdings in St. Lawrence County with the intention of moving with his wife to Clinton, Iowa, where they would live with the couple's surviving daughter, Elizabeth, and her growing family. Elizabeth's recent marriage had made it possible for her to care for her aging parents in her home—a common practice at the time.[2]

Born in 1853, Elizabeth, known to her friends as "Lizzie," or "Tillie," in 1875 married William Austin Bignall, a thirty-three-year-old resident of Gouverneur, New York. The newlyweds moved to Clinton, where Bignall established a grocery and retail tobacco business. The couple started their family and two years later welcomed Lizzie's parents into their home. Joseph, an experienced retailer, may have assisted his son-in-law's mercantile endeavor.[3]

Unfortunately, Margaret Brodie's health did not improve in Iowa, for she died in Clinton on July 17, 1878, at age fifty. Joseph, Alexander, and Lizzie, along with her two small children, accompanied Margaret's body back to Edwards for interment in the local cemetery next to Margaret's youngest son Robert, and eldest daughter Harriet. By a strange coincidence, Margaret's eighty-five-year-old father, James Brown, died in Edwards only two days after the death of his daughter. Consequently, a simultaneous service, described as a "double funeral," was held in the Edwards Union Church, with the two caskets arranged side by side. Following the burial, Joseph and Alexander, concluding that nothing remained for them in New York, made plans to move west, eventually settling in southeast Kansas.[4]

Late in the summer of 1878, with Alexander apparently waiting in New York, Joseph purchased 640 acres of prime farmland in Greenwood County for $1,200 and immediately asked Alexander to join him. The two Brodies soon abandoned their Kansas project, however. Joseph left first. In 1881, after selling the farm to his son for $3,000, Joseph returned to Clinton. Less than a year later, the younger Brodie, who had shifted the emphasis from farming to ranching, sold the property for $7,000 and dropped out of sight.[5]

For the next five years, with one brief exception, few clues indicate Alexander Brodie's location and activities. Some sources suggest he entered the mining business in the Dakota Territory and/or Colorado, but such reports never have been confirmed. Brodie, himself, avoided any clear reference to this obscure part of his life. In a letter to his cousin in Scotland, he dismissed quickly most of his activities in the decade following his 1877 resignation from the army. "I was engaged," he wrote, "first in the cattle business in Kansas for four years, then moving about for sometime and from '87 on, as a mining and civil engineer in Arizona." Strangely, he did not even reveal the peculiar circumstances surrounding a brief return to Arizona in 1883.[6]

On August 6, 1883, acting on an impulsive decision that he later rarely mentioned and apparently never explained, Brodie walked into the recruiting office at Jefferson Barracks, Missouri, and enlisted for five years in M Troop, Sixth Cavalry, commanded by Capt. William A. Rafferty, an 1865 graduate of the Military Academy. If Brodie selected Rafferty's troop expecting to see field duty in the twilight hours of the Geronimo campaign then in progress, he had made a wise choice. M Troop, stationed at Fort Bowie, a three-company post located only fifty-five miles north of Mexico in southeastern Arizona, was ideally located to prevent Apache bands from moving back and forth across the Mexican border. Nevertheless, Brodie quickly became thoroughly disillusioned with his assignment.[7]

Arriving at Fort Bowie on September 10, Brodie learned that he would not campaign with his troop as he had expected. Instead, he had been detailed to the post quartermaster. Captain Rafferty, in his dual role of troop and post commander, concluded it would be a waste of manpower to send a West Point graduate with seven years' experience into the field as a private in the ranks. Brodie, of course, who genuinely enjoyed field duty, resented his captain's decision. Later that same month, he stood glumly on the parade ground watching Rafferty lead his troop out of the fort on an extended scouting mission south into the towering Chiricahua Mountains. Unfortunately, this proved to be only the beginning of Brodie's disillusionment with Fort Bowie.[8]

On November 20, Brodie's service as an enlisted man came to an inglorious end. Leopold O. Parker, captain of F Company, First Infantry, and acting post commander during Captain Rafferty's absence, ordered Brodie arrested and thrown into the post guardhouse pending a general court-martial. The charges are not known, but they must have been compelling, for Rafferty did not rescind Parker's action upon his return three days later. Brodie, meanwhile, pondering from the close confines of the guardhouse the sudden collapse of his second attempt to establish a military career, decided to avoid the stigma of a trial by applying for a discharge. He hoped to benefit from an infrequently used regulation authorizing the Adjutant General of the Army, on an individual basis, to discharge a soldier prior to the expiration of a five-year enlistment.[9]

Fortunately for Brodie, his gamble succeeded. The Adjutant General approved his request and the discharge order reached Fort Bowie before the court-martial board convened. Rafferty, however, did not process the discharge. Instead, it was handled by Maj. David Perry, Brodie's former commander in the Nez Perce campaign, who had been promoted and attached to Fort Bowie as post commander.[10]

Major Perry must have been shocked to find one of his former troop officers from Washington Territory confined to the guardhouse at remote Fort Bowie in Arizona, but there was little he could do to influence the situation. Events had moved far beyond his authority to interfere. Nevertheless, Perry did what he could, making sure for example that Brodie's character was recorded as "excellent" on the trooper's discharge papers—an unusually high recommendation for a man who had served sixty-four days under arrest and confinement. Remembering the traumatic personal tragedies which had so badly shaken Brodie at Forts Colville and Walla Walla, Perry obviously considered the former lieutenant's past services in making his final evaluation. On February 4, 1884, with his discharge in his saddlebags and enlisted military career behind him, Brodie rode out of Fort Bowie into temporary obscurity. For the next four years, his activities are almost completely unknown.[11]

The sudden erratic behavior which characterized Brodie's last few months in the First Cavalry and period immediately thereafter is difficult to explain. Until 1877, his career had progressed as expected. Reputedly capable, reliable, and noted for making sound decisions, he generally was held in high regard by both associates and superior officers. His sudden resignation, spur-of-the-moment enlistment, and subsequent incarceration at Fort Bowie, however, reveal that his personal life had gone awry. Brodie's unusual actions, begun in the summer of 1877, coupled with his later well-known reputation for excessive drinking, suggests strongly that following the death of his wife and daughter he became, as plainspoken Arthur L. Tuttle later expressed it, "a booze fighter."[12]

By 1898, when Brodie had been back in Arizona for approximately ten years, many of his friends believed that he had resigned his commission to avoid a court-martial for excessive drinking. For example, Robert Brow, a Prescott saloonkeeper and former partner with Brodie in a local mining venture, made public that allegation. The problem with Brow's assertion is that absolutely no hard evidence has ever surfaced indicating that drinking played a role in Brodie's 1877 resignation. The discharge at Fort Bowie in 1884 is another matter entirely.[13]

All available evidence suggests that Captain Parker ordered Brodie arrested for reasons associated with liquor. Brodie's early discharge, however, prevented Parker's accusations from becoming a matter of public record. Undoubtedly, Robert Brow and others, responding to rumors, confused the circumstances surrounding Brodie's 1877 resignation with his 1884 discharge. Brodie's alcoholic legacy as an enlisted man inadvertently had become associated with Brodie as an officer.

One conclusion is clear, however. When Brodie again returned to Arizona in 1887 or 1888, he had changed. Somehow, during his four or five year absence, he had successfully put his life back together. Perhaps, during the sixty-four day respite of forced sobriety in the Fort Bowie guardhouse, he had come to realize the folly of his recent behavior. To be sure, Brodie did continue to imbibe—certainly sometimes to excess—but he never again permitted his fondness for liquor to interfere unduly with his business or professional life.

CHAPTER 9

"The Water Is Upon Us"

Brodie's precipitous decline from respected army officer to disgraced private released from the Fort Bowie guardhouse to be discharged must have weighed heavily on the Military Academy graduate. After leaving the army he spent four years struggling to resolve the emotional problems that had plagued him since the death of his wife at Fort Colville. Finally, satisfied that he had regained control of his personal life, he again turned to Arizona.

Details of how he secured the position are not known, but in the summer of 1888 Brodie rode into Prescott as the newly hired assistant engineer of the Walnut Grove Water Storage Company. The firm recently had completed an impressive masonry dam for placer mining purposes in a small valley called Walnut Grove on the Hassayampa River thirty miles south of Prescott. Spanning a narrow channel of the river between two sheer granite cliffs, the 110-foot high structure measured 100 feet along the base and 410 feet across the top. A wooden intake tower in the lake contained hydraulic-operated gates designed to regulate downstream flow through two iron pipes positioned through the bottom of the dam. As Brodie soon would learn, however, the appearance of stability proved illusional. The Walnut Grove project had a checkered existence from the very beginning.[1]

A brainchild of Wells H. Bates, a thirty-four-year-old entrepreneur from New York with a particular interest in mining, plans for the Walnut Grove dam and attending water storage project first took root in 1882. That year, upon surveying the gold-bearing sands along the Hassayampa and its tributaries, Bates concluded that a California-style hydraulic mining operation could be successful provided that an adequate water supply could be developed. Securing the financial backing

New York entrepreneur Henry Spingler Van Beuren financed development of the Crown Point mine and served as president of the Walnut Grove Water Storage Company. Joseph Wittmann collection.

of New York colleagues, he organized under Kentucky law two corporations to launch the enterprise. The Walnut Grove Water Storage Company had the responsibilty to build a dam across the Hassayampa River, and the Piedmont Cattle Company would help secure mineral rights and access to the area by purchasing two large existing ranches.[2]

Construction of the dam commenced in 1886, but unforeseen problems surfaced almost immediately. Within a year, financial difficulties forced Bates to relinquish control of the water storage company to other investors, resulting in personnel changes that rocked the firm for two years. The company also abandoned Bates's original plan of using the lake at Walnut Grove as a direct source of water. Instead, a smaller dam would be constructed fifteen miles downstream. As needed, water would be released from the primary reservoir to the smaller diversion dam, where it would be pumped through wooden flumes to the placer fields some distance away. Assistant Engineer Brodie had the responsibility to oversee construction of the diversion or "lower dam."[3]

Brodie's employment at Walnut Grove coincided with a significant change in company management. In July, a wealthy New York stockholder, Henry Spingler Van Beuren, arrived at Walnut Grove to personally assess company operations. A recent investor and newly elected president of the Walnut Grove Water Storage Company, Van

Beuren took his duties seriously. Before returning to New York a few weeks later, Van Beuren had made it clear that he considered himself to be the driving force behind the Walnut Grove project. Moreover, Brodie had so impressed Van Beuren that the president considered his assistant engineer to be the most capable employee on site.[4]

Under Brodie's aggressive supervision, construction of the diversion dam moved forward rapidly. By the end of the year, his crews had the structure nearly completed, but the following March a late winter storm drenched the Bradshaw Mountains. Swollen with runoff, the Hassayampa filled the main reservoir to capacity and sent dark-colored water racing through the spillway, which quickly became congested with logs and other debris. Workers frantically and successfully cleared the jam, but little could be done to protect the nearly completed diversion dam downstream, which disappeared in a torrent of muddy water as did enough lumber stacked nearby to construct fifteen miles of flume.[5]

Chief Engineer and Superintendent John E. Anderson directed Brodie to rebuild immediately. Constructed of quarried stone, the new diversion dam would be 220 feet long and 44 feet high. But that summer, Brodie unexpectedly accepted a position in El Paso, Texas, with the United States Hydrological Commission. In less than two months, however, Van Beuren summoned him back to Walnut Grove.[6] Apparently upset over a lack of progress at Walnut Grove, Van Beuren tendered the position of general superintendent and chief engineer to Brodie, who immediately accepted. Obviously, Van Beuren had lost confidence in Anderson and for some time had been looking for an opportunity to replace the engineer. As early as the previous December, Van Beuren and Assistant Engineer Brodie had been corresponding directly regarding company matters which should have been handled by the chief engineer.[7]

Assuming his new office on July 31, 1889, Brodie moved quickly to neutralize persistent rumors then rife in Yavapai County that serious structural deficiencies existed in the main dam. Assuring the Yavapai County Board of Supervisors that the structure "is built in a thoroughly solid and stable manner," Brodie emphasized that a safety valve had been installed by cutting a five by twenty-five foot "waste way" through solid rock near the dam on the west side.[8]

As the year came to a close, Van Beuren returned to help push the project to its final conclusion. By nature a "hands-on" type of executive, the millionaire could not resist involvement in decision making on a day-to-day basis. As usual, his devoted daughter, Eleanor "Nell" Cecilia Van Beuren, accompanied him. On this trip, however, Nell brought a traveling companion with her, a slender, dark-haired fourth

Walnut Grove Dam.
Photograph probably taken early 1889 showing the partially filled lake. Joseph Wittmann collection.

cousin from Morristown, New Jersey, named Mary Louise Hanlon. In addition, two employees completed Van Beuren's small traveling entourage: Nell's maid, a forty-year-old Irish immigrant named Hannah McCarty, and coachman Alexander McMillan. Brodie took one look at the twenty-five-year-old Mary Hanlon and liked what he saw.

Shortly before Christmas, with the lower dam and flume system nearly completed, Van Beuren ordered pumps, hoses, and other hydraulic equipment necessary to begin actual mining shipped from California. For the next few weeks, he and his entourage waited at Headquarters Camp, a comfortable house the company had built on the Hassayampa riverbank five miles below the diversion dam. Brodie and James Redington, a newly hired hydraulic engineer from California, who later proved to be a good man to have on hand during an emergency, occupied the dwelling with them.[9]

Advised finally that three carloads of the long-awaited equipment had arrived in Phoenix, Van Beuren asked Brodie, Nell, and Mary Hanlon to accompany him on Tuesday, February 18, 1890, to the territorial capital, where he would arrange to transport the machinery to Walnut Grove. Brodie, who already was actively courting Mary, welcomed the opportunity to entertain the young woman in Phoenix. On Tuesday, however, a light rain fell, causing Van Beuren to delay the trip one day.[10]

By Wednesday, Mary had changed her mind. As originally planned, Van Beuren's departure would leave Hannah McCarty, Nell's Irish maid, the only woman at Headquarters Camp. Hannah confided to Mary that she did not want to remain alone with the men. Reluctantly—very reluctantly—Mary agreed to stay with Hannah. On Wednesday, just prior to Brodie's and Van Beuren's departure, Mary, choking back tears of disappointment, informed Brodie that she would not accompany him to Phoenix.[11]

A disappointed Brodie found the two-day stagecoach trip to Phoenix to be an unhappy experience. Ominous slate gray clouds scuttling in from California hung low to the ground, dumping almost continuous rain, turning to snow at the higher elevations. At Phoenix, Saturday passed without incident, but Sunday afternoon after church, Brodie and Van Beuren received stunning news that the Walnut Grove dam had washed away with considerable loss of life. Brodie reacted immediately, leaving early the following morning on horseback. Van Beuren initially remained in Phoenix, agreeing to meet Brodie at Walnut Grove later.[12]

At Walnut Grove, Brodie found the devastation far worse than he expected. The upper dam had disappeared almost completely, leaving only a clump of masonry clinging to one canyon wall. Two company employees, Assistant Engineer Thomas Brown and James C. Hunt, provided Brodie with vivid descriptions of the dam's collapse. This was the same James Hunt who eighteen years earlier had served as Brodie's troop commander at Camp Apache. Following his forced resignation from the army in 1872, the former captain had remained in the Prescott area, eventually finding employment at Walnut Grove.[13]

Acting Chief Engineer Brown explained that he had made every effort to avoid the tragedy. Upon realizing early Friday afternoon that the spillway and twin discharge pipes could not handle the flood water cascading out of the Bradshaws, Brown ordered a fifteen-man crew to enlarge the spillway, but his effort proved too little and too late. By midafternoon, water began pouring over the top of the dam. Convinced that the structure soon would collapse, Brown mounted Dan Burke, a company blacksmith, on the best horse available and sent him to warn the construction workers and others living along the river below. By 9:00 p.m. with a three-foot wall of water still roaring over the dam, Brown dispatched a second messenger, William Akard. It was well he did, for Akard encountered Burke drunk at a nearby saloon. The alarm, which Brown tried so hard to sound, had not been given, and Akard, in the darkness, did not have time to complete Burke's mission.[14]

With Brown and Hunt watching helplessly in the moonlight, the end came shortly after midnight. A steel cable supporting the intake tower suddenly separated with a loud crack. The tower swayed briefly and then collapsed. At that point the entire dam, apparently moving as a single unit, simply disappeared. A wall of water estimated at fifty to sixty feet high thundered down the canyon, sweeping everything before it. Hunt recalled that the "roar of the water sounded like that of Niagara Falls, only tenfold greater."[15]

Rescue and salvage operations, Brodie learned, had begun immediately. On Saturday afternoon, within two hours after learning of the dam's collapse, Brodie's friend, Yavapai County Sheriff William Owen "Buckey" O'Neill, rode out of Prescott at the head of a relief party. By late Monday, O'Neill's group had located and buried forty victims, including five children. Eleven bodies, stripped of clothing by the violence of the water, were so badly battered that they could not be identified. Most survivors remained convinced that additional bodies would be uncovered in the silt and mud of the riverbed farther downstream, as a number of Walnut Grove residents had not yet been accounted for.[16]

Sheriff O'Neill's efficient relief efforts left little for Brodie to accomplish other than show the company flag and console survivors. His primary personal concern, of course, was the safety and well-being of Mary Hanlon. Upon learning that she had been taken to Martinez Ranch, a few miles below the lower dam site, Brodie headed in that direction. At the ranch, he found Mary and Van Beuren, who had arrived from Phoenix, waiting for him.[17]

Mary, who had reached the ranch Sunday evening, had just finished writing her mother a graphic account of her narrow escape. After Van Beuren, Nell, and Brodie departed for Phoenix on Wednesday, Mary, swallowing her disappointment, concluded to make the best of her situation. She and Hannah McCarty, the Irish housekeeper, intended to enjoy a few relaxing days until Van Beuren returned. James Redington and the Van Beuren coachman, Alexander McMillan, a sixty-year-old Scot with twinkling blue eyes and a fine sense of humor, occupied the house with the two women. The pleasant situation changed that evening when the storm blew in from California. By Thursday, with heavy rain still falling, the river in front of the house began to rise rapidly. On Friday, Mary noticed that Redington and McMillan were watching carefully as the river crept higher. The rain, however, had tapered off. After dark, the two men built a large fire on the riverbank, enabling them to continue their vigil that night.[18]

At 10:00 p.m. Redington appeared for a quick dinner, advising the two women not to go to bed early. An hour later, he returned to inform Mary and Hannah, who had been chatting about Hannah's girlhood in Ireland, that the water appeared to be receding and they could retire.

Martinez Ranch, headquarters of the Piedmont Cattle Company, where Mary Hanlon recovered from the Walnut Grove flood. Author's files.

Nevertheless, Redington assured the women he would continue his watch. Still apprehensive—possibly even harboring a premonition—Mary, before retiring, left a lamp burning in the sitting room and laid out clothes for herself and for Hannah on a nearby chair.

The next sound Mary heard was Redington shouting an urgent warning: "Girls, get up, get up. The water is upon us." Mary immediately jumped out of bed and, without pausing to dress, ran through the open door into Hannah's bedroom. The night of terror had begun.

As Mary explained to her mother, she found Hannah standing immobile in her nightclothes. Hearing Redington call again, Mary dashed through the sitting room toward the front door, imploring her friend to follow. Realizing as she reached the entrance that the maid was not behind her, Mary returned to the bedroom, again calling for Hannah to follow. But the terrified servant refused to move, protesting that she was not dressed. "'Come, come' again I shrieked, but she stood like a statue. Mother, can I ever forget it? I turned and fled, she would not come, petrified by terror."

Meanwhile, the faithful horseman, McMillan, ran to the stables to release the animals. He was not fast enough. As Mary ran from the house, she heard the middle-aged Scot scream as the flood smashed into the stables with a sound "like boards being split." Redington, racing for higher ground ahead of Mary, kept extorting her to run for her life. In pain, terrified and barefoot, the hapless woman stumbled her way up the slope through rocks, brush, and cactus for approximately 200 feet. Below her, "the waters sounded like thunder—louder than thunder and the great boulders of rock as they rolled and split like cannon." Exhausted, Mary suddenly fell, but Redington swiftly turned, picked up his companion and carried her to safety. "To him, Mama," Mary confided, "you owe the little my life is worth."

Pausing on the steep slope above the river, Redington took stock. The night was cold, and Mary's clothing had been ripped to shreds. In fact, her condition may have been worse than she confided to her mother. Brodie family tradition holds that Mary's nightdress had been fastened at the throat with a high Prussian collar. When she reached safety on the ridge above the river, only the collar remained—everything else having been ripped away. Naturally, Mary did not want to confide to her very proper mother that she had scampered nude up a canyon wall while accompanied by a man. At any rate, Redington wrapped Mary in his coat and placed his socks on her swollen, bleeding feet. His efforts to kindle a fire failed, but the engineer noticed flames flickering in the darkness not far away. The pair slowly made their way over the rocky hillside in that direction. They found five men huddled around a small fire trying to stay warm. All five greeted Mary with kindness, wrapping her in their only blanket and positioning her close to the fire. One man gave Mary his socks—Redington's having been shredded during her trek toward the fire.[19]

Just before dawn, several other destitute survivors joined Redington's group, having been attracted by the fire. At daybreak, Redington organized a search of the canyon below. One group soon returned with two women and five children. Mary shared her blanket with three of the youngest. One of the men, who had managed to salvage some provisions, prepared a late breakfast for the entire group. Later, three more men arrived carrying additional food.

On Saturday, Mary spent another cold and uncomfortable night on the mountain, but Sunday morning, Redington awakened her with the welcome news that a group from the Piedmont Cattle Company, bringing food and clothing, had arrived at the river below. One of the ranch hands would take Mary on his horse to the Martinez Ranch.

Working her way slowly down the hillside toward the riverbed, Mary scarcely could believe the devastation that unfolded before her. "Momsey, dear Momsey," she wrote, "never shall I forget the scene that greeted my eyes when we went down to the place where our cozy, happy home had been nothing but a stretch of barren glistening sand. . . . Oh my God, it was awful." At the river, a cowboy waited to take her across the still-flowing stream on his horse. "I put on his overalls and sat straddle behind him with my arms around him," Mary continued. "Surely he will never be held tighter." Late Sunday afternoon, the pair rode into the Martinez Ranch. Mary's two-day ordeal finally ended.[20]

Joining Mary and Van Beuren at the ranch, Brodie expected to depart immediately for Prescott, but Mary wanted to rest a few days first. The delay afforded an opportunity for the two men to discuss the future of the Walnut Grove project. Van Beuren, considering the collapse of the dam to be only a temporary setback, planned to rebuild, but obviously there first would be legal obstacles to overcome. In early March, with Mary well on the road to recovery, Van Beuren's group returned to Prescott.

At the mile-high city, Brodie found that he and Van Beuren were not being blamed for the disaster—at least publicly. Van Beuren's handling of the company financial obligations helped influence public opinion in that regard. Although the company records had been lost in the flood, Van Beuren honored without question all claims for wages due and other alleged company debts.

On March 15, a group of flood survivors, accompanied by the Fort Whipple Military Band, gathered at Van Beuren's hotel to present a testimonial. With Van Beuren, Brodie, and Mary gathered on a balcony, the spokesman, a local judge, praised Van Beuren for paying all company debts. Then, ignoring Redington's actions on the ridge above Headquarters Camp, he surprisingly singled out Mary Hanlon addressing her as a "heroic lady" who had organized rescue efforts the day after the flood. Your conduct, the judge assured Mary, "will live in the memory of our people as long as they remember the fearful disaster." The judge concluded by presenting Van Beuren with a five and a quarter ounce gold nugget, which had been picked up below the dam site after the flood. Van Beuren responded with a few remarks as did Mary, undoubtedly embarrassed by the totally unwarranted praise she had received. Brodie declined to comment in deference to the late hour.[21]

Brodie and Van Beuren found professional engineers across the country to be far less forgiving. Some contemporaries blamed the dam's collapse on faulty overall design. Others pointed to the obviously inadequate spillway. Still another group claimed the break resulted from shoddy workmanship by the contractor and inadequate supervision by qualified engineers.[22]

Remembering the lessons in public relations he had learned many years earlier at Camp Apache, Brodie offered no public speculation as to the cause of the disaster. Privately, however, he expressed his opinion that the spillway had been located too close to the dam. Flood water pouring over the top of the dam for eight hours, he theorized, mixed with the flow from the spillway to create an eddy, or whirlpool, which undercut the center of the structure. Clearly, Brodie had good reasons to hold these thoughts to himself. Both Prescott newspapers had absolved him of all blame, pointing out that he had not been involved either in design or construction of the main dam. But, another consideration existed, which Brodie did not want to surface. True, he had not been involved in the construction phase, but neither had he made any determined effort to correct the design flaws revealed by the earlier flood in March 1889. In addition, the modest effort he had made in December to increase the size of the spillway had proven inadequate. Sometimes, it is prudent to let sleeping dogs lie.[23]

For the record, Brodie did express confidence that the dams would be rebuilt. Company President Van Beuren had taken the same position and soon was using his influence with Eastern capitalists to bring his dream into reality. On several occasions over the next two years he sommoned Brodie back to New York to explain and discuss the Walnut Grove project with prospective investors. Brodie welcomed these trips, which afforded him an opportunity to continue his courtship of Mary Hanlon, who had returned to her home in Morristown.

Before construction of a new dam actually could begin, a number of lawsuits had to be adjudicated. Over the next few weeks, fourteen claims totaling $93,000 in damages were filed in the district court in Phoenix. The highest single claim of $50,000 was entered on behalf of Carrie and Ada Haynes, two minors who had been orphaned by the flood. Charges specified that the company had erected an "insufficient, defective and negligently constructed dam." Judge Joseph Kibbey presided.[24]

In February 1891, Brodie led a sizable delegation of potential witnesses in the trial to Phoenix. The first trial resulted in a hung jury, but the second decided in favor of the company in ten cases, with the remaining four being dismissed. Elated at the result, and eager to get started, Van Beuren arranged with the Farmers' Loan and Trust Company of New York to float a new bond issue to finance the Walnut Grove venture. Meanwhile, back in Arizona, another problem made an appearance.[25]

Internal company opposition to Van Beuren's leadership unexpectedly surfaced. Apparently, a few employees in Arizona joined a group of stockholders attempting to alter the primary thrust of the project from mining to developing hydroelectric power for Prescott. Van Beuren, however, remained steadfast to the original plan, with some modifications. When Brodie, whose loyalty to Van Beuren never wavered, refused to join the dissident group, he found himself targeted for removal.

Convinced that Wells H. Bates, still actively promoting mines in

Yavapai County, and other former company officials had joined forces to unseat Van Beuren, Brodie advised his employer and friend of the situation. "There are none of them [Van Beuren's enemies]," Brodie wrote five months after the flood, "that are against me today can scare me, neither are there any of them that can buy me—not being for sale." Brodie went on to accuse "Mr. Hall," manager of the Piedmont Cattle Company, of having made a bid to replace Brodie as superintendent. Reportedly, Hall had solicited support of the company attorneys in Prescott, assuring them that Brodie "was a goner and they might as well be on the winning side."

Hall soon rued his defection. "Before I get through with Mr. Hall," an enraged Brodie promised, "his hair will be a shade whiter than it is now." The former cavalryman had never backed away from a good fight and he had no intention of doing so now. Hall's days with the Piedmont Cattle Company were numbered.[26]

Even as they struggled to retain control of the company, Brodie and Van Beuren laid plans to rebuild the main dam, but with significant modifications. The new structure would stand 140 feet high instead of 110 feet, and would be built of "solid cement masonry." By the summer of 1891 Brodie reported that he stood ready to begin construction. Van Beuren, however, failed to convince his Eastern investors that the project could be successful, and the bond issue failed. Deeply disappointed, Van Beuren still would not admit defeat.[27]

Rather than stand by and allow the Walnut Grove Water Storage Company to go into bankruptcy, Van Beuren decided to take personal charge of the firm and its assets. In the fall, he arranged a voluntary receivership, secured with a private corporate note covering the entire company debt of $350,000. At the same time, he assumed personal liability for the court-appointed receiver's salary and other expenses required to maintain mineral and water rights. Needing someone on hand in whom he had complete trust and confidence, Van Beuren arranged to have Brodie appointed receiver with a monthly salary of $200. Van Beuren's actions left him in complete control of the company, but he still lacked the funds necessary to resume operations.[28]

The 1890 flood that washed away two substantial dams on the Hassayampa River also appeared to obliterate Brodie's best chance to establish a viable career since leaving the army in 1877. For a dozen years following his resignation, he had experimented with several occupations, but with minimal success. His employment at Walnut Grove seemed to indicate that his fortune had changed, but unless Van Beuren could raise sufficient capital to rebuild the dam, Brodie at age forty-one again entertained no realistic prospect of immediate employment. But Brodie had many friends in Arizona. Some happened to be influential citizens—movers and shakers not only in Yavapai County but in the territorial capital as well. Moreover, he still had a wealthy benefactor in Henry S. Van Beuren, and a young lady in Morristown was writing regular letters to him addressed "Dear Laddie." Maybe, after all, Brodie's luck had taken a turn for the better.[29]

CHAPTER 10

"An Honest and Upright Man"

With the Walnut Grove Water Storage Company in receivership, Brodie faced an uncertain future. Impressed with the Prescott area, he hoped to become a permanent resident, but should Van Beuren fail to rebuild the Walnut Grove dam, he needed to locate an alternative source of income. Mining appeared to be one viable possibility, but he also considered other endeavors, including local politics. Of paramount immediate importance, however, was his desire to continue wooing Mary Hanlon, who had returned to her home in New Jersey.

The Morristown native had been reared in a religious household—although with an unusual twist. Mary's father, the Reverend John Hanlon, a descendant of Irish Catholic immigrants named O'Hanlon, had been born in New Jersey in 1832. At age twenty, he and a brother, Thomas, converted from Catholicism to the Methodist Episcopal Church. Both became ordained ministers in their adopted faith, practicing in New Jersey. An unacceptable religious defection in the eyes of many relatives, the brothers' conversion resulted in a irreconcilable family schism which caused Mary's father and her uncle to drop the "O'" from their name, thus establishing the Hanlon, or Protestant, branch of the family. Never physically robust, Mary's father died in 1875, leaving a widow, Mary Amelia Bonsall Hanlon, with three children: Mary, age eleven; Eliza, eight; and John, five.[1]

Although Mary enthusiastically welcomed his attention, Brodie found that his courtship efforts did not enjoy the smooth sailing he had hoped. Mary Amelia Bonsall Hanlon, mother of the intended bride, had serious reservations about her daughter's interest in a former army officer living in faraway Arizona. The issue had to be addressed. In May

1890, Brodie wrote Mrs. Hanlon to assure her that he was "an honest and upright man." Mary's mother responded quickly, but, in a carefully worded letter, raised several concerns.[2]

The widow Hanlon made it clear that she maintained a close-knit family, making it difficult for her to accept any prolonged separation from her children. Her message could not be misconstrued. Should Brodie win the hand of Mary Hanlon, he would be expected to permit his bride to visit her mother often. Mrs. Hanlon also pointed out that she knew about Brodie's proclivity for alcohol—"his one great weakness." Obviously, he would be expected to get "that dreadful appetite" under control before matrimony could be seriously considered. In that regard, Mary Bonsall Hanlon did not stand alone. Henry Van Beuren shared her concern.[3]

Suspecting that Brodie spent too much time in the collection of Prescott watering holes known as "Whiskey Row," Van Beuren at one point secured a pledge from Brodie to curtail his drinking, and later even asked the company attorney in Prescott to report on his chief engineer's drinking habits.[4]

In spite of her reservations, Mrs. Hanlon did not shut the door completely on Brodie's courtship of her daughter. Should Brodie meet her expectations regarding the use of alcohol, the widow confided that she "would gladly enlarge our little circle and embrace you in it." She also invited Brodie to visit her in New Jersey, where the two could become better acquainted. Over the next two years, Van Beuren frequently summoned Brodie to New York to discuss the Walnut Grove project, affording Brodie the opportunity to visit the Hanlons. Before long, having effectively neutralized his future mother-in-law's objections, Brodie slipped an engagement ring on Mary's finger.[5]

Finding that his duties as receiver of the Walnut Grove Water Storage Company required very little time and effort, Brodie increasingly turned his attention to gold mining, investing in several promising outcroppings in the highly mineralized Castle Creek Mining District south of Walnut Grove. The most attractive opportunity surfaced in the spring of 1890, when Robert Brow, a saloonkeeper at Walnut Grove, purchased three claims located nine miles south of the dam site for $500. Collectively known as Crown Point, the property initially had been located by Charles Thompson, a veteran prospector of the Bradshaw Mountains since 1877. Brow contacted Brodie and George Merwin, a well-known farmer, prospector, and part-time miner, to discuss the future of his recent acquisition.[6]

Quickly reaching an agreement, Brow retained one-third interest in Crown Point for himself, sold one-third interest in the prospect to Brodie for one dollar, and sold one-third to Merwin for $25. The trio agreed that Brodie and Brow would finance development and Merwin would serve as manager. All three partners had high expectations for Crown Point but, for a variety of reasons, Merwin made little headway.[7]

Meanwhile, possibly to help convince Mary A. Hanlon that he had established himself as a respected member of the Prescott community, Brodie threw his hat into the ring of local politics. In 1891, he agreed to become the first appointed colonel of the newly authorized Arizona National Guard. Earlier that year, Territorial Adjutant General Buckey O'Neill convinced the legislature to enact a military code authorizing a ten-company regiment commanded by a colonel. Prior to 1891 several informal militia companies had been formed in Arizona, but no official territorial force had been authorized.[8]

Undoubtedly, the influential Nathan Oakes Murphy, a well-known Yavapai County politician, played a key role in securing Brodie's appointment. Born in Maine in 1869, Murphy and his younger brother, Frank, settled in Prescott in the mid-1880s, quickly becoming involved in mining, railroad building, and Republican Party politics. In 1889, Oakes, as he liked to be called, became secretary of Arizona Territory. The following year, President Benjamin Harrison appointed a new Arizona governor, John R. Irwin of Iowa. Irwin previously had served as chief executive of Idaho Territory, but he had no prior association with Arizona. Consequently, in making his initial appointments, Irwin probably relied heavily on the advice of Secretary Murphy, who recommended that Brodie be appointed colonel of the National Guard.

Although Brodie certainly enjoyed his National Guard affiliation, he retained the position for only one year. In May 1892, apparently for political reasons, the colonel tendered his resignation. The month before, Governor Irwin, who had generated little support in Arizona for his administration, resigned under pressure from Washington. President Harrison replaced Irwin by elevating Secretary Oakes Murphy to the governorship. For unknown reasons, relations between Colonel Brodie and Governor Murphy had become strained, and Brodie did not care to serve with Murphy, who accepted Brodie's resignation with appropriate expressions of regret.[9]

Brodie's brief service in the Arizona National Guard resulted in one long-lasting legacy. In the past, local newspapers commonly referred to him as "Lieutenant Brodie" in deference to his rank in the First Cavalry. Now, they began calling him "Colonel," a new title he would carry to his grave.

Four months after resigning from the Guard, Brodie won by acclamation the Republican nomination for Yavapai County recorder. Brodie's candidacy caught many by surprise. Most Prescott Republicans predicted that he would win easily, but some Democrats hinted darkly that he really did not want the position and, if elected, actually would be nothing more than a figurehead—an allegation which Brodie quickly denied.[10]

Actually, local Democratic speculation regarding Brodie's motive in seeking public office may have been closer to the truth than Brodie admitted. Of course, he intended to serve if elected, but his decision to accept the position may have hinged on his desire to convince the widow Hanlon that he stood prepared to care for her daughter financially and that he had become a man of good standing in the Prescott community. After all, the future of the Walnut Grove Water Storage Company obviously remained in limbo, and Brodie needed to expand his financial interests and income. At any rate, in December, with the results of his easy victory at the polls in hand, Brodie headed east to claim his bride.

As one would expect, the wedding in Haddonfield, where Mary's mother had moved from Morristown, fully reflected the social standing of the Hanlon Family. The bride's uncle, the Reverend Thomas Hanlon, performed the ceremony. Henry Van Beuren and his daughter, Nell, who served as a bridesmaid, attended. Mary's twenty-two-year-old brother, John, stood as best man. None of Brodie's relatives made an appearance. Following the ceremony, the happy couple immediately departed for Arizona, intending to set up housekeeping in a comfortable home that Brodie had purchased in Prescott.[11]

Less than a year later, Brodie received a telegram from his sister, Lizzie, advising him that Joseph Brodie had fallen seriously ill. Turning his recorder's duties over to his two assistants, he left on the afternoon train that same day. Even so, he arrived two days late. His father died of "paralysis" on November 6, 1893, in Knoxville, Tennessee, where he had been living with Lizzie and her second husband, John F. Anderson. In keeping with family tradition, Brodie, his sister, and her three children escorted Joseph's body back to Edwards for burial in the family plot. As far as can be determined, only once would Brodie again return to the place of his birth.[12]

As Brodie's two-year term as county recorder drew to a close, he announced he would not seek reelection. Mary had become pregnant, and perhaps Brodie felt that the recorder's salary, scheduled to change the first of the year, would not be adequate to support a growing family. At any rate, his withdrawal surprised many of his friends, some of whom had been considering him for a higher office—perhaps even governor.[13]

Ten months after Joseph Brodie's death, the long-anticipated addition to the Brodie household arrived. On September 18, 1894, Mary, a small-boned, almost frail woman, successfully gave birth to a healthy boy. Remembering with horror the tragedy that had accompanied the birth of his daughter at Fort Colville seventeen years earlier, Brodie must have been extremely apprehensive as Mary went into labor, but she came through the event in good order. The happy couple named their son Alexander Oswald after the father. Brodie now could complete his term of county recorder without further distraction.[14]

Even before Brodie stepped down as recorder, his relationship with Van Beuren had progressed far beyond the original agreement. As receiver of the Walnut Grove Water Storage Company, Brodie had been charged only with safeguarding the firm's property, mineral, and water rights. Now, sensing an opportunity to expand more aggressively into the mining business, Brodie assumed the additional mantle of acting as Van Beuren's personal agent. Both men hoped to capitalize on a gold mining boom then sweeping the West.

As a result of the Panic of 1893, the United States reinstated the gold standard, thereby causing the nation's silver industry to collapse. Prices plummeted and many silver mines closed. Western miners and mineral speculators, no longer able to sell silver to the United States Treasury, switched their attention to gold, and deposits of the yellow metal in Arizona and elsewhere in the West invited nationwide attention. With potential investors from all parts of the country actively clamoring to invest in Arizona mines, Van Beuren and Brodie eagerly jumped on the golden bandwagon.

Utilizing his Prescott contacts, Brodie surveyed a number of prospects for possible purchase. The best appeared to be the Mayflower, a small but reputedly high-grade deposit located near Crown Point. Impressed with the samples Brodie collected, Van Beuren made the purchase, entrusting his agent to develop the property. Brodie put a small crew on the site and quickly found that he and the normally cautious Van Beuren had been hoodwinked—victims of one of the oldest scams in the mining business. Charles Thompson, the previous owner and the same man who had first located Crown Point, had covered a large pile of low-grade rock on the mine dump with a thin veneer of good ore. Brodie failed to detect the ruse until after the purchase.[15]

It is difficult to understand how Brodie, supposedly an experienced miner, could recommend purchase of a mine "salted" in such a transparent and unsophisticated manner. He probably knew and foolishly trusted Thompson, who was commonly known as the "Patriarch of the Bradshaws," in deference to the many years he had spent prospecting the area. Embarrassed at having been so easily taken in by the subterfuge, Brodie thereafter referred to the promoter as "Horsethief Thompson."[16]

In spite of Brodie's best efforts, his investment in the Crown Point mine also floundered. The initial arrangement of having two partners, Brodie and Robert Brow, provide the working capital while the third part-owner, George Merwin, took charge of development, simply proved unsatisfactory. None of the three had sufficient funds to carry the project and Merwin could make little headway. Finally, after a projected sale of the mine in 1894 to an Ohio investor for $50,000 fell through, Brodie concluded that changes had to be made.[17]

It took two years, but Brodie finally convinced Van Beuren to purchase Brow's share of the mine. At the same time, the millionaire also made overtures to acquire Merwin's interest, but that individual held out until 1897, when he finally relented and sold his portion to Van Beuren for $15,000. Unlike Brow, however, Merwin departed with a bad taste in his mouth, feeling that Brodie, his former partner, had pressured him unduly into selling. For his part, Brodie expressed satisfaction with Merwin's withdrawal. "I believe that the purchase of the Crown Point was one of the best you ever made," Brodie wrote his New York friend, "for I think it outside of Jerome, the largest mine in the County."[18]

Backed by Van Beuren's considerable financial resources, and with Merwin no longer a factor, Brodie personally took charge of development. Proceeding carefully, he followed sound mining principles by blocking out the entire ore body systematically, as opposed to merely following rich stringers, hoping to realize a quick profit. He had some success, occasionally sending gold bars recovered from ore removed during exploration to Van Beuren, who sold them in New York. By the end of 1897, Brodie advised his partner that he had enough ore in sight to justify erecting a ten-stamp mill at the mine site.[19]

In addition to his mining activities, Brodie became involved in community affairs, agreeing, for example, to serve as chairman of the Prescott Citizens Committee, a group organized to find and recommend a solution to the community's long-standing water storage problems. Ultimately, the group failed to convince the town council of the need to develop a reliable water storage facility and a modern sewage disposal system. But, under Brodie's leadership, another citizens' group, composed mostly of locally prominent miners and prospectors, established the Prescott Mining Exchange. With funds raised by subscription, the Exchange opened an office in downtown Prescott in 1896, where interested parties could meet to review displayed ore samples and discuss the relative merits of mining properties then available for sale or lease.[20]

That summer, as Brodie and Mary enjoyed their respected position in the social circles of Prescott, the couple suddenly suffered a terrible and unexpected loss. In July, Alexander O. Brodie Jr. fell seriously ill.

His distraught parents did everything possible to save their son, but nothing could be done. After lingering a week with high fever, the two-year-old died on July 26. Heartbroken, the couple took the body back to Edwards for burial. Apparently, Brodie never again returned to the rural upstate New York community where his mother, father, brother, oldest sister, and now his son lay buried.[21]

The unexpected loss of his son was not the only void in Brodie's life. He had resigned from the army nineteen years before, but he still dreamed of reviving a military career. He knew that under existing conditions, however, he had little chance of returning to active duty. The Regular Army, comprising approximately 25,000 officers and enlisted men, easily could meet current requirements. Attrition in the office corps through retirement lagged, and the annual graduation at West Point provided an abundance of junior officers. Brodie's only opportunity to again don the army blue uniform hinged on the possibility of a foreign war. President William McKinley's election in 1896, however, suggested that winds of change in that direction were blowing in from Cuba.

CHAPTER 11

"No Better Material Can Be Found Than in the Men of This Territory"

Located only ninety miles south of Florida, Cuba long posed a knotty problem for American diplomats. Beginning in the mid-nineteenth century, the Cuban people had launched a series of revolts against their Spanish rulers, generally finding sympathy and support in the United States. In 1898, the issue came to a head when the battleship *Maine* blew up in Havana harbor, providing an emotional rallying cry and excuse for war. Brodie quickly responded, finding a niche in what would become the most famous volunteer regiment in American history—the Rough Riders. Moreover, he would become friends with the irrepressible future president of the United States, Theodore Roosevelt.

Brodie's awareness of the Cuban situation crystallized in 1895, when another rebellion on the island broke out. American newspapers, openly sympathetic to the Cuban rebels, embellished their reports of the fighting with lurid tales of Spanish brutality. President Grover Cleveland, a Democrat, refused to take a strong position, hinting only to Spain that unless that nation could resolve the issue peacefully, the United States, for humanitarian reasons, might be forced to intervene. Republican President William McKinley, who grasped the reins of office on March 4, 1897, at first followed his predecessor's lead in exercising restraint, but soon found his peace efforts hampered by outspoken elements in both political parties demanding immediate intervention.[1]

By the end of McKinley's first year in office, the Cuban situation had become critical. In January 1898, responding to riots in Havana, McKinley dispatched the battleship *Maine* to Cuba on a "good will" mission.

Convinced now that war had become unavoidable and that the president soon would issue a call for volunteers, Brodie thought he saw an opportunity to reenter the army. He would organize a volunteer cavalry regiment composed of Arizona cowboys with himself as colonel and offer its services to the War Department in much the same fashion as volunteer units had been accepted into the Union Army during the Civil War. Convinced that such a romantic proposal would generate widespread support, Brodie confidently began detailed planning.

Deciding to test the local reaction to his proposal first, Brodie found enthusiastic support almost immediately. Exact details are not clear, but reportedly the colonel-to-be frequently gathered his friends at Bob Brow's popular saloon on Prescott's Whiskey Row to work out the details. Former sheriff and newly elected Mayor Buckey O'Neill quickly embraced Brodie's concept of cowboy cavalry. In fact, O'Neill became so active in helping Brodie organize the proposed regiment that some of his friends later assumed incorrectly that he originated the plan.[2]

Realizing it would be premature to make public his proposal until some overt act took place, Brodie proceeded cautiously. Quietly, he and O'Neill contacted several friends across the territory to gauge interest and generate support. The most encouraging response came from James Harvey McClintock, one of O'Neill's journalistic colleagues in Phoenix. Born in Sacramento, California, in 1864, McClintock came to Arizona fifteen years later to find employment on a Phoenix newspaper owned by his brother. He had no previous military experience, but he quickly embraced the possibility of being commissioned in a volunteer regiment. The trio agreed that O'Neill would take charge of recruiting in the northern tier of counties and McClintock would perform a similar role in the south. Quietly, both began gathering names of those who expressed an interest in joining.[3]

Modeled after a regular army regiment, Brodie's command would consist of twelve troops arranged in three squadrons. Each squadron would be commanded by a major, and each troop would be staffed by a captain and two lieutenants. Brodie planned to have the enlisted men in each troop elect their officers. A lieutenant colonel would serve as assistant regimental commander. Brodie never publicly revealed whom he intended to select as his second-in-command, but both McClintock and O'Neill undoubtedly felt they would be considered. All commissions, of course, would be signed by the governor.[4]

Early in February, Brodie traveled to Phoenix to solicit the support of Governor Myron Hawley McCord. A resident of the Salt River Valley since 1893, McCord had been appointed governor four years later by his friend President McKinley. Although McCord entertained military ambitions of his own, he agreed to endorse Brodie's proposal to the War Department.[5]

Having gone as far as he could at that point, Brodie paused to await further developments, which unfolded quickly. On February 15, the *Maine*—for reasons still unclear—blew up in Havana harbor with the loss of 192 seamen. Within hours, an inflammatory press blamed Spain, and public opinion demanded a military response. On February 22, sensing that the moment of opportunity had arrived, Brodie took his plan to the public, informing the Associated Press that he was forming a regiment of cowboy cavalry. Within a week he began receiving inquiries from as far away as California. Meanwhile, Brodie asked O'Neill and McClintock to publicly ratchet up their recruiting efforts.[6]

On March 3, eager to start the ball rolling officially, Brodie telegraphed both Governor McCord and President McKinley requesting authority to proceed with his plan. A week later, he reinforced his telegram to the president with a long handwritten letter. "I feel qualified to assure you," Brodie concluded, "that no better material can be found than in the men of this Territory."[7]

The next six weeks proved frustrating for Brodie. Although relations with Spain continued to deteriorate, the administration did not respond to his request. McKinley, still hoping to resolve the Cuban issue peacefully, did not want to send any overt signal to Spain that he was contemplating military action.

With the president's intentions unclear, Brodie found recruiting difficult. By the middle of April, he had approximately 500 men pledged to enlist—well short of the 1,000 troopers he envisioned. But his concept of a cowboy cavalry had caught hold elsewhere. On March 8, sixteen days after Brodie made his plan public, a member of the Wyoming legislature laid a similar proposal before his governor. Two weeks later, Melvin Grigsby, a Civil War Union veteran and adjutant general of South Dakota, applied for federal authorization to form a cowboy regiment in the West.[8]

Although Brodie found actual recruiting to be slower than expected, Arizona newspapers generally rendered enthusiastic support. On April 29, the Tucson *Arizona Star* prophetically endorsed "Col. Brodie's regiment of ROUGH RIDERS [emphasis added]," predicting that the unit would be highly successful. The name "Rough Riders" at that point did not immediately catch hold, but the *Star's* characterization remains the earliest known application of the term to volunteers in 1898.[9]

Meanwhile, the administration's plan to raise troops encountered unexpected opposition in Congress. At first concerned over the legal ramifications of sending federalized militia (National Guard) members to fight on foreign soil, the War Department initially intended to expand Regular Army units to full strength by filling all existing vacancies. Selected National Guard units would be federalized, but they would be used only to augment coastal defense forces. Under no circumstances would state troops be deployed outside the United States. The politically powerful National Guard, however, determined to participate equally with the Regular Army on the field of battle, called upon friends in Congress to kill the offending proposal. A few weeks later, Congress passed a compromise measure known as the Volunteer Bill of April 22. The new law provided that a Volunteer Army would be created by accepting for unrestricted field duty only those National Guard units that first agreed to be federalized. As originally written, however, the Volunteer Bill provided that only National Guard units could be accepted into the Volunteer Army. Apparently, Congress had slammed the door on Brodie's proposal of cowboy cavalry.[10]

At the last moment, Senator Francis X. Warren of Wyoming saved the day, ramming through an amendment to the Volunteer Bill, which authorized the Secretary of War to organize under federal control three independent regiments "possessing special qualifications." Armed with this unexpected authority, Secretary of War Russell A. Alger decided to form in the West three regiments of Volunteer Cavalry. One regiment would be raised in the four territories of Arizona, Oklahoma, New Mexico, and the unorganized area known as the Indian Territory. A second regiment would be formed in Wyoming and a third in the Dakotas.[11]

Obviously, Brodie hoped he would be selected to command one of the special cavalry regiments, but his overtures in that regard amounted to mere whistling in the wind. The president had larger fish to fry than an obscure mining engineer living in a far-off territory. To lead the First United States Volunteer Cavalry Regiment, as he officially designated the unit to be raised in the territories, McKinley initially turned to Theodore Roosevelt, the bellicose assistant secretary of the navy. Citing his lack of military experience, Roosevelt declined the appointment, requesting instead that his friend Capt. Leonard Wood of the medical corps be named colonel and that Roosevelt be named lieutenant colonel. McKinley concurred and directed Secretary Alger to draw up the paperwork.[12]

Alger initially planned to have the First Regiment consist of 780 men organized into nine troops. Based on population, New Mexico would furnish four troops of 340 men, Arizona and the Indian Territory each would provide two troops totaling 170 men, and one troop of 85 men would come from Oklahoma. All troop officers (captains and lieutenants) would be appointed by their respective governors. Field grade officers (major and higher) would be selected by the president. On April 25, the same day that Congress declared war on Spain, Alger wired the governors to call out their men.[13]

Swinging immediately into action, McCord advised Brodie of the Arizona quota. At the same time, he requested that the War Department authorize Arizona to provide one complete regiment. Alger refused, but at McCord's suggestion, appointed Brodie the senior major in the First United States Volunteer Cavalry and designated Whipple Barracks (formerly Ft. Whipple) the Arizona rendezvous site.[14]

From that point, events moved rapidly. On April 27, Alger increased the regimental strength from nine troops of 780 men to twelve troops totaling 1,000 soldiers. At McCord's request, Alger bumped the original Arizona allocation from 170 to 200 men, but he left the other territorial quotas unchanged.[15]

Disappointed that Arizona would provide only two troops to the First U.S. Volunteer Cavalry, but at the same time pleased at having been appointed senior major behind Colonel Wood and Lt. Col. Theodore Roosevelt in the command hierarchy, Brodie harbored one reservation about the timing of his selection. On April 20, less than a week before Brodie's appointment, Mary gave birth to another son, also named Alexander Oswald. The new father had second thoughts about leaving his wife so soon after she had given birth, but Brodie had waited too long for this opportunity, which probably never would come again. He had to accept. At age forty-nine, he could expect no further consideration for active duty. Mary knew how determined her husband was to reenter the army and she could not—would not—hold him back. Mary may even have seen this appointment as an opportunity for the Brodie family to leave the territory. An Eastern girl by upbringing, she never had acquired a liking for Arizona's rustic environment.[16]

Directed to report with two troops totaling 200 men to Colonel Wood at San Antonio, Texas, the regimental rendezvous and training site, Brodie wasted no time. He immediately requested Governor McCord to appoint O'Neill captain of the troop to be recruited in northern Arizona and James McClintock to command the unit gathered in the southern part. McCord agreed and presented commissions to the two captains at a banquet in Phoenix on April 29, at the same time appointing forty-year-old Joseph L. B. Alexander a first lieutenant in McClintock's troop.

Even before the selection and appointment of the key officers fell into place, Brodie had assigned a quota of enlisted men for each county and asked his recruiters to begin the selection process. In those areas where he had no recruiter identified, he asked the county recorder to function in that capacity. "Notify all [applicants]," Brodie cautioned, "that they must be able-bodied; proper ages, between 18 and 45; good shots and good riders. . . . Get best you can."[17]

Meanwhile, Colonel Wood had the situation in Washington well in hand. Keenly aware that there would be a heavy demand for military supplies and equipment by the Volunteer regiments being called into service, Wood relied on Lieutenant Colonel Roosevelt to ensure that his command stood first in line. Prior to departing Washington for San Antonio, Wood instructed Roosevelt to remain in the nation's capital and use his considerable political influence to ensure that the various supply departments give top priority to filling requisitions from the First United States Volunteer Cavalry. It was a brilliant decision.[18]

Brodie also completed arrangements for work at Crown Point to continue during his absence, naming Mary's twenty-eight-year-old brother, "Jack" Hanlon, acting superintendent. Thoroughly familiar with the operation, Hanlon had been employed as assayer for over a year. Brodie also engaged Robert Bignall, eldest son of his sister, Lizzie, thereby assuring the loyalty and reliability of at least two employees—a precaution critical in a gold mine, where miners could walk away with valuable nuggets concealed in lunch boxes.[19]

On April 29, Brodie greeted the first organized group of recruits to reach Prescott. That afternoon, the train from Phoenix disgorged forty-five men from Maricopa County, the nucleus of McClintock's troop. Brodie had arranged for formal enlistment to begin the next day at Whipple Barracks. Captain Buckey O'Neill, however, had other ideas, convincing the Regular Army mustering officer to enroll him on April 29. By this action, O'Neill probably became the first man in the nation to officially enroll in the Volunteer Army of 1898.[20]

Authorizing two lieutenants, eight sergeants, and eight corporals in each troop, Captains O'Neill and McClintock immediately began selecting their assistants. Apparently, Brodie did not become involved in the process, leaving the decisions to his troop commanders.

With 1st Lt. Joe Alexander already on board, McClintock's troopers elected George B. Wilcox their second lieutenant. Wilcox had served as an enlisted man in the Fourth Cavalry. By a strange coincidence, Wilcox and Colonel Wood previously had soldiered together at Fort Huachuca, where Wood had been assigned post surgeon and Wilcox the senior hospital steward. As his first sergeant, McClintock named Harbo Thomas "Tom" Rynning, a thirty-two-year-old native of Wisconsin who had prior enlisted service in the Eighth Cavalry.

O'Neill selected Frank Frantz, clerk of a mining company at Richinbar, a small community east of Prescott, to be his first lieutenant. Handsome, charming, and single, the twenty-nine-year-old native of Illinois enjoyed a well-deserved reputation as an accomplished ladies' man. O'Neill's second lieutenant slot went to Robert S. Patterson, a rancher from Safford who had raised the Graham County contingent and brought it to Prescott. Neither Frantz nor Patterson had prior military experience.[21]

O'Neill's appointment of First Sergeant William H. Greenwood is a puzzler. Greenwood appeared on Whiskey Row shortly after Congress declared war, announcing that he had come from California to enlist in Brodie's regiment. According to Greenwood, he had served as a sergeant with Brodie at Camp Apache and now sought the honor of again serving with his former lieutenant. Soon reported by the Prescott newspapers, Greenwood's story became one of the many popular legends associated with the Arizona contingent of the First United States Volunteer Cavalry. True, Greenwood had soldiered with Brodie in M Troop, but under circumstances far different from what he related.

A native of New York, Greenwood enlisted in M Troop in 1869 at age twenty-two. Present at Camp Apache when Brodie arrived in 1871, Greenwood, who was a private, not a sergeant as he claimed, deserted four months later near the Zuni villages while assigned to a detachment pursuing deserters. In 1887, Greenwood apparently surrendered himself to military authorities at Fort Bliss, Texas, to be discharged, but the desertion charge remained a part of his record.

Brodie's reason for permitting a former private who had deserted from his troop to enlist as O'Neill's first sergeant never has been explained. But there is even more to the story. At age fifty-one, Greenwood exceeded the allowable age for enlistment by six years. The old soldier easily hurdled that obstacle by informing the mustering officer that he was only forty-four. The official may have been taken in by the falsehood, but the more perceptive members of O'Neill's troop, who quickly came to refer to their top kick as "Grandma," were not. Nevertheless, in spite of his questionable background, Greenwood made an excellent first sergeant.[22]

As O'Neill and McClintock put the finishing touches on organizational details, Brodie completed his own preparations. Taking advantage of a regulation authorizing field grade officers to employ a personal orderly, Brodie hired George Taylor, a well-known Baltimore-born black man, who had resided in Prescott since 1882.

Born in 1842, Taylor enlisted during the Civil War in F Company, First United States Colored Volunteer Infantry. The following year, 1863, he was struck in the right elbow by a rifle bullet at Wilson's Landing, Virginia. Fifty-six years old in 1898 and drawing disability for his Civil War wound, Taylor served with pride, referring to himself as "Major Brodie's varley."[23]

George Taylor served as Brodie's orderly in the Rough Riders. Note the medal honoring Taylor's prior service in a black infantry regiment during the Civil War. Author's files.

On the afternoon of May 4, Brodie marched his troopers from Whipple Barracks into Prescott to be honored at a farewell ceremony in the town plaza. Following the Prescott Brass Band through city streets, muddy from an unseasonably late spring snowstorm, the Volunteers formed ranks in front of the grandstand, where Governor McCord and other dignitaries waited. One writer later described the recruits as a "rough-looking crowd of men in cowboy mufti—baggy pants, galluses, blanket-rolls, wrinkled shirts, sweat-stained hats and trail-scuffed boots." A romantic and popular description to be sure, but actually it could not be further from the truth.[24]

Photographs taken that day reveal clearly that Brodie had not surrounded himself with 200 harum-scarum young cowboys. To the contrary, the recruits averaged twenty-eight years of age, and they were well dressed. The vast majority wore sport coats or jackets with neck-

Arizona's quota of Rough Riders gathered in Prescott on May 5, 1898, prior to departing for San Antonio. Note that contrary to legend, the men generally were well dressed in suits or jackets. Author's files.

ties. A number even turned out wearing three-piece suits. Eighty-four recorded their occupation as rancher or cowboy. Thirty-seven claimed to be miners.[25]

Fortunately for the large crowd standing in the chilly town plaza, the departure ceremony ended quickly. Governor McCord delivered a short, inspirational address and presented to Brodie a beautiful silk flag that had been made for the occasion by a group of women in Phoenix. Brodie accepted with a few terse remarks. Other presentations followed. The most unusual gift came from Brodie's former mining partner and saloonkeeper, Bob Brow, who provided a snarling young mountain lion named Josephine to serve as the regimental mascot. The ceremony completed, Brodie led his men to the town depot, where a special train waited to take them to San Antonio. One enthusiastic newspaperman described the send-off as "the greatest demonstration of any kind ever witnessed in the mountain city." Brodie was pleased.[26]

In retrospect, it is difficult to determine the national impact of Brodie's persistent efforts to form a cowboy cavalry regiment. Although Melvin Grigsby, adjutant general of South Dakota and future colonel of the Third United States Volunteer Cavalry, later claimed he had authored the amendment to the Volunteer Bill of April 22, which made possible three special regiments, a strong case may be presented that Brodie actually initiated the concept. After all, he was the first to publicly push such a proposal, predating Grigsby's similar announcement by a month. Moreover, Brodie's efforts received strong support in Washington from McKinley's friend, Governor McCord, and from Nathan Oakes Murphy, Arizona's influential delegate to Congress. Unfortunately, Brodie lacked the personal influence necessary to be named colonel of the regiment he soon would join. Others would be selected to command the Volunteer force destined to gain lasting fame as the "Rough Riders."

Nevertheless, in some respects, Brodie's appointment as senior major of the First United States Volunteer Cavalry remains a remarkable achievement. Only nine years earlier, he had arrived in Prescott dogged by a reputation as a "booze fighter" who had been forced out of the army. His association with the Walnut Grove Water Storage Company, however, had reversed that perception, enabling him to establish himself as a capable engineer and reliable employee. His subsequent involvement in local politics and community affairs had won many friends, particularly after his marriage to the socially aware Mary Hanlon. One of Brodie's staunch friends, James H. McClintock, may have expressed it best when he stated that Brodie was "held in the highest esteem throughout northern Arizona." Certainly, the 200 men from Arizona who volunteered to follow the major into combat in Cuba shared that opinion.[27]

CHAPTER 12

"The Arizona Squadron Is a Peach"

Although deeply disappointed that he had not been selected to command one of the three special Volunteer Cavalry regiments, Brodie realized that he had probably secured one of the most coveted positions in the Volunteer Army. Clearly, both his superior officers, Col. Leonard Wood and Lt. Col. Theodore Roosevelt, were rising stars in their respective fields of endeavor. Wood would carve a niche in the military and Roosevelt would make his mark in politics. Undoubtedly, both would ultimately be in positions to help Brodie reestablish the military career he had once abandoned, but now so desperately wished to revive. In the interim, Brodie would perform his duty in an exemplary manner, hoping that reinstatement in the Regular Army would be his reward.

Arriving at San Antonio just before dawn on May 7, Brodie's troopers boarded streetcars waiting to convey them to the regimental rendezvous site at Riverside Park three miles south of the city, where a hot breakfast had been prepared for them. Brodie, meanwhile, reported to Colonel Wood, who greeted his senior major with enthusiasm. Pleasantries exchanged, Wood wasted no time in confiding his organizational plan and explaining how Brodie and his Arizona men fit into the overall scheme.

Colonel Wood pointed out that the recent increase in authorized strength from 780 to 1,000 men enabled him to configure his command exactly as a Regular Cavalry regiment. Brodie, as senior major, would command the First Squadron consisting of A, B, C, and D Troops. Nine of the regiment's authorized twelve troops had already been assembled in the territories with officers appointed by the governors. That could not be changed. The War Department, however, had

Officers of the First United States Volunteer Cavalry at San Antonio. Major Brodie, holding the leash of the regimental mascot, Josephine, is seated third from the left in the first row and to the immediate right of Colonel Wood. Lieutenant Colonel Roosevelt (without glasses) is seated on Wood's left. Author's files.

given Wood a free hand to organize the additional three troops, including authority to select the officers required to staff them. Moreover, Wood had approval to enlist approximately 200 new men without regard for territorial affiliation. The recruiting process already had begun. Wood introduced Brodie to Maj. George Morton Dunn and 2nd Lt. Hal Sayre. Both had been commissioned before Wood left Washington and had accompanied the colonel to San Antonio.[1]

A resident of Maryland, where he was known as a "master of hounds," the politically well-connected George M. Dunn had been selected personally by President McKinley to serve as the regiment's junior major. Hal Sayre, a Colorado-born twenty-two-year-old graduate of Yale, had probably been chosen by Roosevelt to be commissioned a second lieutenant and assigned to the first available unit vacancy. Others were en route. Even then, Roosevelt, who had been instructed to remain temporarily in Washington, DC, was gathering a group of noted athletes from Ivy League colleges to be enlisted.[2]

Regarding the three additional troops to be organized, Wood explained that one would be created by dividing Brodie's 200 Arizonans into three troops, instead of two. The second would be formed by separating the 340-man contingent from New Mexico into five troops, instead of the original four. The third new company would be established from scratch primarily, but not exclusively, to accommodate those recruits being gathered from the nation at large.

With these arrangements in mind, Wood named Buckey O'Neill the senior regimental captain and designated his company A Troop. McClintock's command became B Troop. Wood then directed Brodie to immediately transfer a total of sixty-five men from A and B Troops to form a third Arizona company lettered C Troop. At Brodie's suggestion, Wood recommended to the War Department that McClintock's first lieutenant, Joseph L. B. Alexander, be promoted to captain and given command of C Troop. Alexander's officers included 1st Lt. Robert S. Patterson, promoted from second lieutenant and transferred from A Troop, and 2nd Lt. Hal Sayre. In A Troop, Sgt. Joshua D. Carter, one of Brodie's friends who had helped establish the Prescott Mining Exchange, accepted a commision as second lieutenant to replace Patterson. In B Troop, 2nd Lt. George B. Wilcox stepped up one rank to replace Alexander, and 1st Sgt. Tom Rynning won a commission to fill Wilcox's former position. Responding quickly to Wood's directive, Brodie had his command reshuffled by sundown on the same day he arrived in San Antonio.[3]

That same afternoon, Brodie and Wood gathered at the Park entrance to watch square-jawed Capt. Robert Bell Huston from Oklahoma smartly march two lieutenants and eighty enlisted men into the bivouac. A lawyer from Guthrie and a captain in the Oklahoma National Guard, Huston had been personally asked by the governor to form the Oklahoma troop of Wood's regiment. Huston informed one San Antonio news reporter that he had organized his troop by enrolling the six best men in each Oklahoma National Guard company. Colonel Wood designated Huston's unit D Troop and assigned it to Brodie's First Squadron.[4]

In one respect, Brodie found a kindred spirit in the ambitious Huston. Both hoped to parlay their service in Wood's regiment into an appointment in the Regular Army. "This is my opportunity," Huston wrote his wife shortly after arrival, "and I am not wearing out the seat of my trousers sitting around."[5]

Two days later, 340 men from New Mexico marched into Riverside Park. The group's commander, Maj. Henry B. Hersey, had resigned his position as territorial adjutant general in order to organize the New Mexico contingent and become the second-ranking major behind Brodie. Colonel Wood immediately designated the four New Mexico troops E, F, G, and H and assigned them to the Second Squadron under Hersey. Wood then directed Hersey to detach sixty-eight men from the Second Squadron to form a fifth New Mexico company lettered I Troop, which would serve in the Third Squadron commanded by Maj. George Dunn. Dunn's squadron would also include K Troop, which

Wood was creating for individuals from the nation at large and the two troops still en route from the Indian Territory.[6]

Meanwhile, the romanticized concept of cowboy cavalry, or Rough Riders, as the San Antonio newspapers began calling Wood's troopers on May 2, had caught hold all across the nation. Young men (and some not so young) from all walks of life began clamoring to enlist. Many even paid their own way to San Antonio hoping to join. Wood evenly apportioned those he accepted into his existing troops until all companies reached their authorized strength of eighty-five enlisted men. Many of the newcomers were college graduates, and Wood maintained a watchful eye to identify those who demonstrated leadership skills. Two caught his attention immediately: John Campbell Greenway and David Marvin Goodrich.

Well-known for his prowess on the football gridiron and baseball diamond at Yale, the Arkansas-born Greenway resigned a position at the Carnegie Steel Company facility in Duquesne, Pennsylvania, to enlist. Highly impressed with the twenty-six-year-old recruit, who was one of the first Easterners to reach San Antonio on his own volition, Wood assigned him to fill the vacant second lieutenant's slot in I Troop and recommended to the War Department that he be commissioned.[7]

David M. Goodrich, a college athlete fresh out of Harvard, made a similar impression. Born in Akron, Ohio, in 1876, only six years after his father founded the B. F. Goodrich Rubber Company, Goodrich initially enlisted as a private in B Troop. Brodie, always quick to recognize talent, recommended that Goodrich be awarded shoulder straps (insignia of commissioned officers). Wood concurred and assigned Goodrich to D Troop, where a second lieutenant's position had become vacant. As events unfolded, both Greenway and Goodrich made outstanding officers.[8]

Disappointed that no equipment seemed to be available for his troopers other than a few blankets, mess kits, and clean straw for bedding, Brodie raised the issue with Colonel Wood, who explained that everything possible was being done to secure equipment and supplies. Even then, he pointed out, regimental horses were being purchased at a nearby remount station. Moreover, before leaving Washington, Wood had instructed Lieutenant Colonel Roosevelt to remain in the nation's capital and use his considerable political influence to expedite delivery of all equipment, including the .30 caliber Krag-Jørgensen carbines used by the Regular Cavalry. With characteristic energy and disregard for protocol, Roosevelt had descended on Washington bureaucrats almost as if he was already in Cuba leading a charge on enemy fortifications.[9]

"I have been rushing about all day," Roosevelt wrote Wood on

May 9, "making the lives of the quartermaster general and the chief of the Bureau of Ordnances a burden to them." But he made his point. Carbines, revolvers, saddles, cavalry tack, and 80,000 carbine cartridges were on the way. Even so, Roosevelt still expressed dissatisfaction. Contrary to promise, the Ordnance Department had dispatched requisitions by regular mail instead of by telegram. "I feel nearly crazy at my inability to hurry these ordnance stores and equipment faster," Roosevelt complained to Wood, "but all I can do I am doing." In that same letter, Roosevelt revealed his determination to get to Cuba. "I suppose you will be keeping me here for several days longer," he wrote, "but there is one thing, old man, you mustn't do, and that is run any risk of having me left here when the regiment starts for Cuba." On that point he need not have been concerned. Even a novice such as Roosevelt should have realized that it takes more than a few days to recruit, organize, equip, and train a regiment.[10]

Of course, Brodie did not wait for equipment to arrive before implementing a training program. Under his watchful eyes, the Arizona troopers, shouldering wooden staves and broomsticks instead of carbines, immediately began practicing close-order drill. Wood was impressed. "These men are the best men I have ever seen together," he wrote his wife the day after Brodie and Huston arrived, "and will make the finest kind of soldiers."[11]

Brodie had been in San Antonio eight days when the arrival of Lt. Col. Theodore Roosevelt galvanized every man in camp and brought all training and work details to a sudden halt. Early in the morning of May 15, Wood directed Brodie to take command of the regiment, explaining that he was riding into town to greet Roosevelt.

In some respects, Roosevelt's arrival posed a knotty problem for Brodie. From the overall standpoint of training and seven years' experience in the First Cavalry, Brodie probably presented better credentials than either Roosevelt or Wood to command a regiment. To be sure, Colonel Wood had over a dozen years service in the Regular Army, but not as a line officer. Originally, Wood had joined the military as a civilian contract surgeon, later being commissioned a doctor in the medical corps. Nevertheless, early in 1898, Wood belatedly received the Medal of Honor for pursuing hostile Apaches thirteen years earlier into Mexico. Roosevelt, except for his tenure as assistant secretary of the navy, had little meaningful military experience.

Brodie, however, realized both Wood and Roosevelt to be exceptionally competent, competitive, ambitious, and above all politically well-connected men. It would be his role to quietly advise and support his superiors in every way possible, remaining always in the background. Brodie knew that Roosevelt, in particular, would require much subtle help in learning his duties. Brodie obviously could furnish that assistance, but in so doing, he must take no action that could possibly detract from either of his commanders in the critical arena of public opinion. There simply was too much at stake personally for Brodie to risk a faux pas in that regard.

Actually, Brodie knew that Roosevelt cast a shadow over Wood from the very beginning. As early as May 2, one San Antonio newspaper made reference to "Roosevelt's Regiment." Moreover, on May 6, that same paper reported that the regiment was "being organized by the Hon. Theodore Roosevelt." Nothing could have been farther from the truth, of course. While waiting for two troops from the Indian Territory to arrive, and with Roosevelt still handling logistical details in Washington, Wood had organized three squadrons and had made most of the necessary decisions regarding officer selection and assignment. But Wood made no public effort to correct the impression that Roosevelt was the driving force behind the First United States Volunteer Cavalry. [12]

What Brodie probably did not fully understand at that point was the fact that Leonard Wood was no fool. Any favorable publicity the regiment received would bode well for Wood's personal career, as well as for that of his second-in-command. If Roosevelt's personal charisma could enhance the regiment's reputation, so be it. Wood would not rock the boat.

For his part, Roosevelt knew that he had limited knowledge of a lieutenant colonel's duties, but he also possessed unbounded confidence in his ability to learn. All he needed, he felt, was a little time. During his trip to San Antonio, he had assiduously studied regulations governing cavalry operations. Now, eager to take the field and try his hand at conducting mounted drill, Roosevelt eagerly grasped the first opportunity to take charge of all troops that had been mounted and put them through their paces.

Watching Roosevelt position himself before the assembled troops, the Arizona cowboys noted that, compared to Brodie, he did not appear to be a particularly good horseman and he did not have a powerful command voice. But with characteristic confidence and enthusiasm, he began issuing ambiguous and contradictory orders, whereupon the formation dissolved into chaos as the confused troopers, still novices themselves, scattered all over the parade ground. Realizing that he had lost control, Roosevelt, who never remained nonplussed for long, called for Major Brodie, who trotted smoothly into place in front of the harried lieutenant colonel.

"Major Brodie," Roosevelt calmly ordered, "take command of the regiment." Brodie saluted, wheeled his big horse, and barked out several commands that quickly restored order. Roosevelt, who already had formed a favorable impression of the "grizzled old frontier soldier," now realized more than ever that Brodie could help him learn to be an officer. Not long after this embarrassing incident, an appreciative Roosevelt moved to forge a lasting bond with his senior major.[13]

As Brodie later told the story, Roosevelt took him aside and, at Roosevelt's request, the two "shook hands and agreed to stand or fall together." Certainly, Brodie then was in a position to render great service to his lieutenant colonel, but the favor later would be returned many times over.[14]

Roosevelt was not the only man to recognize Brodie's talents. Others, for a variety of reasons, shared his opinion. Brodie's Military Academy background at first concerned some, but that reservation quickly faded. Captain Huston drove that point home when he confided to his wife that Brodie was a "West Point man" who "had been in the West so long he is as plain and common as an old farmer." Still others focused on Brodie's organizational and command achievements. "The Arizona Squadron is a peach," Lt. John C. Greenway of I Troop wrote his brother, "Col. [*sic*] Alex Brodie, an old West Pointer . . . is in command."[15]

Experienced in military leadership, Brodie knew when to enforce regulations and when to let them slide. In that regard, eighteen-year-old Arthur L. Tuttle of Safford, Arizona, benefited from Brodie's willingness to bend a regulation or two. Tuttle's problem took root when he enlisted at Whipple Barracks. Unsure about the legal age requirement, he gave his age to the mustering officer as twenty-one. The falsehood caught up with him San Antonio.

Details are unclear, but apparently at both Prescott and Santa Fe, the mustering officers had enlisted the men into the Volunteer Army as individuals instead of enrolling them by unit. Uncovering the error in Washington, the War Department dispatched the same mustering officers to San Antonio to make the correction. On May 17, both officials set up tables in separate tents and summoned the men individually to complete the paperwork. Upon hearing his name called, Tuttle stepped into the designated tent. Fixing him with a gimlet eye, the officer pointedly asked one question: "How old are you?"

"Twenty-one, sir," Tuttle replied.

"No, you are not. You are only eighteen," came the quick retort, "and I will not enlist you." Actually, Tuttle was of legal age, but the mustering officer intended to stand on principle and consider fraudulent Tuttle's effort to enlist.

Stunned by the unexpected turn of events, which left him stranded far from home with no money and no job, Tuttle decided to capitalize on the cowboy skills he had acquired growing up on the family ranch near Safford. Walking to the other side of the park, Tuttle accosted the chief packer of the regiment's 189-mule pack train and asked for a job. After watching Tuttle demonstrate his ability by throwing the approved diamond hitch on one of the recalcitrant mules, the packer offered the young man employment, but suggested he first discuss the situation with Captain O'Neill.

Trudging dejectedly back to camp, Tuttle encountered Major Brodie who, sensing that something seemed amiss, stopped the would-be recruit and requested an explanation. After listening to Tuttle's story, Brodie led him to the tent where the New Mexico troopers were being mustered. Brodie left Tuttle outside and entered the tent alone. A few minutes later he called Tuttle inside where Roosevelt, who just happened to be present, and the New Mexico mustering officer waited. Obviously, Tuttle realized, Brodie had made arrangements with Roosevelt to have Tuttle accepted. "So, young man," Roosevelt greeted the recruit, "you want to go to Cuba do you?" A nervous Tuttle stammered that he certainly did, and the mustering officer showed him where to sign. Roosevelt, standing with Brodie behind the mustering officer, immediately displayed his flashing white teeth in one of his trademark grins and closed the incident with the comment: "You're in the army now."[16]

Tuttle's experience again reveals one of Brodie's outstanding leadership characteristics. He would stand by his men.

On May 17, the same day that the Rough Riders officially became a part of the Volunteer Army, L and M Troops from the Indian Territory reported for duty. Their arrival completed the regiment, except for a few individual slots yet to be filled. All that remained, in addition to outfitting and equipping L and M Troops, was to continue training and wait for marching orders. The Rough Riders expected to join an invasion force, the Fifth Corps, even then gathering at Tampa, Florida.

Eleven days later, on May 28, Colonel Wood received a telegram directing him to move his regiment to Tampa as soon as possible. Wood quietly handed the directive to an emotional Roosevelt who, reacting as expected, threw his hat high in the air and howled with jubilation. The Rough Riders present took their cue from the lieutenant colonel, and the entire camp erupted with cheering soldiers dancing in the company streets and throwing articles of clothing skyward. Not until taps sounded that evening did the bivouac finally quiet down. Meanwhile, the officers worked late into the night putting the final touches on the movement plan.[17]

Wood planned to have Brodie's squadron, with the pack train, leave on a special troop train the next morning, followed by Roosevelt with the other two squadrons on a second train. The colonel commanding, upon ensuring his regiment was on the move, would follow on a regularly scheduled passenger train. Matters went awry almost immediately. Brodie marched his troopers to the depot as scheduled, but the actual loading turned into a welter of confusion. No loading facilities for the horses and mules existed, and some passenger cars arrived late. Nevertheless, Brodie's cowboys and cattlemen, accustomed to loading stock, managed to get the animals on board. At 3:45 p.m., five hours behind schedule, Brodie's squadron rolled out of San Antonio. Roosevelt, encountering even more difficulty than had Brodie, did not get away until the following morning. Wood, meanwhile, departed as scheduled, leaving after Brodie, but before Roosevelt.[18]

Watching the Texas landscape flash by his train window, Brodie could reflect with pride on his twenty-three-day stay at the Alamo city. During that period he had accomplished every goal he had set for himself and more. His squadron clearly was the best in the regiment, and no one doubted him to be the superior major. In fact, the Arizona men considered Brodie to be the most knowledgeable officer in the command hierarchy. Moreover, he had won the complete confidence—if not yet the friendship—of both Wood and Roosevelt. All that remained for Brodie to prove was gallantry on the field of battle. From all indications, that opportunity soon would materialize, as well.

CHAPTER 13

"I Am All Right"

Nothing in Brodie's military background compared with the vast martial array he found gathering at Tampa. Not since the Civil War had the American army mobilized such a formidable force. Yet, the chaotic conditions were almost overwhelming. "There was," according to Colonel Wood, "no head, no tail." Nevertheless, Maj. Gen. William R. Shafter, Commander of the Fifth Corps at Tampa, eventually embarked 17,000 men to invade Cuba. The ensuing campaign proved to be short and bloody, affording Brodie an opportunity to experience again the rattle of gunfire.[1]

Brodie's leading element of the Rough Riders reached Tampa late in the afternoon of June 1. Colonel Wood arrived with Brodie, having overtaken his senior major near New Orleans, where Brodie's train had stopped to enable the horses and mules to be fed and watered. Upon learning that his regiment had been assigned to the cavalry division, Wood directed Brodie to establish an overnight bivouac next to the depot. Later that evening, Brig. Gen. "Fighting Joe" Wheeler, commander of the cavalry division and anxious to meet the most recent addition to his command, briefly visited Brodie's camp.[2]

Early the following morning, Brodie marched his squadron through Tampa to the designated bivouac site near Fifth Corps Headquarters. Roosevelt arrived later that same afternoon. Tampa news reporters, ignoring completely Brodie's and Wood's arrival, reacted quickly to Roosevelt's presence. By focusing narrowly on Roosevelt, the Tampa reporters helped perpetuate two enduring misconceptions of the regiment which had first taken root in San Antonio. The first dealt with who commanded the First Volunteer Cavalry. Under the caption "Roosevelt's Rough Riders," one Tampa daily advised that

Three typical Rough Riders in C Troop at Montauk Point, Long Island. James Gaughan from Phoenix is on the left, and Elisha E. Garrison of New York on the right. The third man is unidentified. Author files.

"Colonel Roosevelt . . . arrived in the city yesterday with *his* [emphasis added] regiment of Rough Riders." The second erroneous impression dealt with the composition of Wood's command. That same paper advised that the regiment is "comprised of the most highly educated college men, millionaires, sons of millionaires, cow boys and Indian scouts." But the reporters even confused the origin of the "cow boys," having stated earlier that they were Texans. Somehow, the dominant role played by the four territories and the influence of Wood and Brodie in forming the regiment had become lost in the shuffle. Henceforth, in the news columns of Eastern publications, which took their cue from the Tampa dailies, Wood's regiment forever would be known as "Roosevelt's Rough Riders."[3]

Overly enthusiastic Tampa press reports aside, the Rough Riders actually comprised a very small cog in a very large wheel. Over 16,000 men already had assembled at the Tampa seaport, with more units arriving daily. Only a handful were Volunteer regiments and, except for

Wood's command, none were Volunteer Cavalry. General Shafter, busy bringing some semblance of order out of chaos, was organizing two infantry divisions, one cavalry division, and one Independent Brigade. Each infantry division consisted of three brigades with three regiments in each brigade. With only six regiments of cavalry on hand, however, the cavalry division contained but two brigades. The First Cavalry Brigade included the Third, the Sixth, and the Ninth Regular Regiments. The First and Tenth Regulars, along with Wood's First Volunteer Cavalry, composed the Second Brigade, commanded by Brig. Gen. Samuel Baldwin Marks Young. Both the Ninth and Tenth Cavalry were black units.[4]

A native of Pennsylvania, General Young rose through the ranks during the Civil War to colonel of volunteers. Serving in the West after the war, he took command of the Third Cavalry Regiment early in 1898, subsequently receiving a promotion to brigadier general of Volunteers and given command of the Second Brigade of Shafter's cavalry. Fifty-eight years old, he stood six feet and four inches without boots.[5]

Pleased to be assigned to the same brigade as his former regiment, the First Cavalry, Brodie found two of his West Point classmates who had served with him in Arizona still assigned to his former regiment; neither being present at Tampa, however. Capt. Otto L. Hein served on detached duty at the Military Academy, and Capt. Peter S. Bomus, who had seen so much hard service with Brodie at Camp Apache, had been sent to Chicago on recruiting duty. But other officers scattered throughout the Fifth Corps brought back memories—some not so pleasant. For example, William A. Rafferty commanded a squadron of the Second Cavalry billeted with the Independent Brigade.[6]

It would be interesting to know what Rafferty thought of the Brodie situation. Fifteen years earlier he had been a captain at Fort Bowie with Private Brodie incarcerated there pending a court martial. Now, Rafferty had been promoted to a lieutenant colonel, and Brodie sported the shoulder straps of a major assigned to the most famous Volunteer regiment in the army. Such were the vagaries of the Volunteer Army concept.

Wood's regiment had scarcely arrived at Tampa before a totally unexpected turn of events electrified the entire command. A shortage of troopships, according to rumor, would limit each cavalry regiment embarking for Cuba to sail with only eight troops of seventy-five men each. Four troops from each regiment, the rumor specified, would be left behind. Moreover, all regimental horses would remain in Tampa. Morale plummeted. Even Roosevelt became incensed, informing one favorite lieutenant that "positively he would not remain in Tampa in charge of the troops there, but would go with the first division if only as a lieut. or captain." That drastic step, of course, did not become necessary, but the rumor itself proved factual.[7]

Upon being informed officially that he would take two squadrons of four dismounted troops each to Cuba, Wood chose Roosevelt and Brodie to lead the two squadrons. Brodie, in particular, would be invaluable in Cuba. Other than Wood, he happened to be the only field grade officer in the regiment who had faced hostile gunfire. Majors Hersey and Dunn with four troops would remain in Tampa. In selecting the eight troops to accompany him, Wood considered seniority and the political ramifications of his decisions.

Obviously, C Troop from the First Squadron and H Troop from the Second, both being junior companies in their respective squadrons, would remain in Tampa. The situation in the Third Squadron, which would provide two troops to the Florida detachment, proved to be more complicated. The two junior troops both came from the Indian Territory. Clearly, it would be politically unwise to leave both behind. Therefore, Wood designated M Troop to remain, leaving the final selection to be made between I Troop from New Mexico and K Troop, which contained many Easterners. In fact, that company was being called the "Millionaires Troop" by many newsmen because it supposedly contained a large number of rich college men. Moreover, many of the men assigned to the ranks in K Troop were Roosevelt's friends, some of whom he had recruited while in Washington. Obviously, there would be no argument. K Troop would go to Cuba, leaving C from Arizona, I and H from New Mexico, and M from the Indian Territory to serve in Tampa under Majors Hersey and Dunn.[8]

Meanwhile, Brodie considered the possibility of being reunited with his family once the fighting ended. Unlike Roosevelt, who brought his wife to Tampa for a three-day visit, Brodie prudently decided to wait for the war to end before making any effort to have his spouse join him. Mary, having no intentions of waiting in Arizona for her husband's return, already had joined her mother in New Jersey, intending also to visit her younger sister, Eliza, in Halifax, Nova Scotia. Eliza, or "Lila" as she liked to be called, had married Walter Mitchell, a well-known resident of Halifax, who owned several merchant ships operating along the eastern shores of North America and in the Caribbean.[9]

In discussing Mary's situation with Captain Huston, Brodie learned that Huston's wife also had come East to await her husband's return. Huston suggested that should the Rough Riders be stationed in Havana after hostilities ended, the two consider having the women meet in New York and travel to Cuba on one of Mitchell's ships. Brodie liked the idea.[10]

Less than a week after reaching Tampa, Wood suddenly informed

Roosevelt and Brodie that the Fifth Corps would sail for Cuba the next day. All units not on board a transport the following morning, Wood warned, would be left in Florida. In double-quick time, Brodie's troopers broke camp, packed their equipment, drew ammunition, and transferred all horses, revolvers (except for officers' and sergeants'), and other property not needed in Cuba to Alexander's C Troop.

Wood had been told that a train would meet him at a nearby siding at midnight to convey his command nine miles to Port Tampa, where the transports would be waiting. The train did not appear, but after waiting six hours, Wood commandeered a coal train headed in the opposite direction and persuaded the engineer to back his train, now filled with dusty and cheering Rough Riders, back down the track to the port staging area.

Quickly realizing that no functional loading plan seemed to exist, Wood directed Brodie to supervise unloading the coal train while he and Roosevelt searched for someone who could tell them which transport to board. After a short delay, an impatient and obviously agitated Roosevelt returned and advised Brodie that the Rough Riders could take the *Yucatan*—if they moved quickly. Wood had already boarded the vessel, Roosevelt explained, and was bringing it to a nearby wharf. Detailing a rear guard to secure the regimental supplies and equipment, Brodie and Roosevelt hurried the Rough Riders on board, narrowly beating out the Second Infantry and Seventy-First New York Volunteer Infantry, which also arrived to claim the transport. The process may have been irregular, but the Rough Riders had their ship.[11]

On June 13, Shafter's armada, consisting of twenty-nine transports loaded with approximately 17,000 men and a naval escort, steamed out of Tampa. Reaching the eastern end of Cuba, the *Yucatan* encountered a steam launch delivering dispatches and offering the soldiers an opportunity to send their last letter home before landing. Brodie quickly dashed off a short note to Mary, still with her mother in New Jersey.

Brodie's letter reveals that Mary still remained in poor health. She had given birth only two months before and evidently had not yet fully recovered. Brodie showed his concern: "I write today to particularly ask you to take good care of yourself, for you are all I have in the world & I hope you see to it that you always have the advice of a good physician." Generally stoic and unemotional by nature, Brodie went on to convey his strong commitment to his wife. "My heart is with you at all times," he wrote, "and my great fear is that you will overdo yourself in some way or get to fretting too much. . . . My love and a kiss to mother, Lila & the youngster & all my love & a thousand kisses to yourself." He concluded with the obligatory: "I am alright so don't worry over me."[12]

As Shafter's flotilla turned west following the southern coast of Cuba, the Rough Riders realized Santiago to be their objective, and not Havana as some had speculated. Indeed, Shafter had been ordered to seize Santiago and drive the Spanish fleet, which had been bottled up in the harbor by elements of the American navy for almost a month, out of its safe anchorage and into the guns of the blockading warships. Well protected from a direct naval attack, Santiago lay five miles inland at the head of a narrow, twisting bay. Spanish batteries at Morro Castle, an impressive ancient stone fort guarding the mouth of the harbor, and other fortifications reportedly provided adequate firepower to seal the harbor from any attack by sea. Aware that approximately 12,000 enemy troops occupied the immediate area, Shafter delayed selecting a landing site until he could confer with the local Cuban rebels, or *Insurrectos*.

Taking the advice of several Cuban revolutionary leaders, Shafter decided to land his command on the morning of June 22 at Daiquirí, a small hamlet seventeen miles east of Santiago harbor. Another possible landing site existed at Siboney, a village eight miles closer to Santiago, but an iron pier at Daiquirí theoretically facilitated landing at that village. Shafter planned to have the Second Infantry Division hit the beach first, followed by the Independent Brigade and then the cavalry division. The First Infantry Division and corps artillery would be the last ashore. A thirty-minute naval bombardment would precede the landing.[13]

The invasion began as scheduled. At 9:00 a.m., the supporting bombardment lifted and infantrymen from the Second Division scurried down cargo nets into waiting steam launches and long boats. To Shafter's surprise, the Spaniards had evacuated Daiquirí the day before, leaving Shafter's men to come ashore uncontested. Nevertheless, other problems surfaced. The ground swells proved rougher than expected, and the pier too high to be useful.

Colonel Wood, meanwhile, concluded that displaying the American flag on shore would raise morale. Turning to his regimental color-sergeant, six-foot six-inch Albert P. Wright, a cowboy from Yuma, Wood directed him to go ashore and raise the Rough Riders' flag on the summit of Mount Losiltires, a promontory just east of the landing site. As the Stars and Stripes swelled on the morning breeze, the invasion turned into a noisy celebration. Soldiers cheered, steam whistles sounded, and a band struck up "The Star-Spangled Banner." On the *Yucatan*, Captain O'Neill, realizing that the flag now waving over Daiquirí to be the same banner that Governor McCord had presented to Major Brodie at Prescott, proudly reacted: "Howl, ye Arizona men," he shouted, "it's our flag up there."[14]

Early that afternoon, with the Second Division and most of the Independent Brigade on shore, the transports loaded with Wheeler's cavalrymen began inching closer to the beachhead. At that point the Rough Riders, scheduled to be one of the last cavalry units to disembark, benefited from the actions of a former aide to Roosevelt in the navy department. Passing the *Yucatan* on an armed yacht, the aide recognized Roosevelt and obligingly escorted the *Yucatan* to within a few hundred yards of the beach, thus enabling Wood's regiment to land earlier than scheduled.

Brodie and Roosevelt lost no time in getting their men down cargo nets into the landing craft. Most of the boats then headed toward the pier, where Captain O'Neill noticed a launch loaded with black troopers from the Tenth Cavalry suddenly capsize in the choppy surf. Two men heavily laden with equipment obviously were in trouble. Throwing his hat and pistol belt aside, O'Neill, who already had made a name for himself as a capable and resourceful officer, repeatedly dove into the roiling water in a vain effort to rescue the two troopers, who either drowned or were crushed against the pier.[15]

By late afternoon, with the Second Infantry Division, the Independent Brigade, and Young's cavalry brigade safely ashore, Shafter learned that the enemy had abandoned the village of Siboney, eight miles closer to Santiago. Quick to capitalize on the opportunity, Shafter ordered Brig. Gen. Henry Ware Lawton to march his Second Infantry Division from Daiquirí and occupy Siboney. Young's cavalry brigade and the Independent Brigade would remain at Daiquirí and secure the beachhead. The First Infantry Division and First Cavalry Brigade, still on the transports, would sail to Siboney and disembark there.[16]

Uncertain as to what the night and following morning might bring, Brodie established a crude perimeter in his assigned sector on the outskirts of Daiquirí and waited for orders. The troopers spent an uneasy first night ashore, with noisy land crabs crawling through the brush, which occasionally caused a nervous sentry to fire blindly into the darkness. At one point, the faint notes of a lone Spanish bugle drifted in on the night air to remind the troops that the enemy could not be far away. The following morning, the bored Rough Riders began constructing palm-frond shelters for protection from the hot sun and daily afternoon rain. Shortly before noon, the confusing situation suddenly changed. "Fighting Joe" Wheeler aggressively took charge.

The ranking officer on the beachhead, Wheeler had accompanied Lawton's First Division on their march from Daiquirí to Siboney. Upon learning from the *Insurrectos* that the Spaniards had withdrawn from Siboney to occupy a defensive position at a crossroads known as

Las Guasimas on the high ground three miles to the north, Wheeler determined to develop the situation with force. Completely ignoring Lawton, who had his entire division at Siboney, Wheeler ordered General Young to march his Second Cavalry Brigade from Daiquirí to Siboney as quickly as possible and prepare for action. Sensing Wheeler's urgency, Young started his three regiments down the Siboney road immediately. As darkness fell, Brodie and Roosevelt directed the exhausted Rough Riders to establish a temporary bivouac on the outskirts of Siboney near an old railroad bed. Wood, meanwhile, reported to General Young for additional orders.[17]

Returning from his conference with Young at midnight, Wood gathered Brodie and Roosevelt around a campfire to enjoy a hot cup of coffee as he issued his marching order. Two converging roads, Wood explained, led from Siboney to the Spanish position at Las Guasimas. One followed a small valley and the other, actually nothing more than a mountain trail, ascended a parallel ridge just outside Siboney and followed the crest to Las Guasimas. At daybreak the next morning, June 24, eight troops of Regular Cavalry would advance up the valley road, and the Rough Riders would follow the mountain trail. The plan called for the two columns to strike the enemy force, estimated at 2,000 men, simultaneously. In support, the *Insurrectos* had promised Young they would provide guides and eight hundred soldiers.[18]

With approximately five hundred men present for duty, Wood designated Roosevelt's Second Squadron, consisting of F, G, L, and K Troops, to lead the advance. Brodie would follow with A, B, D, and E Troops. Led by Capt. Frederick A. Muller, a German-born, thirty-six-year-old resident of Santa Fe, E Troop had been attached to the First Squadron to replace C Troop. Wood specified that L Troop would lead the advance, cautioning that they would find the body of an *Insurrecto* lying alongside the trail just before they reached the Spanish lines.[19]

Although L Troop had received less training than all other companies available, Wood selected it to lead the advance because of the confidence he had in the commander, Capt. Allyn K. Capron. A Regular officer assigned to the Seventh Cavalry, Capron had been placed on detached service by the War Department to organize the two troops from the Indian Territory. Roosevelt called him "the best soldier in the regiment."[20]

Two hours and forty minutes after a 3:00 a.m. reveille on June 24, Roosevelt finally started his troopers up the steep ridge above Siboney. Two Cuban guides led the way, but the promised 800 Cuban fighters failed to appear. Brodie designated A Troop to lead his squadron, followed by D, E, and finally McClintock's B Troop. Wood set a fast pace, wanting to be in position to strike the enemy in concert with the Regulars who followed an easier path in the valley below. Upon reaching the crest of the ridge, Wood halted the regiment only long enough to deploy L Troop as the advance guard and ordered the march to continue.[21]

Brodie did not like the situation. He had enough experience and common sense to know the danger of marching a column of troops without flank guards down a narrow trail lined with almost impenetrable jungle foliage. Yet, he knew Wood had little choice. Throwing out flank guards in the jungle would delay the Rough Riders to the extent that the Regulars in the valley would attack long before Wood's men would be in position to support them. A gamble to be sure, but based on the information provided by the *Insurrectos*, Wood knew exactly where he would encounter the enemy—provided, of course, they had not moved. In Wood's view, the positive benefits of his ability to attack in conjunction with the Regulars outstripped the danger posed by advancing in column formation.

The ridge sloped slightly down hill once the Rough Riders reached the crest, enabling them to move quickly. Brodie marched at the head of his squadron with A Troop. Suddenly, F Troop, just ahead of Brodie's men, halted and word came down the column to maintain silence and load chambers and magazines. For the next few seconds, only the clicking of breech bolts and magazine covers snapping shut broke the morning stillness. Shortly thereafter, the members of F Troop silently melted into the brush to the left. There followed a message directing Brodie to deploy A Troop to the right of the trail, D and E Troops to the left, and to hold B Troop in reserve. Surprised that his squadron's integrity had been compromised by sending one troop to the right and two to the left, Brodie had just sent O'Neill's men into the brush when a few scattered shots followed by the earsplitting roar of a Spanish volley signaled that the battle had begun.[22]

Brodie then hurried forward to locate Colonel Wood and secure additional orders. Passing haversacks and blanket rolls discarded along the trail, he found his commander coolly standing alongside the footpath holding his horse. Firing had become a steady roar and bullets were buzzing through the trees about them, but no other sign of the enemy could be seen. Wood quickly explained the situation.

Upon being informed by Captain Capron that L Troop had made contact with the Spanish outposts, Wood formed a skirmish line as quickly as possible by deploying his troops in alternating fashion instead of by squadron. Hoping to make contact with the Regulars advancing in the valley below, he had formed his right flank by sending

Roosevelt with G, K, and A Troops down a slope in the direction of the Regulars. Wood then directed Brodie to take charge of D, E, and F Troops and mount an attack on the Spanish right flank through the more open terrain to the left. He also ordered Brodie to bring McClintock's B Troop forward and position it in the center of his skirmish line to the left of L Troop.[23]

Moving through B Troop, Brodie suddenly felt a sharp blow to his right wrist, which spun him around, almost causing him to fall. Numbed by the high velocity Spanish rifle bullet, Brodie initially thought he could continue to fight, but loss of blood and the onset of pain convinced him to reconsider. Sitting down on a log in a small clearing, Brodie fished with his left hand a cigar out of his shirt pocket, but he could not manage to light it until a passing member of B Troop struck a match for him. Someone appeared to apply a dressing and convince him that his wound required treatment at the field hospital in Siboney. Relinquishing command of his squadron to Captain Huston, the ranking officer behind McClintock, who already had gone down with a bullet in his leg, Brodie joined the small procession of wounded moving slowly back to Siboney.[24]

Brodie found conditions at the seaport in turmoil. The Rough Riders' adjutant, Lt. Thomas W. Hall, had seen Edward Marshall, a newspaper correspondent, go down with a bullet in his back early in the battle. Assuming incorrectly that Wood had been hit, Hall seized a nearby mule and dashed into Siboney reporting that the Rough Riders had been ambushed and Wood killed. By the time Brodie arrived to explain the actual situation, the damage had been done. Correspondents in Siboney already had flashed the message home that Wood's command had been trapped and wiped out. To further confuse the situation, General Wheeler, who had observed the Regulars' fight at Las Guasimas, had requested that Lawton send a regiment in support. Unaware of the actual situation, Lawton not only sent reinforcements to Wheeler as requested, but also sent elements of the Ninth Cavalry to assist the Rough Riders. Neither was necessary. Even before the reinforcements reached the battlefield, the Spanish troops had pulled back, abandoning their position at Las Guasimas. Contrary to rumor, Wood was very much alive, and the Rough Riders had won their first battle.[25]

After having his wrist dressed at Siboney, Brodie went aboard the *Olivette*, a hospital ship anchored off shore. Aware that Mary, who had gone to visit her sister in Halifax, knew about his wound from newspapers, Brodie slowly and laboriously pieced together with his left hand a letter of reassurance.

On Board *Olivette*
Siboney, Cuba
June 28, 1898

Dear Mary

I send you this word pencilled by my own good left hand so you will know I am all right—slight wound with broken bone disables the other [hand]—Dr. Pope saw that I had good care & now 4 days after the fight I am on deck only waiting for the bone to unite. I had some friends send you word so you would not be worried by telegram—I am trying to get this [letter] off by a Norwegian attache so I must hurry—I have no news of you for 3 weeks but hope & pray that you are both all right & safe in Halifax—kiss Aleck for me as often as you & I like it & teach him to love his daddy. You know that you, his dear mother & my dear wife, have all my love & esteem & enclosed you will find a thousand kisses. [George] Taylor is with me & sends his regards to you & love to Catherine.

My love to all
your aff. husband
Alex O. Brodie[26]

Three days later, July 1, the Fifth Corps successfully overran the Spanish entrenchments on San Juan Heights, a prominent ridge overlooking Santiago. The Rough Riders, positioned on the extreme right flank of the assault line under heavy fire, first captured a small knoll called Kettle Hill and then swept up that portion of San Juan Heights to their direct front. By nightfall, the entire ridge was in American hands, leaving General Shafter in control of the high ground one mile east of the city. Known as the "Battle of San Juan Hill," the engagement effectively sealed the fate of Santiago, as well as that of the Spanish naval flotilla in the harbor.

Brodie did not acquire specific details of the battle until wounded participants boarded the *Olivette*. It had been another bloody battle, they reported, but the Rough Riders had performed well. In fact, according to some accounts, Roosevelt was the man of the hour. The day before the attack, General Young had fallen ill, and Colonel Wood had assumed temporary command of the Second Cavalry Brigade leaving Roosevelt to lead the Rough Riders. With unbridled enthusiasm, Roosevelt, clearly visible to journalists watching from a convenient vantage point, led the Rough Riders charge first up Kettle Hill and then onto San Juan Heights. From this day forward, Wood's command properly could be called "Roosevelt's Rough Riders." The ebullient New York politician finally had his regiment.[27]

All the battlefield news was not good. Brodie was saddened to learn that a number of men in his squadron had been killed or wounded. A significant personal loss was his good friend, William Owen "Buckey" O'Neill, struck down at the base of Kettle Hill.[28]

A few days later the *Olivette*, now filled with wounded or sick veterans, sailed for New York, where the patients would be transferred to the Fort Wadsworth post hospital. Brodie, however, stayed at the hospital only briefly. On July 11, he received a thirty-day convalescent leave. It is not clear where he spent his leave. Probably, he joined his family in Haddonfield, New Jersey, but he obviously spent a few days in Halifax, as well. Certainly, he visited Henry Van Beuren in New York to discuss the future of Crown Point. At any rate, on August 11, he reported for duty at Camp Wikoff, a new post being constructed on the eastern tip of Long Island.

Following the capitulation of Santiago on July 16, the War Department, fearing an outbreak of yellow fever, transferred Shafter's Fifth Corps to what appeared to be a healthy location on Long Island. Although established primarily as a convalescent center, Camp Wikoff also served as a facility to discharge the Volunteer regiments that had campaigned in Cuba. Construction began immediately, with Major Hersey's squadron and other cavalry squadrons left in Tampa ordered north to help lay out the new camp. Brodie, upon arriving on Long Island, assumed command of Hersey's group.

On August 15, Brodie greeted the veterans returning from Cuba, but it was not the same regiment he had helped put together in San Antonio two and a half months earlier. Death, disease, and injury had extracted a shocking toll. Significantly, Roosevelt came ashore proudly sporting the silver-eagle shoulder straps of a full colonel. General Shafter, after occupying Santiago, had appointed Colonel Wood military governor of the city, thus creating a vacancy for a colonel in the First Volunteer Cavalry. Naturally, Roosevelt won the position.[29]

Roosevelt's promotion triggered a chain reaction. The colonel immediately recommended that Major Brodie be promoted to fill his former position. The War Department concurred, and Brodie's lieutenant colonelcy came through effective August 17. To fill Brodie's vacated major's slot, Roosevelt tapped Capt. Micah J. Jenkins of K Troop. Captain Huston resented the selection, grumbling that he deserved the promotion because he had assumed temporary command of the First Squadron after Brodie went down at Las Guasimas. Nevertheless, Roo-

Lieutenant Colonel Brodie at Long Island. Presumably, Brodie affected the Napoleonic pose to conceal his wounded right arm and wr st. Author's files.

sevelt favored Jenkins, a West Point graduate, commenting that Huston "did well in camp work and everything of the kind, but I used to get impatient with him in action because he was not quick enough." Not being "quick enough" obviously did not mesh with Roosevelt's hell-for-leather style of leadership.[30]

Always quick to point out publicly that he promoted Brodie, Jenkins, and Lieutenants Greenway and Goodrich and several others for gallantry, Roosevelt even had the group pose at Camp Wikoff for a photograph. In that respect, the colonel was reaching too far. He did not have the authority to promote any officer. That prerogative rested solely with the War Department. Moreover, regulations did not authorize promotions for gallantry. As a regimental commander, Roosevelt had the authority to recommend, through military channels, promotion of those officers in his command whom he selected to fill existing unit vacancies. That exactly is what he did. But there is more to the story. Always a politician, Roosevelt realized that the image of promoting subordinates for battlefield gallantry would serve him well with the general public on election day. Waving the bloody shirt takes many forms.

On Long Island, Brodie enjoyed a unique experience he would cherish the rest of his life. Because Roosevelt still temporarily commanded the Second Cavalry Brigade, Brodie served as acting commander of the Rough Riders—an honor that only three men ever would achieve. With the regiment preparing to stand down, however, Brodie had few military duties to perform, affording him ample opportunity to ponder his future. Certainly, the friendship and support of high-ranking officers such Wood, Roosevelt, Young, Wheeler, and others would be invaluable in pursuing his long-standing dream of returning to the Regular Army. But, at age forty-nine, Brodie's brief stay in Cuba had driven home the realization that campaigning in a jungle environment such as Cuba—or the Philippines—was a young man's game. What Brodie needed was a staff assignment as opposed to that of a line officer. Even with the solid political connections he had cultivated, however, such an appointment would take time, and Brodie needed to find employment soon.

Brodie once told Henry Van Beuren that he "did not want anything political." Nevertheless, when Arizona friends contacted him on Long Island suggesting that he consider the Republican nomination for Arizona's delegate to Congress in the November 1898 election, he quickly expressed interest. The benefits promised to be many. If elected, he would reside much of the year in Washington, where he could lobby personally for an army appointment. Moreover, living in the East would be much more palatable to Mary, who had no desire to return to Arizona. Brodie's new friend, Theodore Roosevelt, already had committed to seek the New York governorship, and that decision could possibly benefit Brodie's political future, as well. Friends in high places always are welcome assets.[31]

Planning the First Annual Rough Rider Reunion became one of Brodie's final responsibilities. "The Roosevelt Rough Rider Association" had been formed for that purpose, and Brodie was elected president. He also had the responsibility to ensure that a farewell ceremony at Camp Wikoff honoring Colonel Roosevelt be conducted appropriately.

On September 13, after forming the regiment into a hollow square, Brodie escorted Roosevelt to the center, where a field table had been set up containing a bulky, blanket-covered object. William Murphy, an articulate soldier in M Troop, stepped forward to deliver an emotional address, praising Roosevelt for his role in the Rough Riders. Upon conclusion, Murphy whipped the blanket aside and presented Roosevelt a bronze reproduction of Frederic Remington's famous statue "The Broncho Buster." Visibly moved, Roosevelt responded with a few well-chosen nostalgic comments and asked Brodie to have the troopers file by the table, enabling him to shake each man's hand. Two days later, September 15, the First United States

Volunteer Cavalry ceased to exist.[32]

Brodie's brief service in the Rough Riders during the Spanish-American War proved to be a major turning point in his professional career. In addition to the personal satisfaction gained by his association with what became the most famous Volunteer regiment in the war, Brodie would reap tangible benefits far exceeding his most optimistic hopes and expectations. Like all Rough Riders, he would bask in the long shadow cast by the regiment for the rest of his life. To be sure, there would be controversy surrounding what the command did and did not accomplish, but even those who would attempt to denigrate Roosevelt's contribution—and there would be many—reluctantly would be forced to admit that the regiment sported a distinctly American flavor and forged an exemplary combat record. The First United States Volunteer Cavalry reflected an image of the American West, officered, with very few exceptions, by men from Arizona, New Mexico, Oklahoma, and the Indian Territory. Brodie stood tall in the organization from the very beginning, and the long arm of an appreciative Theodore Roosevelt eventually would reach out and tap him for additional honors.

CHAPTER 14

"I Am Not a Politician"

Notwithstanding the obvious benefits associated with a political career in Washington, Brodie did not agree to accept the 1898 Republican nomination for delegate to Congress easily. Several obstacles had to be addressed before the issue could be resolved. Brodie's relationship with Gov. Nathan Oakes Murphy, who had been appointed to a second term early in the fall of 1898, proved to be a major stumbling block. Brodie and Murphy had a strained relationship going back to 1892, when Brodie resigned from the National Guard rather than serve in Murphy's First Administration. Although Governor Murphy faced some internal opposition, he remained the most powerful Republican in the territory, positioned to block the selection of Brodie or any other Republican candidate for office. Obviously, it would be necessary for Brodie's friends and supporters to wring certain concessions from both the party "boss" and Brodie before the latter's candidacy could be agreed upon.

The second major obstacle to Brodie's run for office hinged on the "Silver Question." Responding to the Panic of 1893, the Democratic Party in the presidential election of 1896 had championed the free and unlimited use of silver to support the nation's currency. On a platform of retaining the gold standard, however, Republican William McKinley had easily won the election. By 1898, the question of "free silver," as it was called, had faded as the dominant issue on the national level, but the concept still garnered strong emotional support in Western states and territories such as Arizona, where mining dominated, or at least heavily influenced, the local economy.

Clearly, the silver issue targeted Brodie's Achilles heel. Should

Campaigning in Safford for Arizona's territorial delegate to Congress in 1898, Brodie is greeted by two former Rough Riders: Corporal Wilbur D. French on his right and Arthur L. Tuttle (arms folded) on his left. Author's files.

he refuse to embrace the gold standard, he would not receive the Republican nomination. But in Arizona he had a reputation as a "silver man," having earlier expressed support for that cause. Brodie knew that reversing his position on such an emotionally charged issue would invite accusations of inconsistency. In this case, however, he had little choice.[1]

Faced with these and other minor difficulties, Brodie's supporters and the Murphy faction of the party worked out a scenario ensuring Brodie's nomination. Col. William Christy, a Civil War veteran of the Union Army and founder of the Valley Bank in Phoenix, appears to have been the driving force behind Brodie's nomination. Born in Ohio, Christy came to Arizona in 1882 at age forty-two. Quickly becoming an influential force in the Arizona Republican Party, he served as territorial treasurer, 1891 to 1893. A reformer, Christy obviously did not see eye to eye with the Murphy faction.[2]

Exact details of the deal made with the Murphy camp are not known, but at least one prominent Arizona Republican (not Christy) visited the Rough Rider at Montauk Point to discuss the conditions of Brodie's nomination and subsequent campaign. For starters, Brodie apparently insisted that his nomination at the Republican convention be by acclamation and that Murphy agree to actively campaign for him.

Conceding the silver vote to their opponents, the Republicans hoped to capitalize on Brodie's personal popularity, his reputation as a war hero, and his support for immediate statehood. The latter issue, however, actually amounted to little more than a "me, too" proposition, as the Democrats also championed admission into the Union as a state. In order to enhance his image as a war hero, Brodie agreed to join his wife and son at his sister-in-law's home in Halifax and remain there until after the nominating convention made its selection. In Nova Scotia, of course, Brodie would be far removed from any contact with the Arizona press, and his absence from the territory would be explained by claiming that he still was recovering from his gunshot wound and "camp" dysentery contracted in Cuba. Clearly, the stage was being set for Brodie's presentation as a wounded veteran returning home in response to the will of the people. Before sailing for Halifax, Brodie arranged to have George Taylor, who had stayed with him throughout the entire campaign, accompany his horse, saddle, tack, and saber back to Prescott.

At the Republican territorial convention in Prescott on September 30, the well-orchestrated nomination of the colonel proceeded without a hitch. In a rousing presentation interrupted frequently by applause, George D. Christy, the twenty-nine-year-old son of William Christy, rose to make the nomination. After first reviewing Brodie's record in Arizona of Indian fighting, ranching, and mining, Christy turned to Brodie's service as a Rough Rider, which "made him an invalid for three long and weary months, and will cost him the use of his strong right arm for the rest of his life." Having disposed of the war hero aspects of his candidate, Christy addressed the statehood issue. "Give us Col. Brodie as our standard bearer, and we will sweep every county from the Mexican border to the snow capped peaks of the San Franciscos," Christy thundered, "and place Arizona in the Republican column to stay, and a new star shall appear in the blue of our banner."[3]

The deed was done. As agreed, Brodie received the nomination by acclamation. Four days later, he telegraphed his acceptance and sailed immediately from Halifax to open the campaign upon arrival in Arizona. Mary and little Alexander temporarily remained in the Mitchell home.[4]

The opposition party, meanwhile, also selected a candidate. Meeting in Prescott, the Democrats on the fifth ballot chose Col. John Frank Wilson, a well-known politician and former Arizona attorney general. Born in Tennessee in 1846, Wilson had fought in the Confederate Army, rising to rank of lieutenant colonel. An attorney by profession, he came to Arizona in the 1880s to open a law office. Known as an accomplished orator and well seasoned in the rough-and-tumble school of Arizona politics, Wilson promised to be a skilled and formidable opponent.[5]

Reaching Holbrook on October 14, Brodie found Governor Murphy with a delegation of supporters waiting to help launch the campaign. To compensate for Brodie's well-known limited oratorical ability, Murphy had selected several effective stump speakers to accompany him. The group included Territorial Auditor George W. "Doc" Vickers, a prominent Tucson judge, and reporter George Smalley from the *Arizona Republican*, a Phoenix newspaper owned jointly by Murphy's brother Frank and Vickers. Ostensibly assembled to assist Brodie, the delegation actually appears to have been dominated by Murphy's friends—not necessarily Brodie's.[6]

Plans called for Brodie to begin campaigning at Holbrook and then swing across the territory by rail, buckboard, or any other means necessary to reach the voters. Insofar as possible, Murphy and entourage would travel with him. As events unfolded, however, it became clear that Murphy did not want to stray far from the convenience of a Pullman car. In fact, Murphy's support for Brodie seems to have been halfhearted, at best.[7]

Delivering the inaugural campaign speech at Holbrook, Brodie revealed what his close friends already knew. Politically inexperienced, the colonel would not be an effective stump speaker without a great deal of coaching. In his speech, Brodie admitted he was not a politician, but, if elected, he promised to work for the "benefit of the whole territory." Regarding his opponent, Brodie stated that he knew Wilson personally, considered him to be a friend and believed him to be an "honorable man in every sense of the word." As for the differences between the two candidates, Brodie advised his audience that "it rests with you to decide who is best suited to represent you." Turning to the campaign issues, Brodie again equivocated: "I am not a politician," he said again, "and you are perhaps better posted on that issue than I am." Continuing on to Flagstaff, which would be the next campaign stop, Murphy and friends convinced Brodie that he could not continue to make such obvious faux pas.[8]

Undoubtedly responding to suggestions from his traveling companions, Brodie agreed in his future speeches to drop all favorable reference to Wilson, but he refused to make any personal attacks on the Democrats. Gradually, as the tour of the territory progressed, he developed a comfortable format for his speeches. At each stop he first would detail his interest in Arizona, then carefully make favorable comments regarding any local Rough Riders, and conclude with an enumeration of the benefits of statehood. He dismissed the silver question as irrelevant in an election for a non-voting delegate to Congress. Even then, although he drew large crowds, he failed to generate the expected support. As one newspaper pointed out: "There was no political enthusiasm in Brodie's reception"[9]

John Wilson campaigned much more aggressively. He carefully avoided making any personal attack on the former Rough Rider, but he challenged Brodie's political qualifications and hammered him hard on the silver issue. At one point, Wilson's supporters, apparently considering it necessary to establish that Wilson "ranked" Brodie, arbitrarily promoted their candidate from lieutenant colonel in the Confederate Army to a fictitious "general." Obviously, Brodie's military record concerned them. Moreover, Wilson did not object to a little mudslinging.

According to one writer, "Wilson ran a campaign of character assassination. He called the editor of the Phoenix *Arizona Republican* an 'eastern peon,' the editor of a Saint John's newspaper 'an idiot' and referred to Murphy as 'that ten-cent governor of ours.'" On the evening of November 5, Wilson nearly made a fatal blunder, apparently authorizing an armed group identified as "the Democratic Brigade of the Rough Walkers" to march in Phoenix. Perceived as an insult to all Spanish-American War veterans, the incident triggered enough unfavorable publicity that the Democrats hastily disclaimed responsibility.[10]

Three days later, November 8, the voters cast 8,212 votes for Wilson and 7,384 for Brodie. Although a fairly close election considering the disparity in voter registration between the two parties, the Republicans expressed disappointment, having felt that Brodie's personal popularity would carry the day. The former Rough Riders were crushed. Over sixty years later, Arthur L. Tuttle scornfully recalled that his favorite commander had been defeated "by a drunken politician." Brodie also expressed bitterness—but for far different reasons. On January 17, 1901, he confided to Theodore Roosevelt that Republican Governor Nathan Oakes Murphy "did more than all others to defeat me and by dishonest means." Unfortunately, he did not elaborate.[11]

In retrospect, it is difficult to determine what role, if any, Murphy played in Brodie's defeat. Significantly, Brodie did not stand alone in his opinion that Murphy had worked against him. One Prescott newspaper, more than once, stated that Murphy intentionally used Brodie's candidacy to control the Christy wing of the Republican Party. The issue is murky, but if Murphy actually cast Brodie in the role of a sacrificial lamb to ensure that no popular rival would rise to challenge his position in the party, he had made his point. Murphy had won the first round, but the fight was not over. Not by a long shot.[12]

CHAPTER 15

"You Have Had Nothing Out of This War But Hard Knocks"

Although discouraged by his failure to be elected Arizona's delegate to Congress, Brodie realized that he never would be truly happy at any occupation other than as an officer in the Regular Army. To achieve that end, he stood prepared to pull any string at his disposal. In the interim, he would continue to develop Crown Point, the future of which never appeared brighter. Henry Van Beuren, responding finally to a recommendation that Brodie had pushed even before going off to fight in Cuba, agreed to finance a stamp mill to process ore at the mine.

Late in 1898, concluding that his best chance to reenter the army would be through a vacant major's position in the paymaster's department, Brodie contacted Col. Theodore Roosevelt, Generals Joseph Wheeler, Samuel Young, Leonard Wood, and even Gen. William Shafter requesting letters of recommendation. All responded with varying degrees of enthusiasm. As to be expected, Roosevelt, who narrowly had been elected governor of New York that November, reacted with gusto, writing two letters to President McKinley praising his former comrade-in-arms. Courtly Joe Wheeler penned a polished endorsement of Brodie, as did Wood and Young. One of the most significant recommendations, however, originated with Roosevelt's close friend, Sen. Henry Cabot Lodge of Massachusetts. There is no evidence that Lodge knew Brodie personally, but obviously responding to Roosevelt's request, he wrote that he had a "great personal interest in Col. Brodie and shall be much gratified if he could receive the appointment which I am sure everyone would feel he greatly deserved."[1]

Early in 1899, armed with the impressive array of recommendations he had solicited, Brodie made formal application directly to President McKinley asking for an army appointment. But something was out of place. Throughout his entire adult life, Brodie prided himself on his well-deserved reputation for honesty, integrity, and modesty, avoiding always any self-serving efforts to glorify his own position or reputation. In his letter to McKinley, however, he claimed an honor he never achieved.

After describing briefly to McKinley his duty in Arizona at Camp Apache, Brodie stated that he had "served during the greater part of the Nez Perce Indian War in Idaho in command of F Troop, First Cavalry." Assuming that the official records of F Troop are correct—and there is absolutely no evidence that they are not—Brodie's claim simply is not true. The Nez Perce campaign began with Capt. David Perry's fight at White Bird Canyon on June 17, 1877, and ended October 5 with Chief Joseph's surrender in the Bear Paw Mountains of Montana. The war lasted approximately three and a half months. Brodie joined General Howard's command in the field on July 18 and reported to Captain Perry that same day. Only ten days later, July 28, he assumed temporary duty at Colonel Wheaton's supply base at Lewiston, remaining there until August 27, when he took a thirty-day leave prior to being discharged on September 30. In short, Brodie actually served only ten days with Perry's F Troop and he never assumed command of that company.[2]

One obvious explanation for Brodie's overstatement is that he simply wanted to increase his chances to reenter the army. Certainly, that is a possibility, but accepting that premise flies in the face of Brodie's well-established and well-documented reputation for honesty and high personal integrity.

Brodie's erratic behavior during the last six months of his army career in 1877 suggests another possible explanation. Following the death of his wife and daughter, he seems to have drifted aimlessly, with no clear purpose or definite course of action in mind. Is it possible that Brodie did, as has often been suggested, seek solace in alcohol to the extent that it clouded his memory of that unhappy period of his life? Did Brodie knowingly lie in 1899 about his role in the Nez Perce campaign, or did his confused memory simply fail him? The exact truth may never be known. But one thing is clear. Brodie knew that the records of F Troop were available in Washington, which easily could verify or refute any allegation he made regarding his service in that unit.

At any rate, having no success contacting President McKinley directly, Brodie returned to Washington early in 1899 to personally lay his papers before appropriate authorities in the War Department. That agency also turned a deaf ear, informing him that no vacancy existed for a man of his qualifications. Greatly discouraged and convinced

Sandy posing with his father's old service revolver at Crown Point. Brodie family collection.

that Secretary of War Russell A. Alger had blocked his appointment because of a prejudice he held against West Point graduates, Brodie returned to Crown Point, leaving his wife and son in New Jersey. Roosevelt, equally disappointed that he had not been able to secure a position for his former lieutenant colonel, as he once had promised, offered condolences: "I am more sorry than I can say that it slipped up on you, old man," he wrote. "You have had nothing out of this war but hard knocks and the consciousness of duty well and gallantly performed."[3]

In Arizona, Brodie again assumed the mantle of Van Beuren's personal representative. Officially still the superintendent and receiver of the Walnut Grove Water Storage Company, Brodie actually supervised and monitored all of Van Beuren's Arizona holdings, including the Piedmont Cattle Company, the Crown Point mine, and several lesser unpatented claims such as the Mayflower and Copper Lyon.

Brodie considered the Crown Point mine—in which he held a one-third interest—to be the most valuable Van Beuren holding. For

Crown Point mine and mill. Entrance to the mine shaft located in the small shed behind the smokestacks. Joseph Wittmann collection.

over two years he had pushed the millionaire to underwrite construction of a stamp mill. Finally, following Brodie's return from Cuba, Van Beuren agreed. That November, Brodie ordered a steam-powered, ten-stamp gold mill and concentrator from the well-known Chicago firm of Fraser and Chalmers.

Considered to reflect state-of-the-art technology, the mill utilized both gravity and mercury amalgamation techniques of ore recovery. A coal-burning engine rated at seventy horsepower provided energy for both the mill and mine hoist. Three fifty-horsepower boilers generated the necessary steam. The complete mill, which cost $7,300 f.o.b. Chicago, soon arrived at the Kirkland railhead, where contract freighters waited to haul it thirty-two miles to Crown Point.[4]

Although he had the mill assembled by the following summer, Brodie delayed putting it in operation until after the First Annual Rough Rider Reunion held June 24-27, 1899, in Las Vegas, New Mexico. Roosevelt personally selected New Mexico as the site of the first gathering, leaving determination of the actual community to Brodie, president of the Roosevelt Rough Rider Association.[5]

Brodie hoped to bring Van Beuren to the reunion, even sending him an engraved invitation tucked into a pocket that he had removed from a regulation army blouse. Brodie probably hoped to use the re-

Brodie with his wife, son, and mother-in-law driving the Crown Point/Prescott road. Brodie family collection.

union as a means to entice Van Beuren to come west, where he could be inveigled to spend a few days at Crown Point. Van Beuren declined the invitation, but Bob Brow, donor of the Rough Rider mountain lion mascot "Josephine," quickly agreed to accompany Brodie to Las Vegas.[6]

Most former Rough Riders considered the reunion to be highly successful, although Roosevelt complained about the small number attending. Festivities included roping contests, horse racing, and of course bronco busting. Naturally Roosevelt became the "crowning attraction" of the event, being called upon repeatedly to deliver speeches. Responding to one such request and possibly caught up in the excitement of the moment, Roosevelt made a comment that brought forth a loud burst of applause from his enthusiastic audience. "All I can say is," a local newspaper carefully quoted him, "if New Mexico wants to be a state you can count me in and I will go to Washington to speak for you or anything you wish." The implication of such a commitment could not have escaped Brodie, who had campaigned on the statehood issue in Arizona the year before.[7]

As a gesture of appreciation, the citizens of New Mexico presented a gold, diamond-studded medal to Roosevelt and a beautifully engraved saber to Brodie. At the business meeting on the final day, the association members reelected Brodie president and authorized the second reunion to be held the following year in Colorado or Oklahoma.

Returning from Las Vegas, Brodie remained at Crown Point only long enough to lay out instructions to Jack Hanlon, acting manager in Brodie's absence, and then headed east. Rumors circulated in Arizona that he had been summoned to Washington to discuss his assuming command of one of the Volunteer regiments then being formed to combat insurrection in the Philippines. That is unlikely. Brodie did not want or seek an appointment with the Volunteer Army. He wanted a position in the Regular Army. Undoubtedly, during his stay in the East, he again tested the political waters in that regard, but his primary purpose in returning to the Washington area in the fall of 1899 seems to have been to bring his wife and son back to Arizona. They had been absent from Prescott for over a year.[8]

Apparently realizing that he would not soon return to active duty, Brodie again directed his full attention and energy toward Crown Point. In October, he ordered the mill started up or "blown in," as the miners expressed it. That same fall, probably for financial reasons, he sold his home in Prescott and moved his family into a "mountain cottage" he had built at the mine site. Mary, of course, hated the move. She had not been able to cope effectively with the hot summers in the relative coolness of mile-high Prescott, let alone in the isolated and barren hills surrounding Crown Point at an elevation of 3,600 feet. Consequently, she continued her practice of spending summers with her mother in New Jersey.[9]

Unfortunately, Brodie's full-time presence at the mine site accomplished little to resolve the two major problems which had plagued the operation from the very beginning—the availability of water and a fuel supply capable of firing the boilers on an extended basis. Except for the Hassayampa River, approximately seven miles distant, the surrounding area contained no reliable surface supply of water. A small spring, or seep, on a nearby hill provided a limited amount, but efforts to increase the flow failed. The mine itself, however, contained water at the lower levels, leading Brodie to put the mill into operation, confident that sufficient water to supply the mill could be pumped from the mine and stored in two large metal holding tanks until needed.

An abundance of soft ponderosa pine covered the higher slopes of the Bradshaw Mountains, but the immediate area contained no extensive mesquite *bosque* or other hardwood capable of generating steam on an extended basis. Brodie chose to purchase Colorado coal from a dealer in New Mexico and ship it by rail to Kirkland. Soon realizing that California oil probably would be more economical, he advised Van Beuren that once the mine came into full production, he would convert to the liquid fuel.[10]

For the next year and a half, Brodie doggedly struggled to put Crown Point on a paying basis, but he never could get the project on track. A shortage of water continued to be the main drawback. Initially, Van Beuren provided a monthly operational budget of $1,600, which he later increased to $1,800. Moreover, Brodie sold all bullion recovered in Prescott to help defray expenses. Even so, Van Beuren lost approximately $1,000 each month, not including Brodie's salary, which came from the water storage company account. In spite of the slow progress, Brodie presented a cheerful front, constantly reassuring Van Beuren that the mine would prove profitable once he developed enough water to operate the mill continuously instead of only ten hours every second or third day, as he had been doing.[11]

Other problems compounded the situation. For example, in February 1901, Brodie's right-hand man, Jack Hanlon, rode into Prescott carrying twenty-six and a half ounces of bullion, which he expected to sell for $500. Returning a few days later, Hanlon reported to a disappointed Brodie that impurities had reduced the value to $200.

The first to see the handwriting on the wall was Robert Bignall, son of Brodie's sister, Lizzie. Early in 1900, Bignall, who had been employed at Crown Point for over two years, resigned to accept employment in the East.[12]

That spring, however, Brodie's fading optimism took a welcome shot in the arm. Two respected brothers, William and Thomas E. Farrish, representing a group of New York investors, expressed an interest in purchasing Crown Point. Tom Farrish presented a solid background, having once mined gold along the Feather River in California. Relocating to Arizona, he first found employment as superintendent of the Toughnut mine in Tombstone. Later, he held the same position at the Vulture mine near Wickenburg. Impressed with the brothers' qualifications and reputation, Brodie opened preliminary negotiations for a sale contingent on an evaluation of the property by the prospective buyers. Brodie proposed a sale price of $300,000 payable in three installments. Advising Van Beuren of his offer, Brodie emphasized that his terms, if accepted, would net him and Van Beuren approximately $125,000 each. Brodie expressed a strong desire to conclude the transaction, but Van Beuren objected to the proposed six-month delay in rendering final payment, and negotiations collapsed.[13]

The end came suddenly, albeit unexpectedly. In January 1901, a strike in the Colorado coal fields brought production to a sudden halt. Brodie quickly advised Van Beuren of the situation, promising that he would burn wood as long as possible to keep the mine dewatered, but on February 28, with no end of the strike in sight, he pulled the pumps and closed the mine. Ironically, the underground shafts and drifts (tunnels) began filling from the same water source that Brodie for over two years had been attempting to develop.[14]

Brodie and Van Beuren fully intended to resume operations once the coal strike ended, but Crown Point never again went into production. Possibly, Brodie had erred by treating the property as a large mine. Instead of attempting to block out the entire ore body, perhaps he should have followed and removed only the stringers and pockets of high-grade ore. Certainly, John Merwin, son of George Merwin, one of the three original partners, took the position that Brodie had mismanaged the property.

Eight years after Crown Point closed, an embittered John Merwin made overtures to purchase the mine from Joseph Wittmann, Van Beuren's heir. According to Merwin, for several years he had been trying to develop two claims adjoining Crown Point on the east known as the Polar Group, which reportedly tapped the same ore body as Crown Point. In his proposal, Merwin revealed that his family still harbored ill will toward Brodie, stemming back to the earlier partnership between George Merwin and Brodie. The younger Merwin claimed that Crown Point had failed under Brodie's direction because of faulty leadership. "The Crownpoint [sic] Mine never had any management," Merwin complained. "Everything was done like a school boy would do when he never seen a mine." According to Merwin, the shaft was too small, the mill not located in the right place, and the property actually required a forty-stamp mill instead of a ten-stamp. Merwin, however, did echo Brodie's long-standing position by offering his own opinion that Crown Point "is the Bigest [*sic*] Gold Mine in Yavapai Co. to day."[15]

Obviously, attempting to acquire his father's former property at a bargain rate, Merwin intended to combine Crown Point with the Polar Group and place both on the open market as a single entity. In order to present the prospect as a large mine with a proven ore body, Merwin felt it necessary to explain why Crown Point had failed. Accusing Brodie of mismanagement would serve that purpose. Wittmann, not impressed with Merwin's logic, refused the sale.

Actually, Crown Point's location in the Castle Creek Mining District seems to have been the kiss of death. In the late 1870s and continuing well over two decades, a veritable swarm of prospectors, enticed by the impressive mineral-stained rocks and outcroppings along Castle Creek, had inundated the area, opening many prospects and erecting a number of stamp mills. All failed. The entire district, from the earliest days to 1926, produced only an estimated $500,000 worth of gold. By comparison, between 1889 and 1910, the Congress mine, located fifteen miles west of Crown Point in the Martinez Mining District, yielded over $7.5 million dollars worth of gold bullion. Undoubtedly,

Brodie's failure at Crown Point resulted from a lack of commercial-grade ore, as opposed to a dearth of water, shortage of cheap fuel, excessive transportation costs, or even, as John Merwin suggested, faulty management.[16]

One result of Crown Point's failure is clear. The mine's sudden demise placed a heavy burden on Brodie's already strained personal resources. As long as he had been able to supplement his $200 a month receiver's stipend with his two-year income as county recorder and the "few thousands" he inherited from his father in 1893, he had been able to live comfortably, anticipating that soon he would garner additional income from Crown Point. In January 1900, he confided to Van Beuren that his savings had been exhausted by "sickness and traveling," probably referring to Mary's extended trips to New Jersey and Halifax, which may have been made, at least in part, for health reasons. Even so, Brodie seems to have gone through a substantial amount of money in a comparatively short period of time. Now, with Crown Point on indefinite hold, he needed to look elsewhere.[17]

Even before Crown Point failed, political winds from Washington heralded significant changes which would directly impact Brodie's future. In the spring of 1900, the power brokers in the Republican Party nominated Roosevelt as President McKinley's running mate in the fall election. Roosevelt did not want the vice presidency, preferring to seek a second term as governor of New York. To that end, he asked Brodie to secure a spot on the Arizona delegation to the party convention in Philadelphia so that he could vote against Roosevelt's nomination. Knowing that Arizona's delegation would be pledged to support Roosevelt, however, Brodie tactfully turned down Roosevelt's request. He did not want to be placed in a position forcing him either to turn against a friend's wishes or burn his bridges with the Arizona Republican Party by ignoring party instructions. Informing Roosevelt that he had withdrawn from consideration as a delegate, Brodie cleverly indicated that he had done so out of consideration for Roosevelt's future. "I wish to go to the Convention four years from now," Brodie wrote his friend, "when I shall have the pleasure of casting my vote for you & not against you." Nevertheless, notwithstanding his protest to Brodie, Roosevelt accepted the nomination for vice president.[18]

For the next few months, Brodie did not publicly involve himself with Roosevelt's candidacy, although he certainly discussed it with his former colonel at the Second Annual Rough Rider Reunion in Oklahoma City that July. He and Mary also were dinner guests at Roosevelt's home in Oyster Bay that summer, and the topic may have surfaced there as well. Following McKinley and Roosevelt's easy victory in November, however, Brodie made his move.

Comfortable with Roosevelt's friendship and relying on the colonel's well-known contempt for self-serving and corrupt politicians, Brodie hastened to establish himself as Roosevelt's confidant and political weather vane in Arizona. In January, he advised Roosevelt that some of McKinley's key appointees in Arizona did not represent mainstream Republicans. Governor Nathan Oakes Murphy, Territorial Secretary of State Charles H. Akers, and others, Brodie asserted, belonged to a "ring" interested solely in the spoils of office. Should these individuals approach Roosevelt seeking positions in McKinley's second administration, Brodie suggested that the vice president-elect "turn them down."

In that same letter, Brodie also cautioned Roosevelt that he probably would be approached by a number of office seekers from Arizona. Some, Brodie warned, might profess to be Brodie's friend. In that event, Roosevelt should ignore them unless they presented a personal letter of introduction from Brodie, who promised to issue such letters only to those he felt qualified and "worthy" of consideration. Ironically, after warning Roosevelt to be wary of office seekers, Brodie ended his letter with the subtle reminder that he still desired an army appointment, if only as a captain.[19]

In that respect, Brodie need not have been concerned. Roosevelt had not forgotten his former comrade-in-arms and even then was actively attempting to locate a position for him. Having no success with the military, he began searching elsewhere. Less than a month after his inauguration as vice president, Roosevelt suggested that Brodie accept the governorship of Arizona. Obviously, Roosevelt had decided that changes in Arizona had to be made and now stood ready to press the issue with McKinley. For reasons still unclear, Brodie turned Roosevelt down, writing that "under no circumstances [would he] take the appointment as Governor at this time."[20]

Meanwhile, as Brodie expected, a number of individuals, hoping to capitalize on his friendship with the vice president, contacted him regarding appointments. Some he welcomed. Jim McClintock, for example, expressed an interest in the territorial secretary of state position and requested Brodie's assistance. A similar situation existed with George Smalley, who wrote Brodie early in 1901 concerning a postmaster's position. Brodie was extremely pleased to be back in contact with Smalley, the reporter who had accompanied him on his campaign for delegate to Congress back in 1898. Although at that time an employee of Governor Murphy's newspaper, Smalley developed a deep respect for Brodie and his view of politics. The feeling became mutual. Brodie held Smalley in high regard.[21]

One of the first tests of Roosevelt's and, to a lesser extent, Brodie's influence in the McKinley administration took place in the summer of 1901. Arizona's Secretary of State Charles H. Akers's term of office was about to expire, and Isaac Taft Stoddard wanted the position badly, even traveling to Washington to personally plead his case. McKinley, affording little time for the opposition to organize, quickly appointed Stoddard. Akers had made a strong bid to be reappointed, but in a confrontation with Stoddard, he amounted to little more than a lightweight in the ring with a heavyweight. He never had a chance. Stoddard had far too much influence for Akers to overcome.

Born in the Empire State in 1851, Stoddard boasted powerful connections in the Republican Party at the national level. His mother was a cousin of William Howard Taft, and he had become a close friend of Sen. Thomas C. Platt of New York, probably while engaged in the insurance business in that state. An attorney by training, Stoddard moved to Arizona in the 1880s, where he invested successfully in Yavapai County mines and became a prominent figure in the local Republican Party. On at least three occasions he expressed an interest in the governorship. In making his bid for the territorial secretary position, Stoddard requested a recommendation from Brodie, who knew him well. Brodie quickly declined, ostensibly because he backed James McClintock for the position. In discussing Stoddard's appointment with McClintock later, Brodie pointed out that he detected Governor Murphy's influence in the selection. "And so Stoddard has won out at last against Akers," he wrote. "Well, I wanted to see you get the place & this appointment looks as though Murphy was yet in control."[22]

Although Roosevelt's ascendancy to the vice presidency injected new life into the Christy wing of the Arizona Republican Party, which had languished following Brodie's defeat in 1898, Governor Murphy still presented a force to be reckoned with. As long as he continued to enjoy President McKinley's support and could freely dispense party patronage in Arizona, he would be difficult to dislodge. Nevertheless, his position was beginning to weaken. Brodie's friendship with Roosevelt was well-known in Arizona, as well as his low opinion of Murphy. Brodie obviously had Roosevelt's ear, and Murphy's position could change at any time. The change came sooner than expected. On September 6, 1901, an obscure anarchist shot McKinley at the Pan-American Exposition in Buffalo, New York. Eight days later, Theodore Roosevelt became president. Now, Brodie—not Nathan Oakes Murphy—had a friend occupying the White House.

CHAPTER 16

"The Overthrow of the Philistines"

Roosevelt had been well-informed by Brodie and others on the political situation in Arizona even before the assassin's bullet propelled him into the White House on September 14, 1901. Nevertheless, he did not move quickly to make changes in the Murphy Administration. Aware that Nathan Oakes Murphy had powerful friends and supporters in the nation's capital, Roosevelt did not want to antagonize them unnecessarily. If Governor Murphy had been willing to play his cards close to his vest and avoid any serious breach of decorum, he probably could have completed his term of office, which expired in August 1902. Maintaining a low profile, however, could not be considered Murphy's strong suit. For whatever reasons, in the fall of 1901 and continuing into the following spring, with Brodie watching silently from the wings, Murphy committed a series of blunders, rendering it difficult for Roosevelt not to take action.

Roosevelt had barely taken office when an embarrassing political scandal rocked Arizona. For several weeks Eugene S. Ives, President of the Council (upper house of the territorial legislature), had been investigating the fiscal conduct of Governor Murphy and Territorial Auditor Dr. George W. Vickers. In October, having completed his investigation, Ives demanded that Murphy remove Vickers from office, at the same time presenting a telegram revealing that the auditor had offered a $500 bribe to control the printing contract for the Arizona Revised Statutes. Responding quickly, Murphy accepted Vickers's resignation, but the issue did not die there. Ives, convinced that Murphy "and his crowd have been plundering the territory for years," was trolling for larger fish. He wanted Murphy's head on a platter.[1]

Councilman Ives also had been investigating Murphy's and Vickers's alleged misuse of a special contingency fund. According to Ives, the two officials had illegally withdrawn over $2,500 from the account. With evidence in hand, Ives called upon Attorney General Joseph L. B. Alexander, the former Rough Rider, to bring charges against Murphy and Vickers. Alexander refused, however, causing Ives to speculate that Alexander was attempting to protect Brodie, an assumption which might well have been accurate. Alexander knew that Brodie, obviously in line to be the next governor, could ill afford to be accused of party disloyalty by involving himself, even indirectly, with any premature effort to remove Murphy, a fellow Republican.[2]

Unable to rouse Alexander to action, Ives took it upon himself to bring Murphy down. Convinced that Roosevelt, once he knew the facts of the case, would remove Murphy immediately, Ives decided to personally lay his accusations before the president. In the interim, he inveigled a fellow attorney to bring suit in an Arizona district court. Known as *Wilson v. Murphy and Vickers*, the suit charged both officials with malfeasance. Democratic papers had a field day, calling upon Murphy to resign and predicting that Brodie would be the next governor. Rumors flew like confetti. Some contained a shred of truth.[3]

Late in October, Arizona newspapers reported that Brodie and William Christy had traveled to Washington intending to convince the president that Murphy should immediately be removed and Christy appointed in his place. Instead, the papers confided, Roosevelt had asked Brodie to accept the position of governor. The newsmen obviously reported Roosevelt's intention accurately, but they missed one important ingredient. The timing was wrong. Actually, Roosevelt wanted the results of Murphy's trial in hand before deciding to either remove Governor Murphy or ask for his resignation.[4]

For the next few months, Brodie studiously avoided any involvement in local controversial issues, but at the same time he quietly laid the groundwork for his expected appointment. Maintaining close contact with Jim McClintock and George Smalley, Brodie subtly intimated that soon he would be in position to exert even greater influence on their behalf than he had exercised in the past. Both still desired political appointments. McClintock hoped to be named secretary of state for Arizona and Smalley had his eye on a postmaster's position. But Brodie had other plans for Smalley, intending to appoint him personal secretary to the governor.[5]

Dispensing advice freely to his friends, Brodie stressed the importance of federal job seekers securing recommendations from local Republicans. In counseling McClintock on that point, Brodie clearly intimated that changes would soon take place. In January, he advised his friend that Governor Murphy's influence in Washington "is nil," and that endorsements from Secretary of State Isaac Stoddard "amounts to but little." Brodie's warning seemed clear: Don't hitch your wagon to a falling star.[6]

Meanwhile, Murphy committed a serious blunder by challenging one of the president's pet projects. Two months into his presidency, Roosevelt enthusiastically supported a Democratic-sponsored irrigation and reclamation measure known as the Newlands Act. Highly popular in water-starved Arizona, the proposal, if enacted into law, would create a federal reclamation service charged with utilizing proceeds from the sale of public lands to construct dams and attending irrigation projects in the arid regions of the West. Governor Murphy, a staunch supporter of states' rights, had a long record of supporting such reclamation measures, but he believed that such undertakings should be administered by the states and territories utilizing federal funds. Armed with a two-page, well-written circular outlining his position, Murphy traveled to Washington in January to lobby against the Newlands Act.[7]

Murphy's motivation in publicly opposing the Newlands Act is perplexing. To be sure, the trip to Washington afforded the governor an opportunity to defend himself personally against Ives's accusation of malfeasance, which formally had been presented to Roosevelt that same month, but it seems strange that Murphy, already treading on shaky ground, would deliberately antagonize the man who unilaterally controlled his tenure as governor. Nevertheless, Roosevelt greeted Murphy cordially and waited for results of the pending trial before deciding the governor's future.

Even as Murphy struggled to bolster his waning influence in the nation's capital, Secretary Stoddard moved aggressively to consolidate his own position. A master in the art of exploiting party patronage to entrench his standing in the Arizona Republican Party, Stoddard for several years had capitalized on his considerable influence in Washington to virtually control the appointment of certain territorial officials—particularly postmasters. In fact, so successful had Stoddard been in that regard that he once bragged to a friend that he and Governor Murphy actually shared that power. With Brodie entering the picture, however, the secretary reluctantly acknowledged that questions from Washington regarding territorial appointments now were "referred to Governor Murphy, Colonel Brodie and myself." Keenly aware that the Brodie-Roosevelt connection threatened his influence and possibly even his position, Stoddard moved to establish an understanding with Brodie.[8]

At Stoddard's request, Brodie met the secretary early in 1902 at the Castle Hot Springs Resort south of Crown Point to work out some kind of arrangement. After first making it clear that he harbored no anti-Roosevelt bias, Stoddard expressed his hope that, regarding territorial appointments, he and Brodie could "pull together in the interests of the national administration." Clearly, Stoddard arrogantly hoped to secure a commitment that Governor Brodie would make no recommendation to Washington regarding appointments without first clearing his selections with Stoddard. Undoubtedly seeing through the secretary's rather transparent subterfuge, Brodie remained noncommittal. On several occasions, however, Stoddard later stated that at Castle Hot Springs Brodie agreed that he would not recommend a former Rough Rider for any position. Even so, Stoddard surely realized that his empire-building scheme had failed. No longer would he be able to control or even significantly influence party patronage in Arizona.[9]

Meanwhile, Brodie decided to take the bull by the horns and lock up Smalley's services while the journalist remained available. In March 1902, he invited Smalley and his family to visit the Brodie home at Crown Point where, admitting he probably would be the next governor, Brodie asked his friend to become his personal secretary. At first Smalley hesitated, but Mary stepped into the breach, informing Smalley that "the code of the Southwest demanded that when a friend called there was no alternative but to go." Mary's argument carried the day, but Smalley returned to Tucson still harboring reservations concerning his decision.[10]

A month later, the twisted story of Murphy's last ill-fated six months in office played itself out. On April 26, Judge Edward Kent, who had served as Assistant United States Attorney in Colorado prior to becoming chief justice of Arizona, rendered his verdict. Kent ruled that the warrants issued by Vickers drawing on the special contingency fund for Murphy's benefit were illegal, but that only Vickers and his bondsmen—not Murphy—had the legal responsibility to reimburse the treasury. Although guilty by association, Murphy technically had been taken off the hook. Nevertheless, Roosevelt, who had received fresh complaints concerning Murphy's personal conduct at a recent banquet in Phoenix, had enough. Seeing the handwriting on the wall, Murphy submitted his resignation dated April 21, 1902, with the request that he continue in office until the end of the fiscal year, June 30. Roosevelt agreed, and shortly thereafter submitted Brodie's name to the Senate for ratification.[11]

Quick to offer congratulations, McClintock, who had been appointed Phoenix postmaster in March, wrote Brodie that, except for Murphy, who "didn't look pleasant," most people regarded Brodie's appointment favorably. A Methodist minister, McClintock confided, even "called to express his joy at the overthrow of the Philistines."

Offering his own brand of advice, McClintock suggested that Brodie should "take to the woods for about a week and then come down. Remember that with honors will come tribulation: You have the experience of your life before you." McClintock closed with the pledge that he stood ready to assist Brodie "in all things."[12]

Accepting McClintock's offer, Brodie asked his friend to assist in preparing the inauguration ceremony. "It is my desire," Brodie confided, "to be allowed to take office in as quiet and nonostentatious a way as possible." Regarding a proposed reception to follow the ceremony, Brodie, keenly aware of possible criticism over such an event, wisely cautioned that he would not "like anything having the sole appearance of being a Rough Rider affair." McClintock concurred and began preparation.[13]

Having great confidence and trust in Secretary Smalley's loyalty and judgment, Brodie informed Smalley that he intended to give the territory "an administration that neither I nor my friends need be ashamed of." He also cautioned Smalley not to trust Secretary of State Isaac Stoddard. "We must be prepared to go in and take full charge of the office," he wrote, and "can afford to seek advice of none, neither Stoddard or any one else." Clearly, in Brodie's eye, he had been given a new command and intended to make the most of it.[14]

As Brodie requested, his inauguration ended quickly. Early in the morning on July 1, 1902, approximately fifty observers gathered in the executive office of the capitol building in Phoenix to witness the ceremony. At precisely 8:30, Chief Justice Kent stepped forward to administer the oath of office to Brodie, who responded loudly and clearly. Ex-Governor Murphy grasped Brodie's hand, offered his congratulations and pledged to assist the new governor in any way possible. After graciously thanking Murphy, Brodie delivered a short, well-composed acceptance speech. Perhaps alluding to his predecessor's reputation, Brodie stated he intended to represent all the people of Arizona, accepting the office "not for the benefit it might do me but for the benefit I might be to the Territory of Arizona." He then kissed Mary and the ceremony ended. Smalley later stated that Brodie's eloquent acceptance was the best speech he had ever heard his friend deliver.[15]

In contrast to his lifelong reiteration that he had no interest in politics, Brodie's well-orchestrated rise to governor reveals that he actually possessed a well-honed working grasp of the political system. Aside from his own personal popularity, Brodie recognized his political base in the territory to be quite narrow. He certainly enjoyed strong backing from the Christy, or reform wing, of the Republican Party, but the bulk of the party initially remained in the Murphy camp. The far more numerous Democrats, united in their contempt of Murphy, but also painfully aware that they had no chance of recovering the governor's chair as long as a Republican occupied the White House, would not support Brodie unless he convinced them that he was a political moderate.

Accurately assessing the situation, Brodie cleverly solidified his position in Arizona even as Roosevelt grappled with the dilemma of when and how to best replace Murphy. Watching Murphy self-destruct through a series of ill-advised decisions, Brodie carefully gave no indication that he supported any effort to undercut Murphy or otherwise split the Republican Party. He succeeded so well that Murphy himself, upon realizing that his days as governor were numbered, stated that Brodie would be his successor. Yet, at the same time, Brodie managed to "keep his skirts clean" of any undue association with Murphy, thereby effectively blocking criticism from the Democrats. He could be proud of his achievements. By the time Brodie grasped the reins of office on July 1, 1902, he was being widely hailed as the man who would revitalize and restore popular government to the Territory of Arizona. In this case, President Roosevelt, often accused of excessive partiality to his former Rough Riders, had made a wise choice.

CHAPTER 17

"Green Enough to Pull Up Corn"

The first six months in office provided Governor Brodie a welcome opportunity to establish his administration without confronting the legislature, which did not convene until the following January. In general, he initially enjoyed bipartisan support across the territory. One Murphy-appointed official drove home that point by offering his resignation with the observation that: "No man in the history of the Territory has even entered these duties under such similar circumstances of good will and confidence." Nevertheless, all would not be a bed of roses. To his surprise, Brodie would find the statehood issue, so very much in the hearts of most Arizonans, to be a nasty thorn in his side for the next two years.[1]

Determined to launch his administration by "showing the flag," Brodie left Phoenix the morning following his inauguration to participate in a July Fourth celebration in the important mining community of Bisbee. Subsequent trips took him to Tucson, Yuma, Safford, Flagstaff, and other communities, where he conferred with local authorities and visited various institutions, such as the University of Arizona in Tucson. Mary, and her precocious four-year-old son, "Sandy," accompanied him. The governor was well received at all locations, but particularly at Yuma, where an enthusiastic crowd led by Mayor Robert S. Patterson, the former first lieutenant in Alexander's troop of Rough Riders, greeted Brodie's party. At Thatcher, a small Mormon settlement near Safford on the upper Gila River, Mary suddenly emerged as a charmer.[2]

In October, at the Academy of Latter-day Saints, a Mormon educational facility at Thatcher, local officials requested that the governor and first lady address the assembled citizens. Brodie responded with a few unrehearsed comments, but Mary delivered a "crackerjack talk" causing the Mormon elders present to "josh" the colonel "because he had a wife who could beat him making a speech." At other locations, Mary's quick wit and conversational ability won many friends and admirers. Obviously, Mary would be much happier living in Phoenix than she had been at Crown Point or even Prescott. She obviously intended to enjoy her role as the governor's wife.[3]

Between trips, Brodie put Smalley to work preparing the annual governor's report to the Secretary of the Interior, freeing him to line up suitable individuals to fill the various appointed territorial positions. Determined to appoint officials who possessed some experience in public service, but not necessarily professional politicians, Brodie refused to consider any man not well respected throughout the territory. None would be tainted by even a hint of scandal or impropriety. As customary, all of Nathan Oakes Murphy's appointees had tendered resignations, but Brodie considered one or two to be able public servants whom he hoped to retain in office. The others he would replace quietly with men of his own choosing.[4]

In July, Brodie announced that the highly respected Judge Edmund William Wells of Prescott had agreed to serve as attorney general. Born in Ohio in 1846, Wells later moved to Prescott, where he invested successfully in mining, cattle ranching, and banking. He also served four years in the Arizona legislature and two years as an associate justice of the Arizona Supreme Court. By a strange coincidence, Wells and Murphy shared the same father-in-law, both having married daughters of a pioneer rancher in Chino Valley north of Prescott. One of the wealthiest men in the territory and obviously not in need of employment, Wells reportedly accepted the position only as a favor to his longtime friend Brodie.[5]

That same month Brodie named Isaac Marshall Christy territorial treasurer. A brother of William Christy, the guiding hand of the reform wing of the Arizona Republican Party, Isaac was born in Ohio in 1844. Proud of his service in the Union Army during the Civil War, he had fought in the battle of Shiloh and "marched to the sea" across Georgia with Gen. William T. Sherman. Arriving in Arizona in 1891, he joined his politically active brother and a nephew, George, who had nominated Brodie for delegate to Congress in 1898.[6]

The resignation of Arizona Ranger Captain Burton C. Mossman enabled Brodie to fill another important position. In 1901, Governor Murphy maneuvered a bill through the legislature creating a fourteen-man force known as the Arizona Rangers to combat the theft of livestock and other criminal activity. Murphy selected Burt Mossman, his longtime friend and former superintendent of the huge Aztec Land and

Cattle Company in northern Arizona, to be captain. The thirty-four-year-old Mossman agreed to serve one term, which expired in August 1902. True to his commitment, Mossman resigned as scheduled, although his departure might well have been triggered by a wave of adverse criticism leveled at Mossman personally and several other Rangers who had been involved in an embarrassing Bisbee saloon brawl on August 11.[7]

Brodie chose Thomas H. Rynning, the former second lieutenant in McClintock's troop of Rough Riders, to replace Mossman. Rynning had no prior experience in law enforcement, but he had demonstrated administrative and leadership skills in the army. Moreover, Rynning was searching for employment, having written Roosevelt the year before requesting a position in the army. Mossman evidently did not support Rynning's selection, later complaining that under Roosevelt a "devastating blight of Rough Riders was spreading over the Southwest." Contrary to speculation, however, Rynning would be one of only two Rough Riders appointed by Brodie to fill a significant position. Moreover, other than Rynning's own statement made several years later, no evidence has surfaced suggesting that Roosevelt played a role in selecting Rynning to lead the Rangers.[8]

Brodie hoped to retain in office Auditor William A. Nichols, a popular and talented public servant, who had replaced the scandal-tainted "Doc" Vickers the year before. Nichols chose instead to be the Republican candidate for delegate to Congress in the November election, promising Brodie he would continue as auditor should his bid for delegate fail. It did, and Nichols remained at his post.

Although Brodie kept Roosevelt fully informed of his key appointments, the president generally refrained from interfering. One notable exception hinged on Roosevelt's determination to find a place for Benjamin Franklin Daniels, a favorite Rough Rider from Colorado who had served in K Troop. Roosevelt initially attempted to appoint Daniels, a former lawman, United States marshal for Arizona, replacing ex-Governor Myron Hawley McCord. In January 1902, following a bitter confirmation fight in the Senate, where Daniels's past underwent heavy scrutiny, the former Rough Rider finally won senatorial approval. A month later, however, new evidence surfaced revealing that Daniels had a criminal record. Surprised at the revelation and incensed at Daniels's lack of candor, Roosevelt demanded his resignation and restored McCord as marshal. Yet the president still desired employment for his friend, and Brodie's forthcoming inauguration provided that opportunity.[9]

Roosevelt and Brodie initially agreed that Brodie would name Daniels superintendent of the Arizona territorial prison at Yuma, but

Roosevelt later changed his mind, and Brodie instead offered Daniels the assistant superintendency. The former Rough Rider quickly refused that position, but when the superintendent's slot became available through resignation two years later, Brodie appointed Daniels without further public outcry or opposition.[10]

Brodie's initial appointments met widespread approval. In January 1903, Attorney General Wells, Treasurer Christy, holdover Auditor Nichols, and Ranger Captain Rynning sailed through the confirmation process in the Council without opposition. Individuals selected to fill lesser positions fared equally well. One critically important territorial official Brodie could not control, however, was the Arizona secretary of state, who served at the pleasure of the president—not the governor.

The incumbent secretary, Isaac T. Stoddard, a thoroughly competent and well-connected politician, had been appointed in the summer of 1901 by President McKinley, and Roosevelt did not want to replace him without good cause. Brodie did not trust Stoddard, and it was common knowledge in Arizona that the secretary was "persona non grata" in the Brodie Administration. Yet Brodie had no choice but to tolerate Stoddard—at least temporarily. Former Governor Murphy, of course, and Stoddard were good friends.[11]

Brodie scarcely had his administrative team in place before two unexpected and potentially serious incidents threatened his administration. One raised the specter of an armed confrontation between a group of Apaches and a number of white settlers living near old Fort McDowell. The second threatened to involve Brodie in a labor dispute. These were highly emotional issues which, unless quickly resolved, threatened far-reaching consequences.

On August 20, Brodie received several petitions from forty-four white settlers living near abandoned Fort McDowell complaining that approximately three hundred Mohave-Apaches had settled illegally on government land along the Verde River, where they were stealing from local residents and otherwise causing trouble. The whites demanded that the Indians be removed. Six days later, a delegation of four Apaches appeared in the governor's office to present their side of the story. According to the Indians, only 150 Apaches had settled near McDowell, and had done so with the express permission of the Indian agent at San Carlos and the Office of Indian Affairs in Washington, DC. Refusing to be drawn into the controversy, Brodie referred the matter to the United Stated Office of Indian Affairs, which ultimately sided with the Indians and complimented Brodie for his unbiased approach to the matter.[12]

Brodie considered the labor dispute at mines in Globe to be potentially much more serious. He knew from personal experience that Arizona miners could be a volatile group, capable of shutting down completely the territory's only major industry. In that event, the disruption of Arizona's economic, political, and social fabric would irreparably damage his fledging administration. Usually referred to as a strike, the situation actually was much more complicated. Hard feelings between employees and management of the Old Dominion Copper Mining and Smelting Company, the dominant mining operation in Gila County, had been increasing for months, but the problem came to a head on September 12, 1902, when the company closed the Globe mines and smelter, citing as justification a shortage of coke necessary to fuel the power supply. Members of the Globe miners union, believing the shutdown to be retaliation for recently increased union activity, refused to accept that explanation. Tension quickly escalated.[13]

Members of the Globe Merchants Association, convinced that the *Globe Times*, a newspaper owned by the union, supported certain unlawful acts committed by union members, voted at a mass meeting to withdraw all patronage from the *Times*. The union immediately responded by calling for a boycott of those merchants who had agreed to withhold patronage. Rumors quickly circulated that the workers planned to flood the mine and had threatened the life of the general manager of the Old Dominion. Brodie dispatched Captain Rynning with a handful of Rangers to assess the situation.[14]

Finding conditions at Globe stable, Rynning, after posting his force in position to protect company property, wired the governor for instructions. Brodie approved Rynning's deposition of the Rangers, but cautioned the Ranger captain not to place his force at the disposal of the civil authorities because they had not yet certified to the governor that they could not control the situation without outside assistance. By quickly dispatching Rynning to Globe, Brodie revealed that he understood the dangers and political fallout of a protracted labor dispute. His days at Crown Point had taught him well. In this case, however, his fears proved unfounded. Eight days later, representatives of the union, the copper company, and merchants association signed an agreement ending the dispute. By the end of October, the Old Dominion had resumed production. The crisis had passed.[15]

Opportunists also surfaced to test Brodie's personal commitment. Shortly after taking office, he received several inquiries regarding investment opportunities in Arizona or Sonora mines. One such request even came from a member of the New York legislature. In every case Brodie, who had no intention of being a "carpetbag governor," stood firm, replying that as long as he remained in office he would refrain from commenting on potential investments.[16]

Although Murphy graciously stepped down when Brodie replaced him as governor, he and his brother quickly surfaced to openly challenge Brodie's position as head of the Arizona Republican Party. In September, at the Republican nominating convention in Phoenix, delegates gathered to select candidates for the November election and define the party platform. Brodie and representatives of the Christy wing of the party came prepared to push hard for the nomination of Auditor William Nichols for the important position of delegate to Congress. The Murphy faction turned out equally determined to secure the nomination for Robert E. Morrison, a highly regarded Prescott attorney who had defended the former governor in the case of *Wilson v. Murphy and Vickers*. The battle lines were clearly drawn.[17]

With the total number of delegates to the convention set at 154, controlling the thirty-four-man block from Yavapai County would be critical for the Murphy supporters, who knew that representatives from the southern counties favored Nichols. Brodie, of course, had strong personal support in Yavapai, but that also was Murphy country. Exactly what transpired behind the scenes is not clear, but one Democratic newspaper reported that Frank Murphy held the Yavapai men firmly in line. Reportedly, he arranged for the group to travel to Phoenix on a private car provided by his railroad company, which was "well stocked with corporation-purchased champagne."[18]

According to another Democratic paper, the Murphy faction unscrupulously coppered their bet by convincing the ten-man Coconino County delegation, whose members were "green enough to pull up corn," that it should support Morrison in exchange for the promise that the next chairman of the territorial Republican central committee would be a Coconino County man. The Coconino group supported Morrison as agreed, but soon found they had been hoodwinked. Contrary to agreement, the chairmanship went to Auditor Nichols of Maricopa County as compensation for losing the nomination for delegate to Morrison. "These Yavapai Murphyits," the paper disdainfully concluded, "are gay deceivers ever."[19]

How accurately the Democratic newspapers analyzed the behind-the-scenes machinations endemic to the Republican convention is not clear, but the Murphy forces eked out a narrow victory. On the afternoon of September 17, with Brodie and Nathan Oakes Murphy seated together on the stage in the convention hall as a sop to party unity, the delegates cast seventy-eight votes for Morrison and seventy-six for Nichols. As arranged, the Yavapai and Coconino delegations stood solidly behind Morrison. Deeply disappointed, Brodie swallowed his pride and agreed to support Morrison. Indeed, he could do little else.

Some Democrats, who had hoped that Governor Brodie's appointment would break Murphy's stranglehold on the Arizona Republican

Party, saw the convention as an unexpected setback. "If they [the 'decent' Republicans] cannot control with a man like Brodie as governor to aid them," one newspaper lamented, "they cannot hope for success when Arizona becomes a state and Murphy dishes out all the fat offices to his henchmen." Murphy, the Democratic organ concluded, "is again the smiling boss, the genial high grand dictator of the Republican Party in Arizona."[20]

Actually, those who criticized Brodie's failure to control the 1902 convention did so prematurely. Brodie had been in the governor's chair for only two and a half months and still was bringing on board those who supported his political philosophy. Murphy, on the other hand, had been the party "boss" for many years and had a long history of skillfully dispensing political favors and benefits to his friends and colleagues—many of whom now stood ready to repay in kind. For Brodie's candidate to surmount such formidable obstacles and lose by only two votes suggests a remarkable achievement. The Arizona Republican convention, scheduled for 1904, when Roosevelt would stand reelection, undoubtedly would be a much more accurate test of the relative strength of Brodie's reformers and Murphy's "Old Guard."

Although he carefully maintained friendly and cordial relations with newspapermen, Brodie refrained from publicly giving any indication, other than statehood, of his long-range plans for Arizona. Obviously, he did not want to be embarrassed by having any premature comments come back to haunt him. He even refused to speculate on any hypothetical legislation, informing one individual that "not even Mrs. Brodie knows what action I shall take on any one specific bill." The first public disclosure of his intention and goals appeared in his eagerly awaited ninety-nine-page annual report to the Secretary of the Interior.[21]

Released in October, Brodie's report at first glance appears to have been little more than a carefully compiled statistical review of the territory. Upon closer scrutiny, however, it becomes obvious that the report could also function as a written justification for statehood. The population of Arizona, Brodie emphasized, consisted of over 122,000 "law abiding, energetic and progressive residents," of which approximately 70,500 claimed native birth. Aggressive steps were being taken to improve education opportunities, and a number of new churches were under construction.[22]

Financial and economic conditions also were improving, Brodie reported. Net bonded and territorial floating indebtedness had decreased over the past year, but assessed valuation had increased. The mining, cattle, railroad, lumber, and agricultural industries were flourishing, but the construction of dams and reservoirs along the Gila, Salt, Hassayampa, and other rivers would enable many more acres of farmland to be brought into production. Brodie pointed out that the Hansbrough-Newlands Act, or National Reclamation Act (originally known as the Newlands Act) which Roosevelt had signed into law earlier that year, made such reclamation projects possible. Admitting that the territorial tax rate exceeded that found in many states, Brodie explained that Arizona's mining industry had not yet been called upon to assume a fair share of the tax burden.

Brodie closed by offering ten specific recommendations, the first two being keystones for Arizona's future. The first, as one would expect, requested the Interior Department to support legislation then before Congress to grant statehood to Arizona, New Mexico, and Oklahoma. The second requested that aid to Arizona irrigation projects through the Hansbrough-Newlands Act be "carefully considered." Other recommendations included an increase in the governor's salary, and additional federal funds to support Indian schools and the National Guard. He also suggested that with statehood, "a hospital for aged and infirm miners" be established. Brodie ended his report with the recommendation that an appropriation be made to control flooding along the lower Colorado River by constructing a levee from Yuma to the Mexican border, and that a reforestation program be established to replace the depleted timber resources. Perceived as an accurate and comprehensive review of conditions in Arizona, Brodie's report received favorable comments across the territory—particularly his pitch for statehood.[23]

Most Arizonans believed that Roosevelt's ascendancy to the White House and his subsequent appointment of Governor Brodie virtually assured statehood. Indeed, few could fault that assumption. After all, Brodie had been an exceptionally strong advocate for the admission of Arizona for over four years and undoubtedly had the president's ear on the subject. Roosevelt, himself, at the First Annual Reunion of the Rough Riders, publicly pledged his support for admission. Moreover, proposed legislation known as the Omnibus Statehood Bill, providing for the admission of Arizona, New Mexico, and Oklahoma, was already working its way through Congress.

With active support from both New Mexico's delegate to Congress and Arizona's Marcus Aurelius Smith, a Democrat, the Omnibus Bill passed the House with little opposition on May 9, 1902. In the Senate, support for statehood came from the powerful Matthew S. Quay, a sixty-nine-year-old Republican from Pennsylvania. Unfortunately, Albert J. Beveridge, a young, opinionated Republican senator from Indiana, stood firmly in opposition—and Beveridge chaired the Senate Committee on Territories.[24]

Late that fall, unable to control his committee, which remained split on the statehood issue, Beveridge managed to postpone action on the Omnibus Bill until the next session of Congress. In the meantime, a four-man subcommittee consisting of Beveridge and three other senators planned to tour Arizona, New Mexico, and Oklahoma on a fact-finding mission to determine the territories' readiness for statehood.[25]

In November, Brodie began making preparations for Beveridge's visit, but the senator sent an alarming message by ignoring Brodie and making travel arrangements directly with Nathan Oakes Murphy's brother Frank, owner of the Santa Fe, Prescott and Phoenix Railroad. Originally, Beveridge planned to enter Arizona from New Mexico via the Southern Pacific Railroad through Tucson, but at the last moment changed his itinerary, instead scheduling his arrival in northern Arizona on the Santa Fe Railroad. He also requested that Frank Murphy arrange to have a private rail car meet his party at Ash Fork, a railroad town north of Prescott. Seeing this as an opportunity to ingratiate himself with Beveridge, Murphy arranged a one-day layover in Prescott, enabling Beveridge to meet with selected local citizens and attend a lavish evening party in Murphy's Prescott home. The following morning, November 17, the group entrained for Phoenix, stopping en route to briefly tour the booming Congress gold mine. A part owner of the mine, Murphy instructed the mine superintendent, obviously a trusted employee, to accompany Beveridge throughout the remainder of his Arizona trip.[26]

In Phoenix, Beveridge found Brodie, former Governors Murphy and McCord, Secretary Stoddard, and other dignitaries waiting at his hotel to host a reception followed that evening by a dinner. The next day, after a tour of the city, the delegation received in closed session testimony from local citizens regarding conditions in Arizona. Just before midnight, Brodie escorted the group aboard a special train bound for Bisbee, with a brief layover in Tucson, enabling the group to visit the University of Arizona. At Bisbee, Beveridge's committee toured the mines and reduction works of the immense Copper Queen Consolidated Mining Company owned by the Phelps Dodge Corporation, departing late that same evening for Las Cruces, New Mexico. Beveridge's fact-finding trip to Arizona lasted just three days.[27]

Although members of Beveridge's group carefully refrained from commenting publicly on their findings in Arizona, most local papers suggested that the territory had presented its case well. Even Brodie publicly appeared to be optimistic, but privately he harbored serious reservations. Beveridge's demeanor from Prescott to Bisbee had not been encouraging. Reportedly, the senator had conversed little, generally dozing quietly in his train seat "with his hat over his eyes and his back to the window."[28]

Remembering his own admonishment "to never trust a Murphy," Brodie must have been concerned with the Murphy brothers' overt involvement in the Beveridge visit. In this case, Brodie and Murphy ostensibly apperared to be allies working for the common goal of statehood, although possibly for different reasons. But by the fall of 1902, Brodie was beginning to have second thoughts—not about the wisdom of statehood—but the timing of the event.[29]

Contrary to the glowing picture of Arizona that Brodie had painted in his annual report, he knew that a five-year drought had seriously impacted both agricultural interests and the cattle industry. Considering the increased financial burden which statehood would bring to Arizona, Brodie concluded that the event should be postponed for two years. Under existing circumstances, however, he had no choice but to keep these thoughts to himself and continue to support immediate statehood vigorously. He would do so to the best of his ability. On November 15, Brodie took his case directly to the president, informing Roosevelt that he would "greatly appreciate" presidential backing of the Omnibus Bill. It was not to be.[30]

Beveridge scarcely had returned to Washington when rumors surfaced that his report to Congress would not favor admission of either Arizona or New Mexico. Mark Smith, Arizona's hardworking delegate to Congress, continued to exude optimism, expressing his hope that Senator Quay's pro-statehood stance yet would carry the day. But the tide was turning. One of the most telling blows fell on December 2, when President Roosevelt, in his annual report to Congress, ignored Brodie's appeal and failed to even mention statehood. Two weeks later, Congress, bowing to Beveridge's skillful delaying tactics, voted to postpone further debate on the question until after the first of the year. Brodie, meanwhile, remained silent on the issue, refusing to make any public comment or speculation.[31]

In December, as the wheels of government slowed in deference to the Christmas holidays, Brodie focused on preparing his first annual message to the legislature, which would convene in January. This would be his first opportunity to publicly lay out his legislative agenda for Arizona, and he knew that both Democrats and Republicans would be watching closely. Nevertheless, he made one executive decision which caught a few Arizonans by surprise. He paroled Pearl Hart, Arizona's notorious female hold-up artist, who had been sentenced to five years in the territorial prison at Yuma.

The strange case of Arizona's bandit queen never has been unraveled. Abandoned by a possibly abusive husband, the young woman stuggled to survive as best as she could in the mining camps of Pinal and Gila counties. In 1897, accompanied by an accomplice known as

Joe Boot, she held up the Globe-Florence stagecoach, removing $790 in cash, a passenger's watch and the driver's revolver. Later captured near Mammoth on the San Pedro River south of old Camp Grant, Hart ultimately began her incarceration at Yuma.[32]

In the fall of 1902, possibly responding to a request from Pearl's sister living in Kansas City, Missouri, the superintendent of the territorial prison recommended that Hart and two other inmates, one female, be paroled. Pearl's release, however, would be predicated on her agreement to leave the territory with funds provided by her sister. Although the superintendent provided no specific reason for his request, except for a veiled reference to the women's section being overcrowded, Brodie approved the recommendation. Fifty-two years later, George Smalley stated that Brodie had pardoned the woman because she had become pregnant, thereby avoiding an embarrassing prison scandal.[33]

After six months in office, Brodie continued to enjoy widespread bipartisan support, successfully maintaining the universal feeling of goodwill which had attended his inauguration. The reform wing of his party stood solidly behind him, and the "Old Guard" Republicans maintained a low profile, offering no premature criticism. The Democrats, elated that the unpopular Nathan Oakes Murphy had been ousted, continued to extend the hand of cooperation. Understanding clearly the political ramifications of his appointment, Brodie had moved carefully to place his administration on a sound footing by surrounding himself with respected, capable, and honest men. The two potential crises that could have proven embarrassing had fortunately blown over quickly, enabling the new governor to face the Democrat-controlled legislature with confidence and no black marks against his record. The future looked bright.

CHAPTER 18

"A Very Good Democrat After All"

On January 19, 1903, the Twenty-Second Territorial Legislature convened in Phoenix. That afternoon, with preliminary organizational details completed, the lawmakers gathered in joint session to meet the new governor. Dressed in a dark cutaway suit with his slightly graying hair neatly combed and mustache carefully trimmed, Brodie strode confidently to the podium before a packed gallery.[1]

Brodie wasted no time explaining his agenda. After first quickly reviewing the overall financial conditions of the territory, the new governor presented a litany of legislative recommendations designed primarily—but not exclusively—to improve the tax structure and streamline internal procedures then in place to safeguard territorial funds. All territorial and county officials still operating on a fee basis, Brodie requested, should be converted to salary. Other suggestions included realigning judicial districts, enacting a primary election law, doubling the size of the Arizona Ranger Company, purchasing and preserving "relics of prehistoric races," and granting increased financial support to the Pioneers' Historical Society, the University of Arizona, and the Normal School of Arizona (now Arizona State University) in Tempe.[2]

Three of Brodie's carefully crafted recommendations struck a particularly responsive chord with both lawmakers and the general public. Previously, Governor Murphy unsuccessfully had urged the legislature to levy a tax on the output of Arizona mines. Brodie revived that controversial proposal, pointing out that for years the mining industry, Arizona's economic power base, had not been carrying a fair share of the tax burden. Now, he argued, the time had come to enact a fair tax

Arizona Secretary of State Isaac Taft Stoddard. A talented and well connected politician, Stoddard unsuccessfully challenged Governor Brodie for control of incorporation fees. Courtesy of Sharlot Hall Museum Library and Archives, Prescott, Airzona.

on ore removed from producing mines. But such a tax, the governor cautioned, should not deter the development of new mines.

Turning to another potentially inflammatory issue, Brodie asked the legislature to study the advisability of replacing the customary ten-hour work day in the mining industry with a mandated eight-hour work shift. Realizing that such a measure would be highly controversial and possibly could negatively impact small mine owners, Brodie stopped short of calling on the legislature to pass such a law, instead requesting only that the lawmakers take "a fair and impartial view" of the question. But Brodie's studied attack on existing procedures in place to process the filing of incorporation fees proved the real bombshell.[3]

Choosing his words carefully, Brodie pointed out that for two years many corporations had chosen to organize under Arizona's liberal incorporation laws intending to conduct business outside the territory. Existing Arizona law specified that all fees and other charges associated with the incorporation process would be collected by the secretary of state personally. Believing that Arizona—and not the secretary—should benefit from these transactions, Brodie urged the legislature to require that any organization incorporating under Arizona law file their articles with the territorial auditor, who would deposit all associated fees into the treasury, instead of with the secretary. In submitting this recommendation, Brodie threw a red flag directly in the face of Secretary of State Isaac Taft Stoddard.[4]

Secretary Stoddard, who had been pocketing incorporation fees for nearly two years, never had been called upon to render a formal accounting of his collections. There were rumors, of course. Some critics estimated that the secretary was drawing as much as $120,000 annually. Others merely stated that he was becoming rich. In any event, a combative Stoddard had no intention of permitting Brodie to kill his Golden Goose. An experienced and well-entrenched politician with powerful friends, he stood prepared to challenge the governor on this issue by any means at his disposal. Brodie had thrown down the gauntlet. The fight was on.[5]

Brodie also informed the legislature that he took his own fiscal responsibilities seriously. A law passed in 1901, he explained, which authorized the governor to spend $750 annually at his own discretion, could not be considered good government. In Brodie's view, public funds should be appropriated only for specific purposes, and vouchers always should be required. Therefore, Brodie promised to leave all such discretionary funds in the treasury untouched.

Except for a handful of Old Guard Republicans, Brodie's address drew accolades from both parties. Many of the governor's progressive recommendations reflected Democratic principles as defined in that party's convention held in Tucson the previous September. The Democrats had gone on record as advocating an eight-hour work day, eliminating the fee system in favor of salaried employees, changing incorporation procedures, establishing uniformity in primary elections, and several other measures endorsed by Brodie. All in all, the Democrats expressed unprecedented satisfaction with this Republican chief executive. "Governor Brodie," one Democratic paper concluded, "seems to be a very good democrat after all."[6]

Hoping to work harmoniously with the legislature, Brodie knew that he needed to cooperate with the opposition party, which outnumbered Republicans twenty-one to three in the House, and seven to five in the Council. Although the Democrats obviously controlled the legislature, they lacked the discipline necessary to close ranks and establish their own agenda. Not only did the Arizona mining and railroad interests maintain powerful lobbies which transcended party lines, but longtime Republican politicians such as ex-Governor Murphy and Secretary Stoddard had cultivated friends and supporters on both sides of the aisle. Reform would not be easy.

Forgoing the customary inaugural ball, the evening following Brodie's address to the legislature Stoddard and his wife hosted an elaborate reception in their home to honor the new governor. Decorations in the dining room consisted of extensive arrangements of Mary's favorite flowers interspersed with small electric lights spelling out "Brodie." All in attendance reported that they enjoyed themselves immensely, and the evening reflected no hint that Brodie and Stoddard were locked on a collision course.[7]

Actually, Brodie and Stoddard had been at loggerheads even before Brodie addressed the legislature. While preparing his annual message to that body, Brodie had requested that all department heads and other key officials submit an accounting of their activities for the previous year, which he intended to append to his own report. Stoddard initially ignored Brodie's request, but upon being informed that the statutes required such an accounting, belatedly complied. Stating that he was filing his report "in compliance with a law which I am unable to learn has been observed in the past," Stoddard, probably reacting to a specific request from Brodie to include details regarding the collection of incorporation fees, stated arrogantly that he was "including also such business of a personal nature connected with the office and to which the Secretary is in no way accountable to the Territory." Technically, Stoddard probably was correct in his position that the collection of incorporation fees as provided by law remained a personal matter, but to imply that he marched to a higher authority than other territorial officials was a mistake. Brodie would not take that challenge lying down.[8]

Responding to Brodie's message, the legislature first tackled the mandatory eight-hour work day for the mining industry. Introduced in the House on January 27, the measure quickly passed with virtually no dissent, but ran into opposition in the Council. Some opponents expressed concern that such a law would result in strikes and other manifestations of labor unrest. Under this proposal, miners would work two hours a day less than they had been before. Would their pay be adjusted accordingly? With the law mute on that question, the issue remained to be resolved by negotiation between mine owners and workers. Brodie and others feared that many small mine operators, already existing on a shoestring budget, would be particularly affected. Nevertheless, in spite of some opposition in the Council, the bill passed with one significant amendment. Instead of including the entire mining industry as originally envisioned, the eight-hour work day applied to underground miners only. Brodie signed the measure on March 10, with the implementation date of June 1.[9]

The day after proposing the eight-hour work shift, the House dropped the hammer on Secretary Stoddard. Representative Lawrence Oscar Cowan of Pima County, a Democrat, introduced a measure known as the Cowan Bill, which removed all incorporation fees from the secretary of state's control, providing instead that all such fees would be collected by the auditor and deposited in the territorial treasury. Assigned to a five-man House Standing Committee on Territorial Affairs, the Cowan Bill provided exactly what Brodie had recommended.[10]

Determined to stop the Cowan Bill in its tracks, Stoddard called upon his friends in the House to kill the measure in committee. Brodie was ready for him, however. He was learning to play the political game, too. The key was public opinion. Newspapers across the territory already were demanding that Stoddard resign, citing as justification the exorbitant amount of incorporation fee money the secretary supposedly was collecting. Finally, attempting to neutralize the criticism, Stoddard, in his belated report to Brodie, stated that the total amount he had collected during his eighteen months and seven days in office amounted to only $15,946.30. Seeing this figure as an opportunity to further weaken the secretary's position, Brodie withheld public release of Stoddard's report for several weeks, thereby affording Stoddard's critics additional time to build their own case without refutation. The ploy succeeded. Fanned by Stoddard's questionable claims of a modest income from fees as opposed to the widely accepted rumors of extremely lucrative payouts, demands for passage of the Cowan Bill snowballed.

Nevertheless, Stoddard won the first round, albeit a Pyrrhic victory. On February 16, a three-man majority of the House Standing Committee on Territorial Affairs, led by a Democrat from Prescott (Stoddard's home town), rendered a report. Praising Stoddard's cooperation and stating that "all of the records and papers of his office" had been examined, the committee recommended that the Cowen Bill not pass.[11]

Obviously prepared for such a contingency, Representative Gus Williams, a Democrat from Graham County, rose to present an electrifying two-man minority report. According to Williams, Stoddard had not presented the official fee books for inspection as the majority report claimed. Instead, Stoddard had informed the committee that he had destroyed the books. However, upon reviewing the few current records available, the minority on the committee found evidence indicating that Stoddard had collected over $3,000 in fees during January and an additional $1,500 during the first three weeks in February. Based on these figures, Williams estimated that Stoddard's annual income from incorporation fees amounted to at least $40,000. At this point, one of the secretary's friends in the House objected to further reading of the minority report, but the damage had been done. Stoddard's official statement that he had collected only $15,946.30 during the previous eighteen months and one week appeared to be a falsehood.[12]

Lawrence Cowan immediately jumped to his feet and offered a resolution creating a special committee consisting of the Speaker of the House and four other members empowered to investigate the secretary's office, with full authority to subpoena all books and records, as well as to take sworn testimony from witnesses. The resolution passed with but one dissenting vote. Five Democrats composed the special committee. None could be considered Stoddard's friends. Watching his support in the House melt away, a frustrated Stoddard sarcastically commented: "That is one hell of a committee."[13]

On March 3, in a bitterly contentious setting, the House again considered the Cowan Bill. The special investigating committee had not yet tendered its findings, but apparently the bill's supporters wanted to move quickly. Again, Stoddard's friends, attempting to delay the final vote, offered procedural objections, an attempted filibuster, and several amendments, one of which exempted the incumbent secretary from the bill's provisions. In the end, however, the delaying tactics failed, and the Cowan Bill passed the House by a vote of fifteen to six, with three members excused.[14]

As the Council prepared to address the issue, the *Arizona Republican*, former Governor Murphy's newspaper, entered the fray to support Stoddard. Pointing out that the secretary's efforts to entice businesses to incorporate in Arizona had been extremely successful, the paper claimed that economic benefits of the incorporation process extended to the counties as well as to the secretary personally. Maricopa County alone, the *Republican* asserted, was receiving over $700 a month in benefits from Stoddard's incorporation activities. The paper also suggested that the Cowan Bill violated an 1886 federal law prohibiting reduction of a territorial official's salary during that individual's term of office. That argument had been raised earlier. Stoddard, himself, had already been advised by at least one attorney that the federal law protected only the fixed salary of officials, but did not extend to the collection of fees.[15]

In the Council, only two Democrats joined Henry Fountain Ashurst to champion Stoddard's now obviously doomed cause. A Democrat from Coconino County, the popular Ashurst was widely touted as a rising star in his party. Born in a covered wagon in the desert of northern Nevada in 1874, Ashurst later moved with his family to northern Arizona, where he became involved in politics. Known for his flamboyant, bombastic oratory, he never failed to entertain his audience. Ashurst's support for Stoddard was well known, but never explained. In fact, one Arizona newspaper suggested that his position on the Cowan Bill could possibly impact negatively on his political future in Arizona, but of course it did not.[16]

Upon receiving the Cowan Bill from the House on March 16, President of the Council Eugene S. Ives, Governor Murphy's former nemesis, moved to suspend Council rules and consider the bill immediately. The motion passed, but not before Ashurst delivered a characteristically emotional half-hour tirade against the measure. Praising Stoddard and denying scornfully that he had "taken the secretary's money" to do so, Ashurst charged that Stoddard's enemies were motivated by envy and, as far as honesty was concerned, Stoddard's critics "had no more idea of honesty than the scarlet women of Babylon had of the immaculate conception." When the bill came up for its final vote, one of Stoddard's two supporters deserted his position and voted for passage. Ashurst, however, and a fellow Democrat from Gila County nailed their colors to the mast and went down with the ship. All five Republicans in the Council voted for the bill. Clearly, in Brodie's view, he had won a significant victory over Secretary Stoddard and those who rode with him.[17]

Following the Council's vote, some newspapers predicted that Stoddard would resign in protest. That proved to be nothing more than wishful thinking. Brodie's troubles with Stoddard had only begun.

Brodie's pet proposal to double the size of the Arizona Ranger force also encountered strong opposition, particularly in the House, where an effort to abolish the Rangers entirely had to be beaten back. That accomplished, friends of the Rangers introduced a bill calling for a second Ranger company. That measure quickly went down in defeat, as did an alternative proposal to double the size of the existing Ranger Company from thirteen to twenty-six men. Representative Stephen Roemer, however, a Democrat from Cochise County, refused to let the issue die. Working quietly and effectively behind the scenes, Roemer gathered enough support to bring the latter proposal back for reconsideration and successfully maneuvered it through the House by the razor-thin margin of thirteen to eleven. The Council concurred by the comfortable vote of nine to three.[18]

Opposition to the Arizona Rangers crystallized for a variety of reasons. Some critics expressed concern that Rangers often displayed an overbearing and unacceptable attitude toward law enforcement, citing as examples the arrest of the notorious bandit Augustín Chacón and the shooting of Lorenzo "Lon" Bass by a Ranger in a Douglas saloon. The Chacón incident raised the issue of illegal apprehension and violation of Mexican sovereignty. Bass's death challenged the Rangers as being too quick on the trigger.

Augustín Chacón was a hard case. In 1895, a court in Solomonville sentenced him to hang for the murder of a Morenci shop holder committed during a robbery. Nine days before the execution, Chacón escaped into Mexico, thereafter frequently crossing into Arizona to rob and steal. In 1902, Ranger Captain Burt Mossman delayed his resignation from the force to follow through on a daring sting operation he had designed to arrest Chacón in Sonora and bring him back to Arizona. The ploy succeeded, and Chacón died by hanging as originally sentenced. Little sympathy existed in Arizona for the notorious desperado, but the legality and propriety of Mossman's actions drew widespread criticism.[19]

The shooting of Lon Bass also raised serious concerns. In the fall of 1902, Captain Rynning moved Ranger headquarters from Bisbee to Douglas, a new community laid out in the Sulphur Spring Valley to accommodate a copper smelter being constructed by the Phelps Dodge Corporation. The smelter would process ore from the company mines at Bisbee and in Sonora. Texan Lon Bass and two partners opened the Cowboy Home Saloon to capitalize on the sudden influx of construction workers, smelter men and cowboys looking for excitement. In January, Bass had words with Ranger William W. Webb, a thirty-five-year-old Texan who had served in Brodie's Arizona Rough Riders. The following month, Webb and another Ranger, hearing gunfire near the Cowboy Saloon, entered the bar to investigate. Bass confronted Webb, a scuffle ensued, shots rang out, and Bass lay dead on the floor. Rynning, who happened to be patrolling nearby on horseback, immediately investigated. Authorities indicted Webb for murder, but a four-day trial in Tombstone acquitted the ranger. Nevertheless, opponents of the Rangers painted Webb as an example of those trigger-happy gunmen who supposedly dominated the Ranger force.[20]

Undoubtedly, some Rangers might have been high-handed and arrogant in performing their duties, but other considerations fostered opposition to the force. Apparently, some county sheriffs, jealous of the Rangers' success, held them responsible for the loss of rewards and other fees normally associated with law enforcement. Actually, the anti-Ranger movement seems to have been rooted more in partisan politics than in Ranger behavior. Many Democrats, apparently viewing the company as purely a Republican entity from the very beginning, stood ready to disband the Rangers at the first opportunity. The vote on Roemer's reconsideration of the bill to double the number of Rangers supports that contention. Of the eight Republicans in the legislature, seven voted to increase the Ranger force, but only fifteen of the twenty-eight Democrats joined them. Significantly, strongest support for the territorial lawmen came from those areas hit hardest by rustlers: Pima, Santa Cruz, Cochise, and Graham Counties. Rynning's troopers found few friends in Yuma, Mohave, and Yavapai Counties.[21]

Brodie never wavered in his support of the Rangers. Convinced that Rynning personally and his troopers in general effectively patrolled the territory, Brodie brooked no undue criticism. Colin Cameron, a prominent Santa Cruz County rancher, learned that the hard way. In November 1902, Cameron wrote Brodie an angry letter complaining about the use of Rangers as cattle inspectors. Brodie reacted immediately. After assuring the rancher that the Rangers were doing "their full duty," Brodie returned Cameron's letter with a caustic notation: "As the tone of your letter of the 25th slightly exceeds the limit, I return the same herewith to you."[22]

Mary Brodie shared her husband's high opinion of the Ranger Company. In some cases, she even acted as a surrogate mother, pleading the case of some errant trooper who had displeased the governor. Yet Mary harbored no illusions about the force, later confiding to her granddaughter that "they were the toughest set of men she had ever seen."[23]

Even the anti-Ranger legislators, however, rallied around Brodie's request to provide relief for the widow of Ranger Carlos Tafolla, who died in a shootout with a band of rustlers in the White Mountains. The legislature voted to pay his widow $600 in $25 a month installments. Two Democrats voted against the measure and one abstained.[24]

In mid-February, a relatively unexpected proposal briefly rocked the legislature. Representative Thomas A. Morrison, a Democrat from Yavapai County, introduced a bill extending suffrage to women in the territory over age twenty-one. Although some legislators at first seemed to treat the proposal as a joke, the bill should not have come as a complete surprise. Two months earlier, the Third Biennial Convention of the Arizona Equal Suffrage Association had met in Phoenix. Chaired by Pauline Marie Schindler O'Neill, the widow of Brodie's friend and fellow Rough Rider Buckey O'Neill, the group announced that a bill granting women the right to vote soon would be introduced. Initially, the announcement drew little public comment, but Morrison's action indicated that the women had made their point. Shortly thereafter, the idea spread and territorial newspapers chose sides.[25]

Brodie, of course, as was his custom, withheld public comment, but he revealed his personal thoughts in a letter to Andrew Kimball, his Mormon friend in Thatcher. Referring to the still-pending statehood issue, Brodie pointed out that "any drastic legislation, or any changing materially of the existing order of affairs in Arizona might be called up in the Senate and act to our disadvantage. To be sure," he continued, "I feel as many others do, that it would be a hard matter to secure the attendance of the good home-loving women of the Territory at the polls on election day." Perhaps, Brodie mused, it would be best to have the women of Arizona vote on whether or not they should be granted suffrage. Fortunately, such ambiguities did not find their way into the mainstream press. Obviously, the suffrage issue did not find a champion in Governor Brodie.[26]

Encountering little opposition, Morrison's bill moved through the House quickly, passing on February 13 by a vote of sixteen to seven with one member excused. Four Democrats and three Republicans voted against the bill. More serious opposition surfaced in the Council, where opponents attempted to kill the bill in committee. That move failed, and the measure passed on March 17, with five Republicans and three Democrats voting in the affirmative and four Democrats standing opposed. Territorial newspapers had a field day, speculating whether Brodie would or would not sign the measure.[27]

Before packed galleries in the evening session on March 19, Brodie delivered his decision to the House. In a carefully worded message, composed in an uncharacteristically stilted, legal style, Brodie vetoed the Suffrage Bill. Probably written, or at least greatly influenced, by Attorney General Edmund Wells, Brodie's veto message argued that the legislature did not have the authority to extend suffrage to women. The organic law of Arizona, Brodie carefully explained, limited Arizona to pass only those laws "not inconsistent with the Constitution and laws of the United States." Arizona's organic law gave every male citizen above age twenty-one the right to vote. The privilege of voting, then, was not a "natural" right, but a privilege "conferred by law." Because the Constitution of the United States mentioned only male inhabitants in regard to voting, Brodie concluded that the Arizona Legislature, in granting suffrage to women, was attempting to enact legislation "not consistent with the Constitution of the United States and the Acts of Congress."[28]

With the reading of the veto message complete, one representative sarcastically moved that "the apology of the Governor be accepted." The chairman ruled the motion out of order and members of the House rose to argue either for or against the veto. Emotions in both cases ran high, but the House soon attempted an override. With a number of women in the galleries "hissing" at each negative vote, the House sustained the veto by a margin of fourteen to eight. Two Republicans and twelve Democrats supported the governor.[29]

Reaction across the Territory surfaced immediately, but not as emotionally as one might expect. The most virulent comment came from the *Arizona Daily Star,* which in a highly unusual parody on Brodie's days as a Rough Rider, screamed in bold headlines:

BRODIE THE ROUGH RIDER

MAKES A LAST CHARGE

THE WOMEN OF ARIZONA HIS VICTIMS

Suggesting that Brodie concocted the legal argument only as an excuse for vetoing a bill he philosophically opposed, the *Star* concluded that the governor simply was seeking "the easiest way out." Without citing specifics, the paper speculated that Brodie may have fallen under the influence of his wife, who was "avowedly antagonistic to the principal [sic] of equal rights." Rejecting out of hand Brodie's position that the suffrage bill violated the organic act, the *Star*, again without explanation, asserted that saloonkeepers and gamblers had taken the lead in opposing suffrage. "As a prominent citizen said tonight," the paper lamented, "the gamblers and saloons win, the women lose."[30]

Other than the *Star*, few newspapers offered anything more than a token condemnation of Brodie's veto. Most appeared to agree in principle with the *Arizona Bulletin*'s comment that Brodie acted as he saw his duty. Moreover, the fact that the House voted fourteen to eight not to override the veto of a bill they earlier had passed sixteen to seven certainly supports the *Bulletin*'s observation that a great deal of quiet opposition to women's suffrage still existed in Arizona. Perhaps some previously outspoken advocates for suffrage, both in and out of the legislature, secretly harbored reservations about the issue and silently applauded Brodie for standing firm. At any rate, for whatever reasons, Brodie's veto did not significantly impact his popularity as governor.[31]

In early February, two special envoys from Utah handed Brodie their credentials, explaining that they had been empowered by the governor and legislature of the state to propose that Arizona cede the area north and west of the Colorado River to Utah. Utah officials had advanced this proposal twice before and Brodie knew full well how this latest delegation would be received. Nevertheless, not wishing to antagonize a neighboring state at a time when Arizona was pleading for statehood, Brodie introduced the two men to the Council with the request they receive "courteous consideration."[32]

Rather than have the Utah delegation meet with the entire legislature, the lawmakers convened a joint committee to hear the Utah proposal. Known as the Arizona Strip or simply "The Strip," the area in question contained approximately 8,000 square miles extending from the Colorado River north to the Utah border. The Utah delegation argued that the Grand Canyon and Colorado River rendered it extremely difficult for Mohave and Coconino Counties of Arizona to administer and provide law enforcement to the isolated and largely unsettled Strip. Utah, the envoys argued, would easily be able to provide those services, as no natural barrier to Utah existed. One Arizona newspaper, watching the situation closely, suggested a religious issue existed, confiding that most Mormon inhabitants of the Strip regarded Utah as "their home" and considered themselves separated from Utah only by an imaginary line.[33]

The legislature acted quickly and as expected. The joint committee unanimously rejected the Utah offer, pointing out that the Strip contained a magnificent stand of pine timber, valuable mineral deposits, and lush grazing land, which Arizona did not want to lose. Having made their position known to Utah, the lawmakers then passed a memorandum to Congress expressing opposition to any Arizona boundary change and emphasizing that the marvelous and majestic Grand Canyon always had been "exclusively an Arizona endowment." The memorandum closed with the assurance that the people of Arizona stood "unalterably opposed to the annexation of any portion of said tract to the state of Utah."[34]

Brodie also became involved in an ongoing administrative problem at the University of Arizona in Tucson, which would plague him for well over a year. Officially opened in 1893, the university was governed by a board of directors appointed by the governor. Duties of the board included selecting a chancellor (presiding officer of the board), hiring faculty, and in the event of an opening, recommending appointment of the university president. Trouble began in the summer of 1901, when the board abruptly and for unclear reasons demanded that President Millard M. Parker resign. The only reason given was a vague accusation that he had made inappropriate remarks in the presence of faculty. In September, with Parker refusing to step down, the board terminated his services, naming history professor Frank Yale Adams acting president. Adams had graduated from St. Lawrence University, Brodie's former school. In May President Roosevelt, strictly for political reasons, wrote incoming Governor Brodie that he wanted Ferris S. Fitch named president. A noted Michigan educator, Fitch had been recommended to Roosevelt by the president of the University of Michigan. Secretary Stoddard, however, acting governor during Murphy's temporary absence from the territory, effectively tied Brodie's hands in the matter by officially confirming Adams's appointment a month before Brodie took office. Adams and Stoddard were boyhood chums.[35]

Stymied by Stoddard's action, Brodie still intended to honor Roosevelt's request. Soon after taking office, he appointed Fitch to the Board of Regents, at the same time arranging to have him elected chancellor. Apparently, Brodie intended to ease Adams out and turn the chancellor's position into a stepping stone to the presidency.

As to be expected, Chancellor Fitch and President Adams butted heads immediately, resulting in a bitter quarrel that spread throughout the entire Tucson community and even beyond. The Tucson newspapers chose sides, both publishing letters supposedly written by students justifying their position. The *Star* supported Fitch, arguing that Brodie had selected him to straighten out the deplorable conditions theoretically existing on campus. Adams, the paper charged, had been responsible for the ouster of the popular Parker, and subsequently gained the presidency only because of his friendship with Secretary Stoddard. Moreover, according to the *Star*, campus discipline had broken down during Adams's tenure, and students had become unduly involved in administrative decisions. In short, the *Star* concluded that during Adams's tenure, the inmates had seized control of the institution.

The *Citizen* endorsed Adams, claiming that Fitch had used his power as chancellor to force Adams out and secure the presidency for himself. The paper considered Fitch to be nothing more than a "carpet bagger," who was disrupting the university for his own personal benefit. "Let [the university] be an institution of learning and not a hospital for political derelicts," the *Citizen* scornfully concluded. Both men refused to back down.[36]

The situation finally came to a head in June 1903, when Adams resigned, privately stating that he had been forced into that decision because of the constant meddling in administrative matters by Chancellor Fitch and the board. Fitch, apparently realizing that he lacked sufficient local support to secure the presidency, resigned a few days later and accepted a position with a mining company in the desert near Quijotoa, sixty miles west of Tucson. The faculty, meanwhile, fed up with the Fitch-Adams machinations, appealed directly to Brodie, requesting that a president with proven administrative ability be appointed. With Fitch no longer in contention and Roosevelt now silent on the issue, Brodie approved the board's presidential nomination of Dr. Kendric Charles Babcock, a native of New York and current assistant professor of history at the University of California. Brodie and Babcock agreed that the new president would exercise full authority over educational policies and administration of the university. The board would be restricted to auditing accounts and attending to business matters.[37]

True to his word, Brodie thereafter supported Babcock fully, even when the student body almost rebelled when the president disciplined a group of students for cutting classes on St. Patrick's Day. Brodie's successful efforts to remove political considerations from administrative decisions at the university were well received.

Meanwhile, as Brodie grappled with problems in Arizona, the fight over statehood continued in Washington. With Senators Quay and Beveridge both holding firm, an increasing number of Congressmen began urging compromise, eventually proposing that Arizona and New Mexico be united in one state called Montezuma. To make the union more palatable, the proposal specified that Arizona would be granted separate statehood upon reaching a population of 300,000 residents.

Mark Smith, Arizona's Delegate to Congress, who had been working diligently in support of the Omnibus Bill, immediately wired the territorial legislature, advising that a critical point had been reached and requesting instructions. Senator Quay, Smith confided, had recommended to him that Arizona accept the compromise. Responding quickly, the legislature telegraphed a resolution to Smith thanking him for his past efforts and assuring him that the legislature, "representing practically the unanimous opinion of the people of Arizona," firmly opposed joining New Mexico. The lawmakers then empowered a joint committee to draft a lengthy response to Smith. Reportedly, the House stood unanimously behind the anti-joint-statehood resolution, but some reservations apparently existed in the Council.[38]

On February 4, the same day that the joint resolution passed, the Council in a bizarre turn of events enacted a "concurrent" resolution accepting joint statehood in principle, with two minor reservations or provisions. Six Democrats, led by President Eugene Ives, voted in favor, with one Democrat excused. All five Republicans cast ballots in opposition. The resolution then was transmitted to a joint committee, where it was tabled. Almost a month later, without any authority to do so, some unknown Council member or members forwarded the resolution to Washington as if it had been approved by both houses, which it had not.[39]

Infuriated, the House responded with still another resolution to Congress, unanimously repudiating the Council's actions and reiterating that the Arizona House of Representatives, for a variety of reasons, had always opposed joint statehood. Naturally, hard feelings between the two legislative bodies surfaced over the issue, but the House had made its point. Congress soon thereafter adjourned without taking action on statehood for Arizona, New Mexico, or Oklahoma.[40]

In retrospect, the joint resolution undoubtedly exaggerated the degree of support for separate statehood, but obviously a solid majority in Arizona preferred to remain a territory as opposed to joining New Mexico. Only two leading territorial newspapers endorsed joining New Mexico. The remainder stood firmly in opposition.

Although Brodie did not publicly become involved in the power struggle between the Council and the House over statehood, he had not changed his mind in that regard. He still considered the timing to be inopportune, and he absolutely opposed any union with New Mexico. Realizing that Senator Beveridge's 1903 fact-finding mission to the Southwest had raised the issue in Congress of undue and undesired Spanish-speaking influence in both Arizona and New Mexico, Brodie moved to separate Arizona from that association. Writing Senator William P. Dillingham of Vermont, who had accompanied Beveridge on his trip through Arizona and New Mexico, Brodie explained that "English is taught exclusively in the [Arizona] schools," and joining Arizona with New Mexico would change that arrangement. "The union of the two territories into one state," Brodie confided, "would throw control of matters into the hands of people un-American in custom, language and feeling. . . ." Even while presenting this damning indictment, however, Brodie refrained from repeating a common complaint in Arizona that New Mexico law required at least four members of a jury to be fluent in Spanish. Obviously, in any context, the racial aspects of combining Arizona with the more heavily populated New Mexico could not be ignored.[41]

As the Twenty-Second Legislative Assembly of the Territory of Arizona adjourned on March 20, 1903, Governor Brodie could look back with a great deal of satisfaction on what he had accomplished. Although most of his legislative proposals had been enacted into law, there had been some notable failures. Efforts to tax the output of Arizona mines, for example, had never gotten off the ground, but other governors before him also had failed in that endeavor. Much of Brodie's success may be attributed to his ability to hold the handful of Republican lawmakers firmly in line, attracting at the same time sufficient Democratic support to carry his programs to fruition. Yet some perplexing anomalies existed in that arrangement which defy easy explanation.

For example, the Arizona Democratic Party in 1902 had gone on record in their territorial convention as favoring statehood, honest government, and fiscal responsibility. Opposition to the Cowan Bill, however, which Brodie designed to correct the most obvious flaw in fiscal procedures, came largely from Democrats. Henry Fountain Ashurst, widely heralded as the brightest ascending star in the Arizona Democratic Party, rejected his party's call for reform by supporting Republican Isaac T. Stoddard. John F. Wilson, Arizona's influential Democratic delegate to Congress, did the same thing. Conversely, most Republicans in the legislature strongly repudiated Stoddard, a fellow Republican. Moreover, some Democrats in the Council, again ignoring their own party platform, attempted to block Republican efforts to provide a unified front opposing joint statehood with New Mexico. Perhaps

Ashurst and other dissident Democrats simply did not want Brodie and the Republicans to receive credit for accomplishing anything positive, but there might well have been more to the story.

An event which occurred in the Council on the last day of the legislative session suggests that much of Brodie's success might well have hinged on his ability to exploit an existing schism in the Democratic Party. President of the Council Eugene S. Ives, a Democrat, became outraged upon learning that Brodie had appointed Burdette A. Packard, a Democratic legislator from Cochise County, to the board of managers of the St. Louis World's Fair. Councilman Ives took the floor to launch a bitterly personal attack on Packard and another Democratic member of the Council, viciously accusing the two men of being closet Republicans, whose vote gave Brodie and his party control of the Council. "I have served in eight assemblies," Ives ranted, "but never until this one, have I seen men elected by a trusting political party turn and go into open conference with the opposition." An unconcerned Packard merely smiled at Ives's tirade.[42]

With the exception of Stoddard and his friends, the Murphy wing of the Republican Party lay low, offering no public challenge to the governor's agenda in order to gauge fully the depth of Brodie's strength. But even then, Brodie began reaching out to Murphy's supporters with increasing success. In the First Cavalry and again in the Rough Riders, Brodie repeatedly had demonstrated well-honed instinctive leadership skills which never failed to cultivate strong friends and develop loyal supporters. That characteristic did not fail him now. One of Nathan Oakes Murphy's most capable followers, Thomas E. "Tom" Campbell of Jerome, switched horses and became such a staunch admirer of Brodie that he named his second son, born in January 1904, Alexander Brodie Campbell. Tom Campbell later became Arizona's first elected Republican governor.[43]

Brodie may not have been a politician, as he always maintained, but his actions as governor reveal clearly that he was learning the game rapidly.

CHAPTER 19

"There is a Moral Side to This Issue"

With the Twenty-Third Territorial Legislative Assembly not scheduled to convene until 1905, Brodie had over a year and a half to address several ongoing issues without legislative interference. The statehood issue had not yet been resolved, the Stoddard matter still smoldered, and Brodie obviously would have a fight on his hands to control the 1904 Arizona Republican Party convention. On the brighter side, however, President Roosevelt had scheduled a visit to the territory, thereby affording the governor an opportunity to discuss pressing political issues face-to-face with his former comrade-in-arms. But several unexpected problems lying quietly back in the shadows waited to surface.

Brodie had anticipated Roosevelt's visit to Arizona since the fall of 1902, when the president launched a barnstorming pre-election trip across the country. An accident in Pennsylvania, however, forced him to delay the Western portion of his political junket until the following spring. Brodie hoped Roosevelt would spend several days in Arizona, but the president, intending to visit every state and territory in the Far West, scheduled only one day to view the Grand Canyon. Nevertheless, eager to visit with a favorite Rough Rider and close friend, Roosevelt suggested that Brodie join the presidential party at Albuquerque, at the same time requesting that Brodie accompany him on a horseback ride alone along the southern rim of the Grand Canyon. Seeing this invitation as an opportunity to discuss matters with Roosevelt face-to-face, Brodie quickly directed Smalley to make the arrangements.[1]

Arriving at the Grand Canyon by train from Albuquerque early on May 6, Brodie and Roosevelt found a delegation of territorial officials, other dignitaries, and a handful of former Rough Riders waiting to greet them. Stepping briskly down from his railcar, Roosevelt enthusiastically hailed Tom Rynning, George Wilcox, the former first lieutenant of B Troop, Charles H. Utting, a resident of Phoenix who had served as a sergeant in B Troop, and Ben Daniels. Still smarting from having been summarily replaced as territorial marshal, Daniels nevertheless came to the Canyon to illustrate that he harbored no ill feelings. Roosevelt replied in kind. "Hello Ben," the president boomed. "Why Ben, I'm glad to see you. I surely am."[2]

Pleasantries exchanged, Roosevelt and Brodie, accompanied by two companions, mounted waiting horses for the scheduled twelve-mile ride along the Canyon rim. Eager to let off a little steam and pleased to be riding again with a favorite Rough Rider, Roosevelt set a fast pace, he and Brodie quickly spurring ahead of their two comrades. Once alone, Brodie later related, "Teddy took off his hat and yelled like a wild Indian."[3]

Meanwhile, approximately 1,000 persons gathered to meet the president. Returning from his breakneck gallop with Brodie, Roosevelt addressed the group. First paying tribute to Arizona's Rough Riders, Roosevelt singled out Alex Brodie and Buckey O'Neill for special recognition. Stating that he had great respect for all former members of his regiment, Roosevelt emphasized that he honored none above "your governor." He first had met Brodie at San Antonio, the president explained, and immediately had made up his mind that "I could tie to him." Pausing for the enthusiastic applause to subside, Roosevelt proceeded to touch on several other topics of local interest, beginning with irrigation.

Admitting that he never before had visited Arizona, Roosevelt expressed confidence that the Reclamation Act, which had passed into law the previous June, would provide an adequate water supply to the territory for many years to come. "I look forward to the effects of irrigation as being of greater consequences to all of this region of yours in the next fifteen years," Roosevelt concluded, "than any other material involvement whatsoever."[4]

Then, directing attention to the spectacular Grand Canyon, Roosevelt continued to strike a responsive chord with his appreciative audience. Emphasizing that in the Grand Canyon Arizona possessed a "natural wonder" unequalled anywhere in the world, Roosevelt challenged the residents of Arizona to leave the scenic attraction "as it is. You cannot improve on it; not a bit." Preserve it, he pleaded, unspoiled for your "children's children." Warming to a favorite topic of conservation, the president went on to caution that natural forests should be protected in the same manner as the Canyon. Forests should be used by ranchers and stockmen for the benefit of all the people of the territory, he theorized, but should not be "squandered."

The president then acknowledged the presence of a handful of American Indians in the audience. Pointing out that a number of Indians had served in the Rough Riders, Roosevelt observed that if "they were good enough to fight and die, they are good enough to have me treat them as square as any white man." Roosevelt may have been taking a risk in expressing such a position in frontier Arizona, but no one seems to have taken offense.[5]

Concluding his address, Roosevelt presented diplomas to recent graduates of the Northern Arizona Normal School in Flagstaff, and then departed with Brodie and a large group to visit a nearby mining camp and again view the Grand Canyon. Upon his return, he sequestered himself for half an hour in his railroad car with a group of former Rough Riders, departing shortly thereafter for California.[6]

The enthusiastic response to Roosevelt's presence in Arizona reflected the reception he would receive at almost all scheduled stops on his tour across the Far West. An extremely effective and forceful stump speaker, Roosevelt repeatedly demonstrated an instinctive ability to focus on those local issues important to each particular audience. Moreover, his personal magnetism won many converts. George Smalley, who never before had met the president, fell under Roosevelt's spell at the Grand Canyon, later explaining to his father those personal traits which had endeared the president to so many Arizonans.

Every man, Smalley confided, who met Roosevelt at the Canyon departed with the same reaction. The president's warm greeting and earnest handshake had made each person feel that Roosevelt had come from Washington specifically just to meet him. Smalley also praised Roosevelt's ability to project the image of a common man and yet, when necessary, assume the mantle of a mature politician. "Teddy moves and acts like a cowpuncher when there is a horse in sight," he commented, "and when he is in a long-tail coat he has the appearance of a statesman." Smalley confided that during one of Roosevelt's horseback rides along the Canyon rim, he had prevailed upon William Loeb, Roosevelt's private secretary, to escort him through the president's sleeping car, which "looked like that of a cowpuncher." Books and blankets littered the bed and a "widebrimmed hat hung from a neckband above the bunk, spurs and leggins were thrown about on the floor and in the opposite corner hung a silk hat." The porter explained the disarray by pointing out the president "liked to have things convenient so he would lose no time."[7]

Although disappointed that the president had not allocated more time to spend in Arizona, Brodie expressed satisfaction with his friend's visit, stating that the presidential party unanimously considered the Grand Canyon visit to be the "most enjoyable day they had experienced since leaving Washington." Yet, one significant point was missing. No one seemed to notice that Roosevelt had made no reference to statehood.[8]

Three weeks after watching Roosevelt's train depart for California, Brodie, accompanied by Mary and son Sandy, boarded a train headed east. As customary, Mary intended to spend the summer at her mother's home in Haddonfield. Concerned with his wife's continued poor health, Brodie secured a thirty-day leave to ensure that Mary reached New Jersey safely and that she had all the necessary care arranged before he returned to Phoenix.[9]

The only worry attending Brodie's extended absence from Arizona hinged on the possibility of repercussions from the law prescribing the eight-hour workday scheduled to take effect June 1. Some rumors suggested there could be trouble in some of the smaller mining camps in Yavapai County, but in general most observers felt there would be no serious problem. Even at Morenci, considered to be one of the most volatile mining communities in the territory, conditions appeared to be stable. Consequently, on May 24, the Brodies departed Phoenix. As provided by law, Secretary Stoddard picked up the reins as acting governor, but the reliable Smalley could be counted upon to maintain stability in the governor's office and keep Brodie fully informed of any significant development.[10]

On June 1, the lid blew off the Clifton-Morenci mining district. Located near the Gila River approximately twenty miles from New Mexico, the isolated area's only outside rail connection went through Lordsburg, New Mexico. Three major mining companies, the Arizona Copper Company, the Detroit Copper Company, and the Shannon Copper Company, operated mines and reduction works either near Clifton or four miles away at Morenci. The largest operation, that of the Detroit Copper Company, a subsidiary of the Phelps Dodge Corporation, produced between 1.3 million and 1.4 million pounds of copper per month. Brodie knew well the superintendent of the Detroit Company, Charles E. Mills, who had taken a leave of absence in 1898 to serve as a private in O'Neill's troop of Rough Riders. Once, when asked by a fellow trooper why he had not become an officer, Mills created something of a legend for himself by replying that he was "too good a private to be spoiled by a commission."[11]

In late May, as the deadline for the new eight-hour law to go into effect approached, representatives from all three companies met with groups of miners to resolve the compensation and working-hours issue. Mexican employees dominated the non-unionized labor force, but a large number of Italian immigrants also participated. Stating that thirty tons of ore produced only one ton of copper, company officials explained they considered mining costs too high to accommodate the workers' demand that they receive the same daily pay for working eight hours that they had been receiving for laboring ten hours. Instead, the three companies offered nine hours pay for eight hours work. The miners refused what they perceived to be a pay cut, and 1,500 underground miners walked out, causing the companies to suspend operations. This in turn idled 2,000 surface employees. At first, the strike appeared to be peaceful and without designated leaders. That quickly changed.[12]

After four days, Acting Governor Stoddard, swayed by rumors that the situation at Morenci had gotten out of hand, ordered Captain Rynning to assemble his Rangers at the mining camp and cooperate with the Graham County sheriff to restore order. Upon arrival, Rynning found that William, or Weneslado H. "Three-fingered Jack" Loustaunau, and several other emerging leaders had effectively organized the strikers. Although a Mexican of French ancestry, Loustaunau had been identified by Rynning and others on the scene as a professional Austrian- or Romanian-born agitator who had been sent from Chicago to stir up trouble. Facing an increasing number of armed miners as a result of Loustaunau's activities, Rynning and the sheriff telegraphed Stoddard for assistance.[13]

Stoddard lost no time responding. On June 9, he ordered Col. James McClintock, commander of the First Regiment of the Arizona National Guard and acting adjutant general, to proceed to Morenci with all available guardsmen. That same day, without first clearing his decision with Brodie, Stoddard wired Roosevelt that 3,000 "mostly foreigners" had gone on strike and advised the president that he had already sent in the National Guard. Apparently, however, Stoddard had little confidence in McClintock's guardsmen, complaining to the president that the Guard's "number [is] small, scattered and undisciplined." Regular troops from Forts Grant and Huachuca, Stoddard pleaded, were needed "immediately." Having sounded the alarm directly to Washington, Stoddard then wired Brodie explaining his actions.[14]

Shocked by Stoddard's telegram, Brodie immediately prepared to depart for Arizona, but before he could entrain, Stoddard telegraphed the welcome news that the Rangers and the National Guard, later assisted by five troops of dismounted Regular Cavalry, had arrested the ring leaders and disarmed the workers. "The strike is over," Stoddard wired. The Mexican employees had agreed to company terms and the Italians were leaving Morenci. Relieved that the crisis had passed, Brodie postponed his return to Arizona until the end of his scheduled thirty-day leave. Mary had suffered some kind of stroke or seizure on her way to New Jersey, and Brodie wanted to remain at her side as long as possible.[15]

Upon returning to Phoenix, Brodie found that Stoddard's decision to deploy the National Guard and request federal troops had few detractors and many supporters. Even the *Arizona Star*, a strongly Democratic paper which traditionally had few kind words for Stoddard, applauded his request for Regulars. Brodie agreed. Thanking Roosevelt for his quick response, Brodie observed that "it is always better to nip these uprisings of mobs in their infancy rather than wait for overt acts to be committed." George Smalley, however, had a slightly different take on Stoddard's behavior, confiding to his father that Acting Governor Stoddard "being green at the biz made the work hard."[16]

Unfortunately for Stoddard, the wave of approval regarding his strike-bearing efforts could little compensate for other problems he now faced. Even as a family tragedy struck his personal life, political walls once again began closing upon him. On June 9, John G. Tinker, secretary of the Maricopa County Republican Press Association, forwarded to Roosevelt a request that Stoddard be removed from office, citing as justification charges that the secretary had engaged in "criminal and improper conduct as an official," and had committed "political treason."[17]

Vague reports of the association's charges quickly appeared in local newspapers, but Stoddard at that point had more pressing matters to address. Six weeks earlier, he had sent his twenty-one-year-old daughter, Florence, east for medical attention. Subsequently diagnosed as diabetic, Florence had gone to stay with her mother's father, Judge Celora E. Martin of Binghamton, New York. On June 17, Stoddard received a telegram advising him that Florence had sunk into a diabetic coma. Stoddard's wife and a son immediately departed for New York, but Stoddard, not one to abandon his post without proper relief, remained in Phoenix only until Brodie returned on June 21. Florence died three days before.[18]

Roosevelt, meanwhile, had forwarded the association's charges to Secretary of the Interior Ethan A. Hitchcock, who sent them to Brodie requesting that he investigate. Well aware of Stoddard's impressive connections with New York politicians, Brodie first wanted to determine Roosevelt's take on the matter before embarking on a possible do-or-die confrontation with Stoddard, a New York native. On July 11, he contacted William Loeb to test the waters. "Do you apprehend," Brodie wrote, "that Mr. Stoddard would cut any particular figure in New York politics?" Assured that the President would stand with him provided that the charges indeed had merit, Brodie launched the requested investigation.[19]

Officially informed by Brodie of the association's accusations upon returning to Phoenix after burying his daughter, an infuriated Stoddard came out with both guns blazing. At Brodie's suggestion he immediately began gathering sworn affidavits defending his position. Tinker, of course, embarked on a similar course designed to discredit Stoddard. On September 25, Brodie submitted a lengthy report with numerous enclosures to Interior Secretary Hitchcock, outlining his findings. Explaining first that he considered the charge of "political treason" and certain other accusations to be of little consequence, Brodie identified three allegations he believed to be serious. First, Stoddard had been accused of maintaining a "corrupt and unscrupulous" lobby to defeat the Cowan Bill. Second, the secretary had made false statements in his official report to Governor Brodie regarding the amount of incorporation fee monies he had collected. The third, and in Brodie's eyes the most serious allegation, charged that Stoddard had "destroyed official [incorporation] fee books" that he had been required by law to maintain. Considering all available evidence, Brodie concluded and recommended that Stoddard be removed from office. Moreover, Brodie requested that Auditor William F. Nichols be named secretary.[20]

In the interim, Stoddard, an attorney by training, began spinning first to Brodie and then directly to Hitchcock a tangled web of hairsplitting legal technicalities and arguments justifying his actions. The charges against him, he constantly reiterated, had been trumped up by his personal and political enemies at the specific request of archrival Charles H. Akers, who still was attempting to regain his former position as secretary of state, a position Stoddard had wrested from him in 1901.

Realizing the alleged destruction of incorporation fee books to be his Achilles heel, Stoddard struck hard to neutralize that issue. In a lengthy written defense of his position addressed to Secretary Hitchcock, he admitted that he had not honored the request of the special committee of the Arizona House of Representatives to review the fee books because he had never maintained official fee books. At one time, Stoddard explained, he had on file "personal account books" detailing fees collected, but these books were "his own personal property" and he had destroyed them because Akers was attempting to obtain the records to identify for his own personal use those corporations which had employed Stoddard as their agent. Stoddard acknowledged that a territorial law required that fee books be maintained, but upon first assuming office in 1901 he had been advised by then Attorney General Charles F. Ainsworth that the law did not apply to the secretary of state. In support of that contention, Stoddard forwarded an affidavit to that effect signed by Ainsworth. He also provided sworn statements from three former secretaries of state revealing that they had not maintained fee books during their tenures of office. As Brodie pointed out, however, these three affidavits actually had little bearing on the matter, as the law authorizing the secretary of state to retain incorporation fees did not take effect until after all three had left office.[21]

Regarding the charge that he had falsified the amount of incorporation fees he had collected, Stoddard took the high road. Arguing that he no longer had detailed records to accurately track the exact amount, he insisted his report to Governor Brodie had been substantially complete and accurate. Brodie, himself, reluctantly supported Stoddard on that point, admitting that it would be impossible to submit a "scrupulously correct report" without the records that Stoddard had destroyed.[22]

Stoddard also admitted that he considered the Cowan Bill unjust and had opposed it only by "persuasion and influence." He flatly denied having maintained a lobby or used any money to defeat the measure. He also provided several affidavits from members of the legislature rejecting Tinker's allegation that he had maintained a "corrupt lobby."[23]

Demonstrating no reluctance to engage in character assassination, Stoddard lashed out personally at his accusers, securing one affidavit asserting that John Tinker's reputation "is that of a habitual drunkard, gambler and unreliable, and unworthy of belief as one who never fulfills any obligation which he can possibly avoid." He characterized another Stoddard critic as a man who had been "arrested and brought before the courts numerous times for larceny, assault, attempted rape and other offenses and is a notorious, disorderly and thoroughly unreliable person."[24]

Regarding his own character and standing in the territory, Stoddard forwarded copies of old letters written on his behalf, at the same time including statements from prominent businessmen referring to his present status. Interestingly enough, one of the older letters Stoddard carefully included was one written by Alex O. Brodie in 1897, endorsing Stoddard's application for governor. At that time, Brodie stated that he found Stoddard "qualified" for the position.[25]

The prominent businessmen Stoddard asked for endorsements could ill-afford to become involved directly in the Brodie-Tinker-Stoddard imbroglio, but they could—and did—comment favorably on Stoddard's handling of the Morenci strike, and requested that he be retained in office. The superintendent of the Copper Queen Consolidated Mining Company at Bisbee, the presidents of the Oriental Mining Company and the Poland Mining Company in Yavapai County, and the Arizona Copper Company at Morenci all supported Stoddard.

Even Cleveland H. Dodge, representing the immense Phelps Dodge Company, headquartered in New York, wrote a letter praising the embattled secretary. Quite probably, Stoddard requested a letter signed personally by Cleveland Dodge for political reasons, knowing that Dodge and Roosevelt had been boyhood chums.[26]

Had Stoddard's status been determined in a court of law, it is possible that his spirited defense might well have carried the day, but that would not be the case. The final determination of his future hinged solely on President Roosevelt's decision regarding the propriety (or impropriety) of the secretary's actions. Realizing the insecurity of his position and aware that Brodie stood against him, Stoddard returned to Washington in the early fall to present his defense personally to Hitchcock, confident that the secretary's recommendations would carry much weight with Roosevelt.

Meanwhile, Arizona newspapers, which apparently still had not located copies of the press association's charges, based their surprisingly accurate assessments on what information had been leaked. Clearly, what meager support Stoddard once enjoyed with the local press no longer existed. Even the *Arizona Republican* now left him twisting alone in the wind. Pointing out that Stoddard had gone to Washington to confer with Secretary Hitchcock, the *Republican* concluded the trip to be an exercise in futility, predicting that the president would support Brodie. Significantly, the *Republican* also declared that Stoddard had made a critical blunder in the first place by ignoring the advice of his friends and fighting the Cowan Bill.[27]

Following a long meeting with Stoddard, Hitchcock submitted his final report to Roosevelt. Obviously irritated by Stoddard's sanctimonious response to the association's charges, Hitchcock sided with Brodie. Regarding the destruction of fee books, Hitchcock dismissed Stoddard's contention that the books were personal property, concluding instead that the law required such books be maintained and by destroying them, Stoddard not only violated the law, but had committed a "criminal offense *as well*." Hitchcock also stated that Stoddard had admitted to him that he had "for his own selfish and sordid purposes exerted such power as he could command to influence the Members of the Legislature to defeat [the Cowan Bill]." Moreover, based on information provided by Stoddard himself, Hitchcock concluded that Stoddard actually had collected $41,000 in incorporation fees and not $15,946.30, as he had reported. Convinced, therefore, that Stoddard had failed to "maintain the honor of the service and protect the interests of the public," Hitchcock recommended that Stoddard be "immediately dismissed from his office."[28]

George Smalley could not have been more pleased. Anticipating that Roosevelt now would move quickly to remove Stoddard, he confided to his father that "he [Stoddard] is corrupt," and about to "swing out of the official family." Smalley's assessment, however, proved premature. The secretary had one more sharpened arrow in his quiver. He still had powerful friends in New York, and 1904 was an election year. While in the East to defend himself, Stoddard had asked a number of New York politicians to intercede on his behalf.[29]

Although Brodie wanted Stoddard out of office, his exact position regarding Stoddard's alleged corruption is not clear. There is no doubt, however, that he believed the secretary walked a narrow line, once confiding to Roosevelt that "there is a moral side to this issue which I feel should be considered." Brodie felt that Stoddard regarded his office "solely as his personal property . . . and has used it for the greatest possible personal pecuniary gain."[30]

Meanwhile, an obscure individual with an entirely fresh take on the matter entered the picture. In June, one E. F. Garrison, a resident of Connecticut with business affairs in Arizona, advised Roosevelt that during a business trip to the territory, he had learned from a reliable source that Brodie long had desired to file charges against Stoddard, but for unclear reasons had failed to do so. Garrison assured Roosevelt that Frank Murphy, "leader of the anti-Brodie faction of the [Arizona] Republican Party," could be persuaded to make a deal. Explaining that the Murphy Republicans stood in full sympathy with the movement against Stoddard, Garrison suggested that cutting Stoddard loose to fend for himself would serve as a starting point to "bring two very influential men [Brodie and Murphy] together." Brodie, of course, had absolutely no interest in cooperating with the Murphys, but Garrison's letter does suggest that many Eastern politicians had become accustomed to viewing Arizona as a fertile ground to accommodate New York and New England party patronage. Obviously, they did not want that to change.[31]

Brodie's best opportunity to nudge Roosevelt into implementing Hitchcock's recommendation to replace Stoddard surfaced in December, when Brodie traveled east to bring his family back to Phoenix. During his absence from Phoenix, the ever-vigilant Smalley observed Stoddard enter Tinker's office. Curious, Smalley accosted Tinker and learned that the secretary had offered Tinker $250 cash to sign a paper without first reading it. Interpreting the offer to be an attempted bribe, Tinker refused. Smalley immediately secured an affidavit to that effect and, fully aware that Brodie had scheduled several meetings with Roosevelt to discuss the Stoddard issue as well as other pressing matters, forwarded the affidavit to Brodie, who handed the document to the president. Nevertheless, even with this new evidence in hand, Roosevelt did not commit himself. Deeply disappointed, Brodie turned to other concerns such as the content of his annual report to Secretary of the Interior Hitchcock.[32]

Completed early that fall, Brodie's 1903 report presented a comprehensive 264-page summary of conditions in Arizona. Of primary importance to the continued growth of Arizona, Brodie carefully explained, was the need to develop additional water resources which would be provided by the National Reclamation Act—and statehood. Brodie devoted thirty-six pages to the benefits of agriculture and improved water storage and distribution capabilities. Only two pages contained a discussion of statehood, but they were strongly written. "Arizona seeks admission as a state," Brodie concluded. "She seeks it on her own merits, but she seeks it as Arizona."

The Salt River long had been recognized as the key which could unlock agricultural development of the valley surrounding Phoenix. In 1889, James McClintock and two friends had identified an ideal location for a large dam between two towering, sheer rock cliffs at the confluence of Tonto Creek and the Salt River. Located eighty miles east of Phoenix, the locale soon became known as the Tonto Site.

The first serious step toward constructing the Tonto Dam, as it became known, occurred in 1900, when the Phoenix Board of Trade formed a committee on water storage—a forerunner of the Salt River Valley Water Users' Association—to study the feasibility of storing and distributing water throughout the valley. One of Brodie's friends, Benjamin Fowler, quickly became a primary supporter of the ensuing plan. A Civil War veteran from Massachusetts and a graduate of Yale, Fowler moved to Arizona in the late nineteenth century for his health. Purchasing a ranch near Phoenix, he quickly involved himself in community affairs, including water development. Convinced a dam on the Salt River to be absolutely necessary, Fowler spent the winters of 1901 and 1902 in Washington, where he lobbied continuously and effectively in support of the National Reclamation Act. Returning to Phoenix, he became president of the Salt River Valley Water Users' Association, and applied his considerable talents toward convincing Secretary of the Interior Hitchcock that the Salt River Project and Tonto Dam should be the first federal effort to develop water resources as authorized by the act.[33]

Convincing Hitchcock to authorize the Tonto Dam to be built first proved to be a formidable undertaking. Most of the arable land in the Salt River Valley, already in private hands, could not legally be irrigated with water provided by the federal government until the affected landowners first collectively agreed upon a comprehensive water distribution plan. Moreover, Arizona was competing with proposed similar projects in Montana, Colorado, Wyoming, and Nevada. To further complicate the situation, some Arizona residents disagreed with the Salt River Valley Water Users' Association, arguing instead that the first federal dam constructed in Arizona should be at San Carlos on the Gila River east of Globe.[34]

In fact, Hitchcock finally selected the Tonto site to be the first. Why he did so still is not entirely clear. Certainly, Benjamin Fowler and others played a key role in the decision, but many years later Rough Rider Captain Joseph L. B. Alexander gave full credit to Brodie. According to Alexander, Brodie related to him that in a meeting with Hitchcock during one of his trips to Washington, Brodie learned that the secretary did not favor the Salt River Project because of the land-ownership question. Brodie appealed to Roosevelt, who summoned Hitchcock to meet that same evening with him and Brodie to discuss the situation. At that meeting, Roosevelt informed the secretary that in consideration of his long friendship with Brodie, he wanted the first dam authorized by the Reclamation Act to be built in Arizona. He then left the room, directing Brodie and Hitchcock to work out the details. Hitchcock raised no further objections, agreeing that construction soon would begin on what would become Roosevelt Dam on the Salt River.[35]

Unlikely support for Alexander's explanation comes from the recollections of Democrat Thomas F. Weedin, an opinionated newspaper editor and territorial legislator from Florence. In 1912, Weedin informed a subcommittee of the United States House of Representatives that in 1903 he had visited with Roosevelt at the Grand Canyon to argue that the first dam in Arizona be constructed at the San Carlos Site. At that meeting, Roosevelt agreed to withhold any final decision on the matter until he could verify the facts justifying the San Carlos location that Weedin had presented. But before that could be accomplished, Weedin bitterly complained, Brodie traveled to Washington and convinced Roosevelt to authorize construction of the Tonto Dam.[36]

Together, Alexander's and Weedin's accounts indicate that Brodie should be credited with locating what became Roosevelt Dam. The statements of both men reflect accurately Brodie's success in calling on Roosevelt for favors, although the governor consistently expressed reluctance to admit publicly that such an avenue from Phoenix to the White House existed. Brodie seldom sought publicity for himself, and in this case probably would not have objected strongly to others receiving credit for what he privately had accomplished. Alexander stated that he had refrained from commenting on Brodie's role in securing the Salt River Project until other key players involved in the selection process had died. Alexander's rationale in making that decision is not clear. Perhaps he wanted to avoid embarrassing anyone still living who had claimed responsibility for securing approval of the Tonto Dam. At any rate, by the fall of 1903, approximately 200 workers were laying out a wagon road to the designated location. Residents of the Salt River Valley were elated.

After one full calendar year in office, Brodie continued to enjoy widespread bipartisan support across the territory. He had made no critical mistakes, and his good luck had not yet failed him. The use of the National Guard and federal troops to break the Morenci strike easily could have proved embarrassing, but any adverse fallout from that incident descended on the shoulders of Acting Governor Isaac T. Stoddard and not Brodie, who was in New Jersey when the strike occurred. In general, the mining industry continued to flourish, and the drought finally was beginning to break, portending well for local agriculture and cattle interests. Brodie's efforts to remove the unpopular Stoddard from office had not been successful, but most political observers laid that failure on the Washington bureaucracy, and not on any lack of effort by Governor Brodie.

Unfortunately, virtually nothing had been accomplished regarding statehood. In fact, the chances of Arizona soon becoming a state appeared to be fading rapidly. In his annual report to the Secretary of the Interior, Brodie stated that Arizona would not accept joint statehood with New Mexico. That may have been the deciding factor. The feeling in Congress, as reported in the Arizona newspapers, indicated that nothing regarding statehood now would be accomplished until after the 1904 elections. Oklahoma seemed to have a slim chance of securing a new star in the nation's flag, but separate statehood for Arizona and New Mexico had been taken off the table. All Arizona residents could do at this point would be to ask Delegate John F. Wilson, who had replaced Mark Smith in the election of 1902, to continue to push the matter to the best of his ability.[37]

CHAPTER 20

"He Has Deported Himself with Propriety"

Brodie's final fourteen months in office effectively assured his political legacy in Arizona. Except for statehood, almost everything he had worked to achieve since becoming governor would fall into place—although not without further effort on his part. A significant contribution was securing for Roosevelt a committed delegation to the 1904 Republican National Convention. Roosevelt had relied upon Brodie to control the Arizona Republican Party, and that confidence had not been misplaced. The roots of the Progressive Movement had been carefully planted and nurtured in the future Copper State.

Putting the festering Stoddard matter temporarily on hold early in 1904, Brodie focused his attention on the Republican territorial convention, scheduled to convene in Tucson on March 8 to select the six-man delegation to the national nominating convention. Although President Roosevelt faced no serious national challenge to his nomination, a few die-hard holdouts across the country still hoped that Ohio Senator Marcus A. Hanna would step forward to lead the anti-Roosevelt faction. To that end, they intended to pack the national convention in Chicago with sufficient uninstructed delegates to possibly unhorse the Rough Rider in some kind of coup engineered in the proverbial smoke-filled back room. In Arizona, the pro-Hanna faction, led by Frank Murphy, organized the fight to secure an uninstructed delegation. Brodie, absolutely determined that Arizona Republicans would appoint a pro-Roosevelt, or instructed, delegation, rallied his forces in opposition.[1]

Having decided to remain in Washington until after the Arizona convention, Nathan Oakes Murphy relied upon brother Frank to lead the fight in Arizona. In February, Frank threw down the gauntlet, publicly endorsing Roosevelt for president, but at the same time carefully tempering his endorsement by insisting that the Arizona delegation be uninstructed. Such a position, Murphy explained, would leave the delegates free "to act for the best interests of the Territory."[2]

Some Arizona Democratic newspapers quickly rejected Frank Murphy's explanation, suggesting that he intended to arrange an uninstructed delegation headed by brother Nathan for the sole purpose of supporting Hanna. One paper, well-aware of Brodie's determination to stop the Murphys in this regard, predicted there would be a "battle royal in Arizona for control of the Arizona Republican delegation."[3]

Responding to Frank Murphy's challenge, Brodie came out swinging. "I am thoroughly opposed to the idea of sending delegates to Chicago uninstructed for Roosevelt," the governor began. Convinced that Roosevelt's nomination in Chicago would be by acclamation, Brodie explained that Arizona would have no voice in Roosevelt's selection unless it sent committed delegates to Chicago. By choosing a committed or instructed delegation in support of Roosevelt, Arizona would send a message across the nation that the territory strongly supported the president. Obviously, the battle line was clear, and Brodie stood prepared on this point to fight the Murphys to a finish. Within two weeks, however, Hanna's unexpected death eliminated the only man who had even a remote chance of challenging Roosevelt's nomination. Nevertheless, the question of an instructed versus an uninstructed delegation had become a test of power that remained to be fought out in Tucson.[4]

Considering southern Arizona to be Brodie country, the Murphys concentrated their efforts in Maricopa and the northern tier of counties, where Frank Murphy's railway and mining interests provided a long-standing economic power base. In February, not willing to concede anything to his opponents, Brodie made a quick trip to Flagstaff and other northern communities to challenge the brothers on their home turf.

Some Democrats, predicting that Brodie would not enjoy the clear sailing at the convention that he expected, indirectly suggested that the governor's long-standing aura of personal popularity had begun to fade. The statehood issue again had surfaced, forcing Brodie to defend both himself and his friendship with Roosevelt. Moreover, rumors circulated that "women suffragists," seeking revenge for Brodie's veto of the women's suffrage bill, planned to disrupt the convention.[5]

The first sign of actual trouble for Brodie surfaced in early March, when the Associated Press unexpectedly released a telegram sent by Bernard S. Rodey, New Mexico's delegate to Congress, stating that

Roosevelt now definitely supported joint statehood for New Mexico and Arizona. A week later, on the very eve of the Arizona convention, a second letter from Rodey asserted that the president, at the next session of Congress, would actively support a bill granting joint statehood. If Rodey's letters constituted a political ploy designed to embarrass Brodie at the Arizona convention, the timing could not have been better.[6]

Stunned by Rodey's revelations, Brodie had little time to orchestrate damage control. He quickly wired William Loeb to determine the validity of Rodey's claim. On March 8, however, with no reply from either Roosevelt or Loeb in hand, Brodie faced the delegates gathered in Tucson to pour oil on the troubled waters as best he could.

Speaking calmly and unemotionally, Brodie assured his Tucson audience that Rodey's statements did not accurately reflect Roosevelt's position. During the president's visit to the Grand Canyon, Brodie revealed, he and Roosevelt had discussed statehood at great length. At that time, Brodie had made it absolutely clear that the people of Arizona stood firmly for separate statehood or nothing. Roosevelt responded by assuring Brodie that he would not involve himself in the matter, leaving the question of statehood solely in the hands of Congress. In his own personal opinion, Brodie concluded, "Nothing is going to be done with Arizona by Congress for at least three years."[7]

In spite of the dire predictions cast by some Democrats, the 1904 Arizona Republican Nominating Convention proved a rousing Brodie success. Even the "suffragists" failed to appear. The Murphy faction never had a chance, having been soundly rejected in the county conventions. Arriving in a festive mood, the delegates in Tucson cheered Brodie vigorously at every opportunity, standing on chairs and waving handkerchiefs to celebrate their victory. Brodie had carried every county except Gila. The longtime Murphy stranglehold on Yavapai County had been shattered by a thirty-vote majority at the county convention. In Maricopa County, two Murphy stalwarts apparently resigned as candidates for the Arizona delegation rather than go down with the sinking Murphy ship. The predicted "battle royal" had degenerated into nothing more than a sandbox squabble. In Tucson, the convention selected Brodie to lead a six-man delegation to Chicago, instructed to vote for Roosevelt and to make every effort to secure a plank in the party platform calling for separate statehood. Rough Rider Ben Daniels secured a spot as one of the delegation's six alternates.[8]

George Smalley, keeping his father well-informed of the fight to control the convention, quickly trumpeted Brodie's victory, proudly pointing out that the governor "had received the finest ovation I have ever seen at Tucson in the convention."[9]

Controlling the Arizona Republican Party turned out to be only one significant political victory Brodie achieved in March. Early that month, Roosevelt finally resolved the long-standing Stoddard quagmire. The president wanted to remove the secretary earlier, but the issue had become woven into the fabric of an internal New York Republican Party power struggle involving, among other considerations, party patronage. The problem of removing Stoddard hinged on Roosevelt's relationship with the aging New York Senator Thomas C. Platt, then involved in a bitter fight to regain his former position as the undisputed boss of New York Republican politics, and with Governor Benjamin B. Odell Jr. Platt and Secretary Stoddard were good friends and political allies.[10]

Learning late in the summer of 1903 that John Tinker had filed charges against him, Secretary Stoddard enlisted backing from his father-in-law, Judge Celora B. Martin, Senator Platt, New York Governor Odell, and George W. Dunn, chairman of the New York Republican Party. All informed Roosevelt that they had investigated Tinker's charges and found them unsubstantiated. But the issue was not that clearly drawn. Dissension existed in the ranks. By 1900 Governor Odell, formerly one of Platt's protégés, had challenged his former mentor for control of the state Republican party. Roosevelt watched the ensuing struggle with concern. The year 1904, of course, was an election year, and the president desperately wanted to maintain party unity in the key state of New York—at least until after the voters went to the polls in November. "My effort has been to keep Governor Odell and you together," Roosevelt told Platt in 1903: "I do not want a division in the party just now." Obviously, Roosevelt did not want to take immediate action on the Stoddard matter for fear of entangling himself in the Platt-Odell power struggle at such a critical point.[11]

Early in 1904, however, Odell forced the issue, affording Roosevelt an opportunity to break the deadlock without antagonizing either faction. Governor Odell arranged to have George W. Dunn, an extremely loyal and longtime Platt lieutenant, removed from his position as chairman of the New York State Republican Party. By finding a position in Arizona for the ousted Dunn, Roosevelt obviously would render a favor to Platt, but at the same time would not antagonize Odell, who had replaced Dunn with a man of his own choice. In short, Stoddard had become expendable, caught up in a power struggle in which he found himself grossly overmatched and the outcome of which even Judge Martin could not influence. Negotiating through Platt, Roosevelt set the wheels in motion to remove Stoddard.[12]

Realizing that he must either resign or summarily be removed, Stoddard, in a last-ditch effort to negotiate the conditions of his resignation, requested a statement from Roosevelt to the effect that the investigation into his conduct as Arizona secretary of state revealed no evidence of wrong doing. At one point Stoddard thought he had secured such a concession, but after consulting with the attorney general, the president dashed cold water on that hope. Platt, realizing that he had done all he could to help Stoddard, then advised the secretary to submit an immediate and unqualified resignation. The deed was done effective April 1, 1904.[13]

For unknown reasons, Roosevelt did not immediately turn to Dunn, instead requesting Brodie's opinion of Garrett H. Ryan, an obscure individual then living in Arizona. Brodie dismissed Ryan quickly, pointing out that he was a young man with little experience who had only recently come to Arizona for his health. Then, reflecting the growing resentment in Arizona against outsiders or "carpetbaggers" being appointed to territorial positions, Brodie objected strongly to the practice of farming out territorial appointments among "Eastern Senators and Representatives." In conclusion, Brodie expressed his hope that Auditor William Nichols would be named secretary.[14]

Actually, Ryan never had been a serious contender. On the same day that Brodie penned his rejection of Ryan, Roosevelt advised Brodie that probably he would appoint Dunn to succeed Stoddard. He did not offer further explanation, however, merely assuring Brodie that Dunn's appointment "may be an absolute necessity." A Phoenix newspaper provided additional information.[15]

Revealing how far Stoddard's tentacles reached into the Phoenix community, a Democratic paper, The *Phoenix Enterprise*, attempted to put a positive spin on Stoddard's resignation. The *Enterprise*, asserting that the embattled secretary still commanded powerful influence in Washington, accurately explained that Dunn's selection had been contrived to placate both Platt and Odell. The *Enterprise* then delivered a deliberate slap at Governor Brodie. With Dunn in office as secretary, the paper claimed, Roosevelt would recognize Dunn as the "head of the administration party in Arizona and will look to him to undertake the work of reorganization." Moreover, the paper declared that Stoddard personally had arranged with Platt to have Dunn named his successor. Realizing that the *Enterprise's* article would be no more palatable to Roosevelt than it had been to him, Brodie forwarded a copy to the president, with the contemptuous observation that the news column in question was "inspired [by] and is the mouthing of Secretary Stoddard."[16]

Concerned about Dunn's possible appointment, Brodie sent a four-page letter to the president explaining why Dunn would not be acceptable. Brodie began by pointing out that since becoming governor he had endeavored to please the people of Arizona, the president, and himself by "giving the Territory of Arizona a straightforward, honest and fair administration." He had been eminently successful, as evidenced by the fact that he had secured, against strong opposition, an instructed delegation to support Roosevelt at the nominating convention in Chicago. He had also been selected by acclamation to lead the Arizona delegation. Never in the history of Arizona, Brodie confided, had "the Republican party been so united or had such a grand chance of success as it will have in the coming [territorial] election this fall."

In order to maintain the political momentum he had generated, Brodie went on to explain, an "Arizona man of prominence and standing" must be appointed to replace Stoddard. To appoint an outsider would place Brodie in an "embarrassing position insomuch as my constant fight has been to secure good, honest honorable Arizona men appointed to office." As the successful leader of the Arizona Republican Party, Brodie argued that his recommendation should have a strong bearing on dispensing local patronage. He then reiterated that the reliable Auditor Nichols should be appointed secretary. I have delivered for you, Brodie seemed to be saying; now you should deliver for me.[17]

The impact of Brodie's arguments on Roosevelt's final decision is not clear, but Dunn apparently withdrew from consideration. With no other strong candidate in the field, Roosevelt informed Brodie that he would appoint Nichols. Brodie viewed this decision to be not only a political victory, but a personal triumph as well. He never had trusted Stoddard, fearful that as acting governor during Brodie's absence he would handle the reins of power unwisely. Now, with the reliable Secretary of State Nichols in office, Brodie could put those fears behind him.[18]

Brodie immediately selected Treasurer Isaac M. Christy to replace Nichols as auditor and named Edward Elliot Kirkland treasurer. A native of Hannibal, Missouri, Kirkland came to Arizona in the late 1870s. He later operated a general store near Prescott and soon became friends with Brodie, then developing the nearby Crown Point mine. Honest and reliable, Kirkland made an exceptional treasurer. It had taken him nearly two years, but Brodie finally had his complete administrative team in place. "The last vestige of corruption [has been] wiped out," an elated Smalley wrote his father.[19]

Even while coping with the fallout of Stoddard's resignation, Brodie took time from his busy schedule to entertain Sir William John Menzies, a highly respected cousin from Edinburgh. A noted financier, Menzies in 1873 had organized the Scottish-American Investment Company, the first corporation formed in Scotland to invest solely in the United States. A subsidiary company later loaned £1,225,000 to the Arizona Copper Company, and Menzies had come to inspect the company holdings in Morenci. On a previous trip to the United States, Menzies had visited Cadet Brodie at West Point, and Brodie now took pleasure showing his cousin the attractions of Phoenix.[20]

The following month, an attempted escape at the Yuma Territorial Prison demanded Brodie's attention. On April 28, a group of inmates led by the notorious "Three-fingered Jack" Loustaunau, who had been sentenced to a term at Yuma following the Clifton-Morenci strike, attempted to seize Superintendent William Griffith and Assistant Superintendent George Wilder to use as hostages. Griffith bravely ordered a guard posted on a nearby wall to open fire. Armed with a shotgun loaded with buckshot, the officer fired three shots, injuring three prisoners and wounding Wilder in the thigh. Meanwhile, responding to Griffith's request for assistance, William C. Buck, a convict from Globe serving a life sentence for murder, grabbed a kitchen carving knife and ran to aid the two officials. During the ensuing melee, Griffith managed to escape, arm himself, and help subdue the convicts. Two weeks later, after conferring with Superintendent Griffith, Brodie issued a full pardon to Buck, who had been seriously wounded during the struggle.[21]

As was her habit, Mary Brodie intended to spend the summer of 1904 in New Jersey, but ever-present health issues forced her to delay departure until May. In fact, her physical well-being had become such an issue that her husband for several days had not even made an appearance in his office. Nevertheless, on May 16 Brodie, accompanied by Mary and his now six-year-old son Sandy, entrained for Haddonfield, where Brodie intended to spend the next two months, leaving only to attend the Republican National Convention in Chicago that June. With Secretary Nichols steering the ship of state during his absence, Brodie for the first time felt comfortable in leaving the territory for such an extended period.[22]

In Chicago, the Arizona delegation led by Brodie received little public attention, but the Arizona governor still made his presence known. Quietly meeting with Senator Henry Cabot Lodge and several other power brokers behind the scenes, Brodie convinced the group to eliminate from the Republican Party platform a proposed plank endorsing joint statehood—by any criteria a significant achievement.[23]

The convention itself turned out exactly as Brodie had predicted: Roosevelt won the nomination by acclamation. Proceedings completed, Capt. William H. H. Llewellyn of New Mexico and three other former Rough Riders at the convention joined Brodie in forwarding a telegram congratulating their former commander:

> *Your comrades of 98, delegates to this Convention congratulate you on this, one of the greatest events in American history.*

Every soldier of your regiment will be on duty from now until you are elected president. May God bless you.[24]

Before Brodie returned to Arizona, *Cosmopolitan* magazine asked him to write an article describing the benefits of the National Reclamation Act to the West. Seeing this as an unexpected opportunity to publish an illustrated promotional tract for Arizona, Brodie asked Smalley to ghostwrite the article. As requested, Smalley described in detail the Tonto Dam, pointing out that the Salt River Project ultimately would provide sufficient water to irrigate 250,000 acres, which would boost cattle and agricultural production in the valley to more than $1.5 million annually. Smalley concluded with the prediction that a recently approved proposal to construct a diversion dam for irrigation purposes near Yuma, known as the Colorado River Project, promised to be equally successful. Brodie turned the $100 contributor's fee over to Smalley.[25]

The remainder of the summer proved a busy period for Brodie. Less than a month after returning to Phoenix, he again headed east, having been summoned to represent Arizona on the formal nominating committee scheduled to meet with Roosevelt at the president's estate at Sagamore Hill in Oyster Bay, Long Island. Brodie, with other members of the committee, met at the Waldorf-Astoria Hotel in New York and traveled by special train the next day to Oyster Bay. The Speaker of the House, crusty Joseph B. "Uncle Joe" Cannon, presided over the affair, attended by 175 guests. Following Roosevelt's brief acceptance speech, the guests and committee members enjoyed a luncheon at the president's home. Brodie then took advantage of this opportunity to spend a few days in New Jersey with Mary, whose health had not measurably improved.[26]

Although Mary's poor health remained an ongoing issue for many years, Brodie never publicly revealed the nature of her illness. Occasionally, some reports suggested she had a heart attack or some kind of seizure, but no formal diagnosis ever was made public.

Back in Arizona once more, Brodie put the finishing touches on his 1904 annual report to the Secretary of the Interior. Consisting of 131 pages of narrative and twenty-six of statistics, the report highlighted the progress Arizona had made in the previous year. The mining industry particularly had flourished, Brodie emphasized, with annual production of copper increasing from 150 million pounds to 230 million. Agricultural interests had fared less well because of the extended drought. In that regard, however, relief would soon be provided by the Salt and Colorado River Projects. The amount of taxable property on the tax rolls had increased significantly, and the floating territorial debt of $92,341.90 from the year before had been eliminated.

Brodie ended his report with ten recommendations, one more than he had listed in 1903. In both reports, the plea for statehood headed the list, but this year Brodie added a supporting recommendation explaining the need for separate statehood. Two other recommendations dealt with securing increased federal assistance for irrigation projects.[27]

Brodie then turned his attention to the Arizona Republican Party convention, to be held in Prescott that September. Some Democratic newspapers, failing to recognize how firmly Brodie had grasped control of his party, predicted the Murphy brothers again would challenge the governor, just as they had routinely done in the past. It did not happen. The Murphys had thrown in the towel. Nathan Oakes was not even in the country, having sailed on an extended trip to the Mediterranean with a new bride. Brother Frank basically remained in low profile during the convention, surfacing only to support the party's decisions. Consequently, Brodie's candidate for delegate to Congress, Benjamin H. Fowler, won the nomination with only token opposition. As one would expect, the delegates passed resolutions endorsing the National Reclamation Act, separate statehood, and the administrations of both President Roosevelt and Governor Brodie. Some observers commented that the 1904 Republican convention remained remarkably free from internal bickering and infighting.[28]

Actually, the Murphys may have conceded the convention to Brodie only with the intention of orchestrating a challenge later. As Smalley earlier had pointed out, the Murphy brothers had made their fight with Brodie a personal vendetta, and the slanted manner in which Nathan Oakes's newspaper, the *Arizona Republican*, reported the Arizona Republican convention supports that conclusion. Describing in glowing terms the adulation which supposedly greeted Frank Murphy and Robert E. Morrison, Nathan Oakes Murphy's longtime supporter, at the convention, the *Republican* dismissed quickly the delegates' reaction to Brodie's presence. Clearly, Murphy's newspaper, under the guise of factual reporting, attempted to cast the Murphys and their friends in the best possible light, implying that at Prescott they decisively trumped Brodie's personal popularity. Perhaps the Murphy brothers suspected that Brodie's Arizona career soon would end and were planning accordingly.[29]

As expected, the Arizona Republicans worked diligently to elect Fowler. Charles H. Akers, the same man Stoddard had elbowed aside as secretary of state in 1902, skillfully organized effective and well-financed Fowler Clubs in all major communities. Fowler campaigned aggressively, traveling across the territory delivering speeches, shaking hands and in general reaching out to voters. Except for a brief trip to

New Jersey to visit Mary, who had suffered a relapse, Brodie hit the campaign trail as much as time would permit, visiting such diverse places as Morenci, Bisbee, and Flagstaff. On the very eve of the election, however, a potentially serious incident with religious and racial overtones surfaced at Clifton and Morenci, forcing Brodie to suspend active campaigning.

Earlier that summer, the Sisters of Charity in America, a Catholic children's relief society based in New York, acting in conjunction with the New York Foundling Hospital, arranged to place forty foundlings (orphans) in Clifton and Morenci homes. Unfortunately, upon the children's arrival in October, miscommunication and misunderstandings among the three sisters in charge of the orphans, a local priest, and Anglo residents of the two communities quickly surfaced. In New York only orphans with light-colored hair and fair skin had been selected in order to better blend with their intended adopting parents. In Morenci, however, the local priest assigned all the children except one to Mexican families. Rumors reflecting strong racial prejudice immediately raced through Clifton and Morenci, charging that the selected Mexican families were unacceptable. Some orphans, according to a rumor, had been given to women in the "tenderloin district," some to drunks, and others had even been sold. Committees of angry Anglo residents, mostly Protestants, seized nineteen children who had been placed in Mexican homes and relocated them with Anglo families for adoption. The remaining twenty-one were handed back to the sisters, who returned them to New York. But the tragic story did not end there. The Foundling Hospital filed suit, demanding that the entire group of forty be returned.

Meanwhile, the *Los Angeles Examiner*, *Leslie's Weekly*, and other publications across the country picked up the incident, reporting with little accuracy that the children had been sold or given to persons of poor reputation. At least one magazine published a photograph depicting a foster Mexican family posing with an orphan in front of a dilapidated home. Roosevelt asked Brodie to investigate.[30]

Three days before the polls opened, Brodie arrived in Clifton-Morenci to conduct the requested investigation. After discussing the situation with local officials and visiting several Mexican homes, the governor rendered his report. Admitting that the issue had religious connotations, Brodie stated that the final disposition of the seventeen foundlings still in Arizona should be determined by the courts and not by the governor or the president. Roosevelt did not concur, taking the position that the foundlings should be returned to the sisters and later directing Brodie to support that decision. The president's request arrived too late. The suit already had been filed.[31]

Actually, Brodie appears to have been more concerned with the possible political fallout from the foundling question than with the merits of the case. He later informed Secretary Loeb that he purposely delayed any action on the matter until after the election. "It was a very nasty case from the beginning," Brodie wrote, "and no doubt endeavors were made to mislead the President and the public through the press."[32]

The courts responded quickly. Only two months later, in January 1905, the Arizona supreme court ruled that the Anglo families legally had adopted the seventeen foundlings in question. Brodie attended the emotional hearing, having guaranteed the safety of any Sister who returned to Arizona as a witness. Tensions ran high, but no serious trouble surfaced.[33]

By election day, November 8, the Arizona Republicans optimistically felt that Fowler had a good chance to carry the election, but the landslide victory that retained Roosevelt in the White House did not extend to Arizona. Marcus A. Smith, the Democratic candidate for delegate to Congress, prevailed— 10,394 votes to 9,522. The *Arizona Republican* concluded that Smith's popularity and the overwhelming disparity in party affiliation among the population had proved too large an obstacle for Fowler to overcome. Yet the Republicans did manage to take one step forward. When the newly appointed Governor Brodie faced the legislature in 1903, he found five Republicans and seven Democrats in the Council and three Republicans with twenty-one Democrats in the House. In 1904, Republicans gained one seat in the Council and three in the House. A modest step forward to be sure, but a gain, nonetheless.[34]

That same month, Brodie took another leave, intending to bring Mary and Sandy back to spend the winter in Phoenix. As usual, he took this opportunity to visit with Roosevelt, now firmly established as president in his own right. Exactly what the two discussed is not known, of course, but a rumor soon circulated in Arizona that Brodie had been summoned to Washington to be rewarded with an appointment as paymaster in the army, and that James McClintock would be the new governor. In Minnesota, George Smalley's father had picked up a similar rumor even earlier, writing his son on August 18 that his sources indicated that Brodie had applied for a position of military recorder. Actually, these speculations were not far from the truth, but Brodie, upon returning to Phoenix in December, informed one reporter that he had no intention of resigning.[35]

On January 16, 1905, Brodie appeared before the Twenty-Third Legislative Assembly to deliver his annual message. Devoting the bulk of his speech to taxation and finances, he began by praising the economic advancement Arizona had recorded in the last two years, emphasizing that even greater progress could be expected now that the Tonto Dam and Yuma Irrigation Project had been approved. The mining industry still dominated the economy, Brodie admitted, but agriculture and the cattle industry had managed to hold their own even as the drought continued. Turning to taxation, Brodie pointed out that the tax base had increased significantly in the last twelve months and recommended that the overall system of taxation be reviewed accordingly. Brodie still felt that the mining industry should be called upon to carry a fair share of the tax burden. He also suggested that the current practice of suspending taxation on new railroad lines for a given period of time be discontinued.

Other comments included praise for the Arizona Rangers and the National Guard. Then, apparently still sensitive to thinly veiled suggestions from some quarters that Stoddard had not been treated fairly, Brodie could not resist putting final closure on the incorporation fee collection controversy. Income from incorporation fees received by Auditor Nichols between March 19, 1903, and December 31, 1904, Brodie carefully reported, amounted to $57,369. To his credit, however, Brodie did not belabor the point. Avoiding any direct comparison of Nichols's figure to Stoddard's claim that he collected only $15,946.30 in eighteen months, Brodie satisfied himself with the observation that he found Nichols's report to be "most credible, valuable and interesting." Nevertheless, Nichols's accounting left little room for argument. Brodie and his friends who had pushed the Cowan Bill through the legislature were totally vindicated.[36]

As one would expect, Brodie's 1905 message to the legislature reveals that he had acquired a more comprehensive grasp of Arizona's political structure and customs than he had revealed ealier. As before, his address was well-received by the general public.

Four days later, news broke from Washington that Brodie had been appointed assistant chief of the records and pension office with the rank of major. Roosevelt had alerted Brodie earlier to the possibility of the appointment, but Brodie knew that significant opposition to his appointment had suffered in the nation's capital. At age fifty-five, Brodie was considered by many to be too old for active duty. Moreover, others with military aspirations and strong political connections in Congress were actively seeking such appointments—which required senatorial confirmation. Competition for all such positions remained keen.[37]

Initially, at least from Roosevelt's perspective, a position in the records and pension office appeared to be a good fit for Brodie. The present chief would retire in May, enabling the assistant chief, Maj. Edward S. Fowler, to be promoted to lieutenant colonel and advanced to the position of chief. Brodie then would replace Fowler. Problems surfaced when the Senate, for unclear reasons, refused to confirm Fowler, who had been serving as acting assistant chief since the previous August. In addition, the Army Appropriations Bill, then being debated in the House of Representatives, provided that the position of assistant chief be eliminated upon the next vacancy. Roosevelt, realizing that he had to move quickly while the office still existed, withdrew Fowler's name and submitted Brodie's instead. Brodie had hoped to continue as governor until July 1, but under these conditions he had to accept quickly. One of Roosevelt's friends, Senator Redfield Proctor of Vermont, agreed to shepherd Brodie's appointment through the confirmation process.[38]

Candidates eager to replace Governor Brodie surfaced immediately. Roosevelt, obviously hoping to forestall any internal Republican power struggle in Arizona by naming a replacement quickly, initially turned to Arizona Supreme Court Chief Justice Edward Kent, reputedly a friend of the president since their days together as students at Harvard. But Kent declined the offer, informing Roosevelt that he preferred to remain on the bench. Roosevelt then briefly considered James McClintock, Joseph L. B. Alexander, George Wilcox, the former first lieutenant of B Troop in the Rough Riders, and Benjamin Fowler, who soon emerged as the front-runner.[39]

Alarmed at Fowler's rapidly expanding power base, Brodie met with Judge Kent to assess the situation. Admitting that he had declined the governorship, Kent informed Brodie that he would recommend Fowler for the position—as had the Murphy brothers. Only four months earlier, Brodie enthusiastically had supported Fowler's bid to be elected delegate to Congress, but now, aware that Kent had joined forces with the Murphys to endorse Fowler, he rethought his position. The exact sequence of events still is not clear, but following his defeat for delegate in November, Fowler had traveled to Washington to lobby for separate statehood. There, he apparently fell under the influence of Nathan Oakes Murphy, who had gone to the nation's capital for the same purpose. Concerned with the long-range implications of the apparent Kent-Murphy alliance, Brodie appealed directly to his friend the president.[40]

Knowing that Roosevelt held Judge Kent in high regard, Brodie, in a long letter to the president, proceeded tactfully and carefully. First admitting that he knew of Kent's refusal to accept the governorship, Brodie implied that he also considered Kent's desire to stay in his present position to be a wise choice. "Judge Kent," Brodie stated, "has made the best chief justice in all probability the Territory has ever had." That said, Brodie explained that he and Kent totally disagreed on Fowler. Although he had donned kid gloves in commenting on his relations with Kent, Brodie had no similar compunction about discussing Fowler or the Murphys. "The appointment of Mr. Fowler," Brodie bluntly and somewhat egotistically wrote, "or any other except a man known to be friends to me would be considered with apprehension and the first step towards the return of the Murphy regime to power." Fowler, Brodie went on to explain, "is considered here a Murphy man as he has unfortunately allied himself with them."[41]

Brodie then proposed an alternative. Judge Edmund William Wells, he pleaded, would be the best possible choice for governor. Wells had been raised in Arizona and "his appointment would be more than satisfactory to the people of the country." Brodie concluded by expressing his deep appreciation for Roosevelt reinstating him in the army.[42]

A week later, Roosevelt penned a terse response to Brodie's letter: "In view of certain matters do not deem it advisable to appoint Wells." Quite possibly, Roosevelt did not wish to involve himself unnecessarily in an internal power struggle between Brodie's friends and the Kent-Murphy faction. After all, Brodie was as good as gone from any position of strong influence in Arizona. At any rate, on February 10, Roosevelt asked the Senate to ratify Arizona's Attorney General Joseph H. Kibbey as the new governor. Up to this point, Kibbey had not surfaced as a viable candidate.[43]

Brodie had no reason to criticize Roosevelt's selection. A native of Indiana, Kibbey moved to Florence in 1888 as legal adviser to an irrigation company. Appointed associate justice of the Arizona Supreme Court a year later, he quickly established a reputation as an expert on water rights. In 1904, Brodie appointed him attorney general, replacing Ed Wells, who had resigned. The origin of Kibbey's influence with Roosevelt is not known.[44]

Meanwhile, completing his plans to leave the territory, Brodie tendered his resignation effective February 14. That afternoon he met with both houses of the legislature, emotionally thanking the members for the many courtesies they had extended to him and assuring his audience that he would always hold Arizona in high regard. At midnight he officially relinquished his office to Acting Governor Nichols, who would serve until the Senate confirmed Judge Kibbey.[45]

Three days later Brodie, accompanied by his family and by Mary's mother, who had been visiting her daughter, departed Phoenix on the first leg of their journey to Washington. Stopping for several days in Prescott, Brodie arranged to have Mary's brother, Jack Hanlon, appointed receiver of the Walnut Grove Water Storage Company and superintendent of the Crown Point mine. Brodie wanted to remain in Prescott longer, but he was needed in Washington, having agreed to organize and command the Rough Rider honor guard at Roosevelt's inaugural parade in March.[46]

Brodie's departure from Arizona drew mixed reactions. Most newspapers editorialized that he had been an effective and honest public official. Some praise came from unusual sources. For example, *El Mensajero*, a Spanish newspaper published in Phoenix, reported that "Governor Brodie . . . is by far the most popular Governor Arizona has had." Of course, most papers were not willing to go that far, one commenting that "while not a strong or brilliant Governor, he has deported himself with propriety." But compliments came from other sources, as well. The Arizona Rangers contributed generously for the purchase of an expensive stock saddle, a gift to the man who had been their staunch supporter and advocate. The Democratic legislature appropriated $500 to purchase and suitably engrave a cavalry saber as a fitting tribute to the former Rough Rider.[47]

Although Brodie entered the governor's office with little political experience in a traditional sense, his two-and-one-half year term revealed that he not only possessed finely tuned natural instincts in his own right, but he prudently surrounded himself with politically astute friends and advisers who could be relied upon to help guide him through the intricacies of public office. Some Arizona pundits initially questioned his ability to challenge Nathan Oakes Murphy's well-oiled machine, feeling that Murphy, a well-entrenched master politician, boasted far too much political acumen and experience for Brodie to overcome. Even Roosevelt harbored early reservations concerning Brodie's lack of experience. All were wrong. By seizing firm control of the Arizona Republican Party and cooperating effectively with the Democratic-controlled legislature, Brodie realized far more success than anyone had predicted.

Easily dispensing with several minor political stumbling blocks early in his gubernatorial career, Brodie had faced his first critical challenge when Secretary of State Isaac Taft Stoddard called in his markers to contest the far-reaching implications of the Cowan Bill, which Brodie had pushed through the legislature. Ultimately prevailing in the ensuing confrontation, Brodie successfully broke the Phoenix-New York-Washington connection, which for years had capitalized on Arizona as a convenient dumping ground for "carpetbaggers" whom one newspaper categorized as "political derelicts." Certainly, Brodie's success in breaking the practice of sending job-seekers to Arizona would be one of his most important achievements. But other significant events marked his incumbency, as well: Utah's attempted land grab of the Arizona Strip failed; Arizona's delegation to the National Republican Convention had been instructed for Roosevelt; and the legislature enacted into law several progressive measures that Brodie had recommended. In addition, Brodie's behind-the-scenes influence in securing Roosevelt Dam and the Yuma Reclamation Project created long-term benefits lasting even to this day. But there were failures, as well.

The statehood issue is murky at best, but that question tested Brodie's ability to reconcile his own personal beliefs with those of his constituents. Although he possibly reconsidered later, at the time of his inauguration in 1902, Brodie did not consider Arizona to be ready for admission. He wisely refrained from making his position public, however, knowing that the residents of Arizona wanted statehood, and they wanted it immediately. Putting his personal beliefs aside, therefore, Governor Brodie did everything in his power to secure a new star in the nation's flag. At one point he even requested that the board of supervisors in each county petition Congress to that effect. But, without support from the White House, he could make little headway.

In retrospect, President Roosevelt apparently favored joining Arizona with New Mexico to create one state, but as a concession to his friend Brodie and most Arizonans, who strongly opposed such a union, the president refrained from interjecting himself into the controversy. That decision left Senators Matthew S. Quay and Albert J. Beveridge free to decide Arizona's political future without presidential influence. By keeping the president neutral on the sidelines, Brodie and his supporters garnered enough influence late in 1904 to nip in the bud a very real threat by Congress to join the two territories. Even then, Brodie could not convince Roosevelt to enter the fray in support of separate statehood. Finally, in February 1905, Congress, tired of the constant bickering, rejected the joint-statehood bill, leaving Arizona and New Mexico still knocking futilely on the statehood door. Roosevelt, true to the promise he had made to Brodie at the Grand Canyon, refrained from publicly advocating joint statehood as long as Brodie remained in office. Beyond that, there were no promises.

Still unanswered is the question of Roosevelt's motivation in selecting Brodie to be governor of Arizona. It might well have been nothing more than the simple desire to provide employment for a faithful friend who had faced the Spanish rifles with him in Cuba. But there might have been extenuating circumstances. Did Roosevelt ask Brodie to accept the governorship expecting that he would establish in Arizona a pro-Roosevelt Republican Party, and if Brodie succeeded, did Roosevelt agree to reward him with a position in the Regular Army? There is no hard evidence that such a bargain had been struck, but the overall chain of events does suggest that some kind of prior understanding between the two had been brokered. In any event, few could argue that the Brodie Administration did not set an enviable standard for honesty, integrity, and overall benefit to Arizona.

CHAPTER 21

"When We Pass Over the Great Divide"

Brodie's long-desired return to the army in 1905 coincided with significant changes then taking place in the nation's military establishment. Responding to lessons learned in the Spanish-American War and aware of developing conditions in Europe, the War Department had altered significantly the traditional command structure that existed during the Civil War and the period immediately following. Most significantly, a General Staff Corps had been created to coordinate overall activities, initiate important contingency planning for future operations, and modify tactics as required by a worldwide proliferation of new weapons and other technological innovations. Returning to active duty at the advanced age of fifty-six, Brodie may not have fully realized that times had changed and that the Civil War generation was being pushed aside by younger officers with fresh ideas.

Before settling into his billet in the records and pension office early in 1905, Brodie had one final duty to perform at the request of his friend in the White House. Roosevelt had asked him to assemble and command a detachment of thirty former Rough Riders to escort the president-elect at the inaugural parade on March 4. Selecting the designated number of participants, Brodie designed a snappy uniform consisting of khaki riding "britches" and blouse, a Stetson army hat, buckskin gauntlets, blue flannel shirt, blue silk handkerchief, and flat brass spurs. Brodie assured Roosevelt that he had chosen the men carefully to ensure a balanced representation of the regiment based on geographic considerations and troop affiliation. Roosevelt approved Brodie's overall concept, but he pointed out one glaring inconsistency.[1]

For unknown reasons Brodie, a consummate Westerner by choice, showed unprecedented favoritism toward the relatively few Eastern-

Major Brodie, commander of the Rough Riders' 1905 presidential inaugural honor guard, congratulates President Roosevelt. This photograph clearly reveals the close friendship which existed between the two men. Brodie family collection.

ers who had served in the Rough Riders. Fully half the regiment, approximately 550 men, came from New Mexico and Arizona, but Brodie selected only five from each of those two territories to serve in the honor guard. Thirteen of the thirty members, however, came from New York and Boston, which together had provided only 62 men for the regiment. Recognizing the disparity, Roosevelt suggested that the representation from Arizona and New Mexico be increased at the expense of Boston and New York. Apparently, Brodie did not accept the recommendation, however, retaining instead the original allocation.[2]

Even more perplexing is the manner in which Brodie filled the premier honor positions of wheelmen—those four individuals designated to ride alongside Roosevelt's carriage, two on either side. Only eight of the fifty-five officers who ever held commissions in the Rough Riders came from the East, but all four wheelmen Brodie selected represented that region: Lieutenants John C. Greenway, David M. Goodrich, Robert Harry Munro Ferguson, and Captain Woodbury Kane. All four were Roosevelt's favorites, but Greenway and Goodrich actually owed their commissions to Col. Leonard Wood, who had plucked them from the enlisted ranks at San Antonio to receive shoulder straps. Kane and Ferguson had been Roosevelt men from the very beginning. A native of New York and a friend of Roosevelt since their days together as students at Harvard, Kane originally served as an enlisted man, but worked his way up to captain in command of K Troop.[3]

Ferguson's friendship with Roosevelt also preceded his enlistment in the Rough Riders.[3] The third son of a Scottish "laird," Robert Ferguson had been sent to America as a young man to find his own way in the world. Subsequently becoming a ranch partner with Roosevelt in the Dakotas, he frequently accompanied the future president on extended hunting trips. Although he once had served briefly as a commissioned officer in the British Army, Ferguson enlisted in the Rough Riders, remaining a sergeant until late July when Roosevelt selected him to fill a vacant second lieutenant position in D Troop. Describing some of the officers from New Mexico as "feeble folk," Ferguson nevertheless expressed overall pleasure with his service as a Rough Rider. "Next to going with our own Highland laddies," he wrote his Scottish mother, "it's been a great joy to have fought with our distant cousins across the sea."[4]

The contributions of easterners to the leadership and fighting ranks of the Rough Riders always has been overemphasized, and Brodie's selection of the honor guard only perpetuated that erroneous perception. Roosevelt wanted a balanced representation reflected in his honor guard, but for unknown reasons failed to strongly convey that desire to Brodie.

As some expected, Brodie's assignment to the records and pension office proved short-lived. Reporting for duty early in 1905, he accepted his expected promotion to lieutenant colonel on June 10, receiving shortly thereafter orders directing him to report for duty at military headquarters in Manila, capital of the Philippine Islands. Undoubtedly, Brodie had been watching the Philippine situation closely, anticipating that sooner or later he would be stationed there. During the Spanish-American War, United States forces had seized Manila and shortly thereafter assumed responsibility for the entire former Spanish colony.

Unlike the Cubans, who accepted American occupation with little open resentment, the Filipinos reacted differently. Tension between American forces and the Philippine "Army of Liberation," which had been fighting the Spaniards for several years, gradually escalated. Upon realizing that the United States did not intend to immediately extend independence to the islands, Emilio Aguinaldo, commander of the Philippine Army, unleashed his forces against the Americans late in 1898. After experiencing several decisive defeats in pitched battles, Aguinaldo reverted to guerrilla warfare, which he had employed very effectively against the Spaniards.[5]

Recognizing the Philippine situation to be much more complex than a simple military challenge, the United States wisely attempted to simultaneously address both military and civil aspects of the American occupation. Quickly reinforcing units already in the islands to suppress the insurgency by force of arms, the army organized the Philippine Division with three subordinate geographical commands designated departments. Division headquarters remained in Manila on the large island of Luzon.

At the same time, President McKinley created a five-man non-military Philippine Commission to help the native Filipinos establish an effective central government, revive the economy, and assist local governments. Under the effective leadership of Chairman William Howard Taft, the commission soon made remarkable headway in providing a stabilizing civil influence throughout the Philippine Archipelago.[6]

By 1905 the Philippine Division had succeeded quite well in suppressing insurgent activities except for occasional small, isolated skirmishes, predominantly in such Moro-inhabited islands as Mindanao in the south. Certainly, Manila and immediate surrounding areas appeared to be stable, with local governments gradually expanding control. Under these conditions, Brodie felt secure bringing his family with him—a decision he soon would regret.

The Brodies no sooner reached Manila when seven-year-old Sandy entered a hospital suffering from chronic dysentery. Greatly alarmed, Brodie—who earlier had lost two young children to sickness—vented his frustration to George Smalley: "I am so worried over Sandy's illness," the colonel confided, "that I can hardly write." Fortunately, the boy recovered, but Mary, thoroughly disillusioned with the islands, took her son back to Haddonfield as soon as the lad could safely travel. In one respect, Sandy's illness may have been a blessing in disguise. Brodie's alternating duty stations at Manila and Iloilo would have made it very difficult for him to have enjoyed a normal family life.[7]

Initially, Brodie found no permanent assignment available for him in Manila, but he joined two other officers assigned temporary duty on the controversial Board of Church Claims, which met periodically in Manila to resolve a nasty religious issue. Perceived by many Philippine natives as hated symbols of long-standing Spanish oppression, the Spanish priests, or "friars," had become victims of retaliation after the rebellion against Spain broke out. The rebels killed many priests and drove most of the remainder into Manila where, afraid to return to their parishes, they remained even after the Spanish authorities withdrew and the United States assumed control. In 1900, recognizing the friars' precarious position to have far-reaching implications extending even to the Vatican, President McKinley asked Chief Commissioner Taft to investigate. Learning that the friars actually had clear title to a vast amount of good agricultural land, which they no longer could administer, Taft concluded that the only fair solution would be to have the United States purchase the church land in question and either sell it outright or rent it to the Philippine people.[8]

In 1901, at McKinley's request, Taft traveled to Rome and personally convinced the Pope to accept his plan. Subsequent negotiations authorized the United States to purchase approximately four hundred thousand acres of church land for almost $7,500,000, and to distribute it among the Filipinos. The Church Board of Claims had responsibility to investigate all allegations of damages, forfeited rent, property line disputes, and related matters, reporting their findings to the Philippine Commission for settlement.[9]

Brodie had served only a short time on the church board when he received a permanent assignment as military secretary (later redesignated adjutant general) of the Department of Visayas, with duty station in the city of Iloilo on the island of Panay. The department encompassed the islands of Panay, Samar, Leyte, and several smaller islands clustered in the center of the archipelago between the Department of Mindanao to the south and Luzon to the north. Unfortunately, Brodie's permanent assignment did not relieve him of his responsibility on the board of claims. For the next two years, he would be required to frequently travel by ship back and forth between Iloilo and Manila.[10]

Other than the boring trips to Manila, Brodie enjoyed his duty at Iloilo, particularly after Mary joined him in 1906. Sandy remained with his grandmother in New Jersey. But Brodie did not relish serving on the church board, considering it to be "an interminable job besides being most irksome." Nevertheless, he continued with that assignment until the board dissolved on March 12, 1907.[11]

As he had promised the Arizona legislature upon resigning as governor, Brodie maintained interest in the territory, eagerly awaiting letters from George Smalley, James McClintock, and others describing conditions in Arizona. Advised at one point that a developing relationship between the Murphy brothers and Judge Edward Kent would again bear watching, Brodie felt compelled to express his concern in a letter to William Loeb, President Roosevelt's private secretary. He began by reminding Loeb that the Murphys harbored a "strong hatred of the President." That established, Brodie went on to caution that the brothers were attempting to reestablish themselves as a force in Arizona politics. With that in mind, Brodie expressed his sincere hope that the Murphys' "recommendations will have but little weight in Washington." Then, eager to dispel any suspicion that he entertained any personal bias in the matter, Brodie pointed out that while governor he had "squared" his account with the Murphys to his own satisfaction.[12]

Within the same letter, Brodie advised Loeb that a schism in the officer corps threatened morale. "Ever since I have been back in the service," Brodie lamented, "I have felt that there was a little feeling of unrest over the passing of younger men over the heads of their elders in length of service." In making this observation, Brodie hit the nail squarely on the head. Developing conditions in Europe and unrest in Mexico had caused the War Department to turn more and more to younger officers, such as Maj. Gen. Leonard Wood, to lead the army into the Twentieth Century.[13]

The separation from his son also concerned Brodie. Now eight years old, Sandy, in Brodie's view, needed the guidance of his absentee father. In several letters to his son, Brodie praised the lad's reported scholarship achievements and admonished him to always obey his grandmother. Describing pleasant conditions and events in the Brodie household, such as Mary's interest in scouting the countryside for curios and antiques, Brodie assured Sandy that times were good. Yet, in one letter, he permitted an uncharacteristic touch of nostalgia to surface, reminding Sandy that he had a brother, Oswald, who had died many years before "and will be there to meet us when we pass over the great divide." The colonel made no mention of Sandy's little half-sister, Kate, buried and apparently forgotten in faraway Walla Walla.[14]

Brodie's tour of duty in the Philippines did not officially end until the fall of 1907, but during the previous January, as it had so many times before, Mary's health became an issue. In February, at Brodie's request, Maj. Gen. Leonard Wood, now commander of the Philippine Division, citing Mary's "nervousness," requested that Brodie be given a three-month leave to visit Japan and China prior to being reassigned to the United States. But even that respite did not help. Falling ill in Japan, Mary insisted the couple return to Manila before sailing for San Francisco on July 1.[15]

Both Mary and her husband looked forward to the colonel's new assignment. Eager to locate somewhere with a cool, healthful climate, Brodie briefly considered the Presidio of San Francisco, but instead eventually requested assignment to the Department of Dakota. The War Department granted his request, appointing him department adjutant general with duty station at St. Paul, Minnesota.[16]

Brodie found his duties in St. Paul much less demanding than his previous assignment. Consisting of approximately 170 officers and 2,400 enlisted men, the Department of Dakota's responsibility extended to installations in North Dakota, Montana, Minnesota, and Wyoming, but Brodie found no onerous travel requirement as he had in the Philippines. His office staff consisted of six well-trained civilian clerks who knew their jobs. But Brodie did not intend to be completely deskbound in St. Paul. He would find a way to remain active.[17]

A new regulation, reflecting the War Department's increased emphasis on officer fitness and education, required all field grade cavalry officers to successfully complete an annual three-day timed trail ride. Although still an unusually skilled horseman, Brodie eased the rigors of his annual test by purchasing from a breeder in Virginia a large, easy-gaited Morgan saddle horse. His preparation paid off. Throughout the remainder of his military career, Brodie never failed to easily satisfy the riding requirement.[18]

As an officer on active duty, Brodie could not directly involve himself in politics, but he followed national events closely. Roosevelt, honoring a pledge he had made four years earlier, declined to be a presidential candidate in 1908, selecting instead William H. Taft to be his replacement. Brodie privately backed Taft, if for no other reason than personal loyalty to his friend in the White House. To Brodie's satisfaction, the Arizona Republicans, ignoring the Murphy brothers' opposition, sent a pro-Taft delegation to the Republican National Nominating Convention. In the general election that fall, Taft easily defeated the Democrat, William Jennings Bryan.[19]

A month before Roosevelt's term as president ended, Brodie, obviously motivated by a wave of nostalgia, wrote a long letter congratulating his former commander. Assuring Roosevelt that his record as president would equal "the best" of those who preceded him, Brodie expressed his deep personal satisfaction in having served in the Rough Riders and thanked his friend for appointing him governor of Arizona and arranging for his return to the army. "My loyalty to you," Brodie concluded, "only ends when what is mortal of me shall be laid away in the churchyard." Yet, Brodie's letter contains one passage which is difficult to understand. Brodie still remained in good health, but apparently he envisioned some dark specter hovering over the future. "I am reaching an age," he wrote, "wherein there are certain uncertainties which will in all probability preclude my ever seeing you again." Brodie was wrong. He and Roosevelt would have several future opportunities to relive past triumphs and speculate about the future.[20]

After turning the reins of government over to President Taft in 1909, Roosevelt embarked on an extended big game hunting trip across Africa. Returning early the following summer, he found the Republican Party in shambles. During his absence, the Old Guard had re-emerged to challenge Roosevelt's reformers, and Taft had proved unable or unwilling to suppress their resurgence. Dismayed with President Taft's apparent lack of leadership, Roosevelt launched a speaking tour of major cities to rally support for the Progressive movement. One of his scheduled stops was in St. Paul.

In Minnesota, Roosevelt, eager to reach as large an audience as possible, agreed to address the Second Annual Conservation Congress and the ever-popular Minnesota State Fair. Both organizations were scheduled to convene in St. Paul on the same September day. Over 40,000 people, including the governors of five Western states and other important politicians, promised to attend. Both President Taft and Roosevelt planned to make an appearance, but the two men did not meet face-to-face. Taft arrived first, reaching St. Paul early on September 5. After delivering the opening address to the conservation congress in the morning, Taft greeted the crowd at the fairgrounds that afternoon, departing the city shortly thereafter. Roosevelt arrived the next day.

Emulating Taft's agenda, Roosevelt first addressed the conservation congress and then the state fair. In his two speeches, Roosevelt reiterated many of those personal characteristics of a good citizen which Brodie had come to admire. Calling upon the "average man" to lead his life with honesty, courage, and common sense, Roosevelt pledged that government should embrace a national commitment to the principles embodied in the Golden Rule and Square Deal. Before departing St. Paul that evening, Roosevelt attended as guest of honor a formal dinner hosted by Colonel and Mrs. Brodie.[21]

The Brodies spared no effort in their desire to entertain the former president. Mary thoroughly enjoyed this type of activity and she made the most of it. Dressed in a stunning lavender brocade gown, Mary supervised the seating arrangement, placing herself next to Roosevelt, directly across the large round table from her husband. Twenty-four guests attended, including the commander of the Department of Dakota, the governor, both with their wives, the Archbishop of St. Paul, Gifford Pinchot, and Benjamin Fowler from Arizona. No one made a speech nor proposed a toast, but all those present reportedly enjoyed the evening.[22]

The presence of Gifford Pinchot at the National Conservation Congress came as no surprise. A staunch conservationist, the Connecticut-born Pinchot had been appointed chief of the division of forestry at age forty-three. Under his supervision, the forest service added millions of acres to the national forest system. Roosevelt and Pinchot were good friends and political allies, but the chief forester soon clashed with Roosevelt's successor, President Taft, over the question of withdrawing water power sites from private use and other issues. The situation finally became so acrimonious that Taft replaced Pinchot. For this and other reasons, Roosevelt decided to challenge Taft for the Republican presidential nomination in the election of 1912. Failing in that effort, Roosevelt openly broke with Taft, founding the Progressive "Bull Moose" Party.[23]

Brodie, of course, could not campaign actively for Roosevelt in 1912, but he could and did offer moral support. It is not clear if Brodie truly embraced the philosophy of the Progressive movement or merely supported his friend, but he assured his Rough Rider comrade that he was "with you body and soul for the crusade you are making for civil & political righteousness." But the Bull Moose campaign was doomed to fail. In November, the Democratic candidate, Woodrow Wilson, easily won the election in the electoral tally, but with considerably less support in the popular vote. Brodie was crushed, although being a rather astute observer in politics, he probably was not surprised. Writing Roosevelt from his new duty station in San Francisco, Brodie rationalized the outcome: "You made a wonderful fight."[24]

Two months before the disappointing 1912 election, Brodie received the welcome news that he had been promoted to colonel and assigned to San Francisco as the adjutant general of the Division of the Pacific. No stranger to San Francisco, Brodie had spent time there when stationed as a second lieutenant across the bay at Benicia Barracks.

In general, the colonel and Mary enjoyed their brief stay in San Francisco, where they often entertained friends from Arizona such as George Smalley and his family. Another old friend to stop by was Tom Campbell, a supporter from Yavapai County who had once broken with the Murphys to become a staunch Brodie stalwart. Campbell proudly brought his son, Alexander Brodie Campbell, to visit with his namesake. One of the most perplexing aspects of Brodie's San Francisco assignment, however, hinges on the treatment of Kate Reynolds Brodie, now interred in the post cemetery.[25]

The tragic story of Kate Brodie took an unusual twist after Lieutenant Brodie left Fort Colville in 1877. In conjunction with the closing of that post in 1892, Kate's remains reportedly were exhumed for reburial in the cemetery at the Presidio. Every extant account of the woman—including the 1870 census—records her name and middle initial as Kate M. At the Presidio, however, authorities burried her under the name Catherine R. Brodie, and recorded the date of her death as March 26 instead of March 25. Certainly, if Brodie had been aware of these errors, he would have made appropriate corrections. But he failed to do so, suggesting that Brodie never visited the final burial site of his first wife. In his defense, it is possible that he did not know that Kate's remains had been relocated from Fort Colville. Nevertheless, it appears that when Brodie departed Washington Territory back in the late summer of 1877, he forever turned his back on Kate M. Reynolds Brodie, the woman who had given birth to his only daughter.[26]

As Colonel Brodie's mandatory retirement age approached, he and Mary spent many hours discussing their future. Brodie wanted to settle in Arizona—probably in Prescott. Mary, absolutely determined that this would not occur, insisted that the family take up final residence in Haddonfield. Not only did she consider New Jersey to be much more healthful than Arizona, but her aging mother, her brother Jack, and other relatives resided there. Following Henry Van Beuren's death, Jack had severed his Arizona connection and returned to Haddonfield, where he successfully entered the banking business. Faced with Mary's unflinching determination, Brodie finally gave up the struggle and agreed to retire in the Garden State.[27]

Officially discharged on November 13, 1913, Brodie actually left the service in July, having accrued four months' unused paid leave. Shortly after arriving in Haddonfield, Brodie purchased an attractive older residence which he described to Smalley as a "pretty, old Quaker, Colonial home." Mary's health improved rapidly, and the couple enrolled Sandy in a military boarding school in Pennington, New Jersey. Now as tall as his father, Brodie's sixteen-year-old son soon stood at the head of his class academically. After rearranging their new home to suit their own tastes, Mary and the colonel laid plans to visit friends in Arizona and even Brodie's ancestral origins in Scotland, but for various reasons postponed both trips until it became too late.[28]

Extremely proud of their son, Brodie and Mary eventually would be disappointed with his selection of an occupation. The colonel desperately wanted Sandy to pursue a military career, either by way of West Point or the Naval Academy. Mary stood equally determined that the boy would emulate her father and become a man of the cloth. Probably as headstrong as either of his parents, Sandy ignored their pleas, and following a brief period as a miner in the Little Jessie mine in Yavapai County, Arizona, sought employment as a commercial artist.[29]

Although mentally still alert and vibrant at the time of retirement, Brodie was beginning to slip physically. Writing his old friend

George Smalley, he explained that he often fell asleep in his chair and complained about a general lack of energy. "I feel myself," he once confided, "feeling something as an old horse turned out to grass must [experience]." He frequently mused about his days in Arizona, reminding Smalley of the "good work" they had accomplished while he had been governor. He also had not forgotten the Murphy brothers, bragging that he and Smalley "took pleasure in plucking a few of [their] tail feathers."[30]

Watching foreign affairs occupied much of Brodie's time and interest after retirement. In particular, the revolution in Mexico and attending troubles along the border with that nation gave cause for concern. In 1915, only one year before General John J. ("Black Jack") Pershing stormed into Mexico with several thousand cavalrymen, Brodie wrote Smalley that he feared a war with Mexico to be imminent—a prospect he personally did not relish.[31]

Even more serious was the possibility of the United States being sucked into the raging European inferno. Early in 1917, Theodore Roosevelt wrote the Secretary of War requesting authority to raise a division of volunteers for possible deployment against Germany. The Secretary denied the request, but for the next few months Roosevelt continued to lay preliminary plans to create a modern and expanded version of Rough Riders. Brodie, almost two years shy of his seventieth birthday, knew that he was too old for field duty, but the nostrils of the old warhorse flared briefly one more time, upon being advised by Roosevelt that he "could be of assistance in helping raise the division and manage the home depot." Other former Rough Riders also answered Roosevelt's call. John C. Greenway agreed to command a regiment, and George B. Wilcox consented to serve as a major. David M. Goodrich may have been pledged as well. But President Woodrow Wilson, who had won a second term in 1916, had no intention of giving a political rival an opportunity to gain additional honor on a European battlefield.[32]

Actually, Roosevelt's plan to revive the Rough Rider concept remained a rosy, pie-in-the-sky proposal which had virtually no chance of success. The Secretary of War knew it. The president knew it. Probably even Roosevelt, if he admitted the harsh truth, knew it as well. The original First United States Volunteer Cavalry had been a unique aberration, probably formed at the only point in American history where the political, cultural, and military stars were in line to make such an endeavor possible. That moment would never come again.

Uncertain about the future of Roosevelt's planned division, Brodie decided to explore other avenues. On March 20, 1917, only two weeks before Congress declared war on Germany, Brodie fired off a terse handwritten offer to the Adjutant General of the Army. "In the event of war between the United States and any foreign country," Brodie wrote, "I ask that my services be considered as available for active duty." There is no record that he ever received a response, but fourteen months later, the question of Brodie's services became moot.[33]

On May 10, 1918, with Mary and Sandy at his side in the Haddonfield family home, Roosevelt's "grizzled old frontier soldier" finally laid down his saber. Cause of death was not made public. Within hours, Mary began receiving condolences from her husband's former comrades-in-arms and many friends scattered across the nation. One of the most touching came from George W. P. Hunt, the Democratic governor of the state of Arizona, who wrote: "I have just learned with much sorrow of the passing of Colonel Brodie. . . . There are many reminders in this state of the wise administration of Governor Brodie in that trying time when Arizona, having outgrown the territorial form of government, had not yet achieved statehood."[34]

Honoring Brodie's military service, he was buried in the Arlington National Cemetery, clasping a sprig of Highland heather sent by a cousin in Edinburgh. His regulation military headstone, of course, records no more than his name, rank, and dates of birth and death. Regulations prohibited anything more descriptive. But many years later, former Rough Rider Private Arthur L. Tuttle provided his own unvarnished epitaph, recalling that his former commander "never looked down on any one." What could be a more fitting tribute?[35]

Afterword

Alexander Oswald Brodie generally is remembered in Arizona as a Rough Rider and one of the last territorial governors, but the full extent of his contributions are neither generally known nor appreciated. This oversight may have occurred because Brodie's seven years of service in the First Cavalry, and civilian activities immediately thereafter, offered no clue that he would render outstanding service in Arizona, or anywhere else, for that matter. Brodie's initial army assignment to Camp Apache in 1870 afforded several opportunities for the young officer to make a name for himself, but he failed to do so. Even participation in Colonel Crook's famous 1872-73 campaign into the Tonto Basin accomplished little to establish his reputation as a field soldier. Brodie emerged from the Tonto Basin as the only participating lieutenant from Camp Apache who failed to receive a brevet promotion. Upon resigning his commission in 1877, Brodie appears to have been perceived as a capable officer, but certainly not an outstanding one.

A decade after leaving the army, Brodie finally emerged from obscurity. As superintendent of the Walnut Grove Water Storage Company and trusted associate of the New York entrepreneur Henry S. Van Beuren, he soon gained a reputation in northern Arizona as a man of action and a capable engineer. Fortunately, his developing reputation remained untarnished by Territorial Arizona's most destructive natural disaster—the collapse of the Walnut Grove dam—because he had not been involved in the design or construction of the ill-fated structure. In spite of his best efforts at the Crown Point mine, however, Brodie found no more success mining for gold along the Hassayampa River than he had achieved in the army.

For approximately a dozen years following the Walnut Grove disaster, Brodie expended a great deal of effort and money attempting to develop the Crown Point mine, but the voluminous personal papers of Van Beuren during that period reveal a curious lack of professionalism on Brodie's part. Normal mining practice required weekly or monthly progress reports detailing the extent of underground work completed, and the amount of ore and overburden removed to be discarded or stockpiled for milling. Moreover, detailed assay maps, showing cross sections of the mine with the location and assay results of each sample taken, should have been prepared. Apparently, Brodie did neither. Although he wrote Van Beuren frequently describing conditions at the mine, Brodie seems never to have established a systematic method of record keeping. Why Van Beuren, an experienced businessman, did not require formal reports is not known.[1]

A similar situation existed at the Crown Point mill. As best can be determined, Brodie never prepared periodic milling reports or flow sheets indicating hours of operation, tonnage of ore pushed through the mill, and value of gold recovered. Consequently, there is no way to verify Brodie's oft-repeated opinion that the Crown Point mine would be profitable once he developed a water supply capable of supporting full operation of the mill on a daily basis.[2]

The Spanish-American War dramatically changed Brodie's life, transforming him from a struggling mine operator with a solid, albeit localized, personal reputation into the senior major of the most famous regiment of American volunteer soldiers in history. Today, Brodie's association with the Rough Riders is well-known, but he never received credit for his role in making the regiment possible. Undoubtedly the first man to propose publicly that cowboys be recruited into a volunteer regiment in case of war with Spain, Brodie lacked the political clout necessary to convince the War Department that his plan had merit. Nevertheless, his concept of cowboy cavalry caught hold in the minds of better-known and more influential individuals across the nation, who ultimately pressured Congress to authorize the First United States Volunteer Cavalry. Clearly, Brodie, more than any other single individual, opened the door for Theodore Roosevelt's charge to everlasting fame up San Juan Heights in Cuba.

Brodie's own performance of duty in the Rough Riders was superb. Upon joining the regiment, he quickly convinced both Col. Leonard Wood and Lt. Col. Theodore Roosevelt that he possessed the military background and personality required to help blend a diverse group of individualistic volunteers, largely from the West, into a cohesive fighting force in a very short time. Roosevelt, recognizing Brodie's ability from the very beginning, later commented on several occasions that at San Antonio he perceived Brodie as a man "I could tie to." And tie he did. Six years later, searching for a reliable and honest man to restore popular government to Arizona Territory, President Roosevelt turned to his friend Brodie. Obviously, Brodie found his service in the Rough Riders to be a convenient horse he would ride as far as it would carry him for the rest of his life.

Arizona's forty-nine-year transition from territory to statehood mirrored a pattern common to the trans-Mississippi West. Early territorial governors often established "rings" to develop a working power base. In Arizona, the first few governors initially ignored normal party affiliation and forged an effective coalition, or "ring," embracing northerners, southerners, miners, freighters, and prominent local Mexican-Americans. This arrangement turned Arizona's developing cultural and economic foundation away from Spanish-speaking, agriculture-dominated New Mexico, aligning Arizona instead with Anglo California. By the late 1870s, this functioning coalition began to crack as newly arrived residents introduced the traditional political division between Democrats and Republicans. As Arizona's population continued to diversify, governors became increasingly one-dimensional, catering to pet economic interests such as mining or railroading. However, they continued eagerly to seek federal subsidies to finance economic development.

By 1902, Arizona again had changed course. Under Governor Nathan Oakes Murphy's leadership, Arizona backed away from demanding the continued infusion of federal funds earmarked for specific purposes. Instead, Murphy argued that the territory had the right to decide how federal funds could best be utilized. In other words, the concept of "states' rights" was being offered as an alternative to blindly accepting subsidies based on simple federal paternalism. Murphy believed that Arizona should be granted statehood and allowed to choose its own path of economic development by controlling its own water resources and avoiding the restrictions embodied in Roosevelt's conservation plans. This uncompromising belief ultimately cost Murphy his job, and opened the door for Brodie's gubernatorial appointment.[3]

Throughout his adult life, Brodie never faced a more daunting challenge than the Arizona governorship. Establishing a Progressive or reform-oriented government in Arizona shortly after the turn of the century could not have been easy. Democrats controlled the legislature, and local mainstream Republican leadership, accustomed to controlling the executive branch by manipulating party patronage, entertained no intention of sharing power with Brodie or anyone else not in sympathy with their agenda. It turned into a bitter fight, but Brodie gradually prevailed, easing into office anti-machine politicians who supported reform and honest government.

By the time Brodie left office in 1905, the face of Arizona politics bore little resemblance to what had existed when he took the governor's oath. For nearly five years prior to his appointment, the territory had been dominated by Nathan Oakes Murphy and his friends, who had built a formidable machine in Arizona by controlling patronage through their considerable influence with Eastern politicians. The Democrats, other than complain about perceived corruption, abuse of power, and a seemingly never-ending procession of carpetbaggers, could do little to stop the Murphy juggernaut. The reform wing of the Republican Party remained equally critical of Murphy, but lacked the organization and leadership necessary to mount effective opposition. Brodie, active in the Territorial Republican Party for many years and having briefly served as adjutant general in Murphy's first administration, knew well the character and vulnerability of the men he would challenge.

Exploiting his personal popularity, his close friendship with President Roosevelt, and existing Democratic opposition to his predecessor, Brodie first established credibility as a reform governor by arranging for the replacement of Secretary of State Stoddard and several minor officials widely suspected of corruption. In every case possible, he replaced Murphy's supporters with capable local residents of unquestioned integrity and honesty—men such as Territorial Treasurer Ed Kirkland, who served honorably and well until Arizona achieved statehood in 1912. At the same time, Brodie cultivated support from many Democrats by pushing legislation designed to streamline territorial government and implement needed reforms. He also played a key role in defeating joint statehood with New Mexico.

Above all, Brodie convinced the Arizona Republicans to reject Murphy and his "Old Guard" opposition to Roosevelt, accepting instead many of the president's Progressive concepts. Quick to take advantage of the Newlands Act, Brodie secured federal authorization for the highly popular Roosevelt Dam on the Salt River and the Yuma Reclamation Project on the Colorado. As a result of Brodie's groundbreaking efforts to align the Territory with Roosevelt, the "Bull Moose" movement later was given a reasonably good chance to succeed in Arizona. In sum, scandal-clean Alexander Oswald Brodie, by changing dramatically the direction of the Arizona Republican Party, became one of the most effective of the territory's sixteen governors.

Endnotes

Chapter 1

1. Roosevelt to Lodge, May 25, 1898, Morison, et al., *Letters of Theodore Roosevelt*, vol. 3, pp. 832-833. Lodge, a close friend of Roosevelt from Massachusetts, served three terms in the House of Representatives before moving to the Senate in 1892.
2. Maclean, *Highlanders*, pp. 42, 227-228; Dr. Stephanie Blackden to the author.
3. Brodie and Pitcairn Genealogical Tables in Watson, *Alexander Cowan*.
4. Murphy and Mannion, *Friendly Sons*, pp. 26, 59-60.
5. Manley, "Alexander Macomb," pp. 1-8. Born near Belfast, Ireland, on July 27, 1748, to Scot immigrants, Macomb later settled near Detroit, Michigan, where he became wealthy in the fur trade.
6. Watson, *Alexander Cowan*, pp. 43-45. One of Joseph Pitcairn's relatives, Maj. John Pitcairn of the Royal Marines, commanded the British troops at Lexington on the morning of April 12, 1775. He died on Bunker Hill six weeks later.
7. *Ibid*.
8. Durant and Pierce, *History of St. Lawrence County*, p. 442.
9. Freeman, *Edwards*, pp. 6-7; Manley, "Alexander Macomb," p. 2.
10. LaVerne H. Freeman to the author. Cited hereafter as Freeman Notes.
11. Brodie to Watson, January 13, 1913, Brodie Family Papers. Cited hereafter as BFP.
12. *Ibid.* Efforts to trace this Alexander O. Brodie through the United States Bureau of the Census records indicate that at least two Alexander O. Brodies lived in New York, but the specific Brodie in question cannot definitely be identified until 1850. Clearly, Alexander O. Brodie was a resident of New York long before that date. In 1850, he was living in that city with his wife, Eustacia, who was twenty-nine years younger than her sixty-two-year-old husband. Brodie reportedly owned real estate valued at $150,000. The childless couple returned to Scotland prior to his death in 1856.
13. *Ibid.*
14. *Ibid.*; Freeman notes.
15. Brodie Genealogical Tables in Watson, *Alexander Cowan*.

Chapter 2

1. Durant and Pierce, *History of St. Lawrence County*, p. 442-446. Although descendants of Joseph Brodie today pronounce the name "Brodie," Joseph apparently preferred "Broad-ie." David B. Dill, Jr. to the author.
2. Freeman Notes.
3. *St. Lawrence Plaindealer*, February 20, 1868; Brodie to Watson, January 13, 1913, BFP.
4. Tuttle Interview.
5. Brodie to Watson, January 13, 1913, BFP.
6. *Ibid.*; Ambrose, *Duty, Honor, Country*, pp. 128-129. Brodie's appointment

actually came through in 1865, but regulations prohibited cadets from entering the academy until age sixteen.
7. *United States Military Academy Register, 1870.*
8. *Regulations for the U.S. Military Academy*, 1866, p. 30; Brodie to Watson, January 13, 1913, BFP.
9. *United States Military Academy Register, 1870*. By way of comparison, Cadet Francis V. Greene, ranked first in Brodie's class, posted a composite score of 2270.5. The class "goat," Levi P. Hunt, recorded 957.0. Brodie's score of 1592.1 put him solidly in the middle of the class.
10. Hein, *Memories of Long Ago*, pp. 52-53; Ambrose, *Duty, Honor, Country*, pp. 162-163.
11. Hein, *Memories of Long Ago*, pp. 60-61.
12. Utley, *Frontier Regulars*, pp. 12-14.
13. *Ibid.*, pp. 11-17. Cavalry companies unofficially were called troops until 1883, when the term became official.
14. *Army and Navy Journal (ANJ)*, November 26, 1870, p. 232; Gillem to the United States Adjutant General (USAG), September 2, 1872, Records of the U.S. Regular Army Mobile Units (RUSRAMU), Letters Sent, vol. 5. Cited hereafter as First Cavalry Letter Book. A native of Tennessee, Gillem graduated from the Military Academy in 1851, subsequently seeing combat in Florida during the Second Seminole War (1851-52) and in the Mississippi Valley with the Union Army during the Civil War. Assuming command of the First Cavalry in 1871, he served in that capacity until his death in 1875 at age forty-five. Cullum, *Biographical Register*, vol. 2, pp. 285-286.
15. Hein, *Memories of Long Ago*, pp. 60-61.
16. Angel Island Post Return, October 31, 1870.
17. *San Diego Union*, October 19, 1870; San Diego Barracks Post Return, October 31, 1870.
18. San Diego Barracks Post Return, October 31, 1870. Royal E. Whitman, born May 11, 1833, in Maine, served in the Civil War, rising to rank of colonel, Thirtieth Maine Infantry. Later, accused of excessive drinking and other infractions committed in Arizona, he endured three court-martials before leaving the service in 1871. See Altshuler, *Cavalry Yellow*, pp. 365-366.
19. San Diego Barracks Post Return, October 31, 1870; Altshuler, *Cavalry Yellow*, p. 36. Originally established in 1849 on the west bank of the Colorado River in California, Fort Yuma controlled the important Yuma Crossing near the confluence of the Colorado and Gila Rivers. Brandes, *Frontier Military Posts*, pp. 81-86.

Chapter 3

1. A native of New York and 1846 graduate of the Military Academy, George Stoneman served both in the Mexican and Civil War, where he attained the rank of major general of volunteers in the Union Army. In 1865 he reverted to his permanent rank of lieutenant colonel and assumed command of the Department of Arizona on May 3, 1870.
2. Thrapp, *Conquest of Apachería*, pp. vii-x. For details on Cochise, see Sweeny, *Cochise*.

3. Davisson, "Fort Apache," pp. 62-67.
4. Fort Yuma Post Return, November 30, 1870; Hein, *Memories of Long Ago*, pp. 73-74. Camp Grant, located on the San Pedro River approximately fifty miles northeast of Tucson, was established in 1860. Fort Bowie, laid out in 1862, controlled the important spring of reliable water in Apache Pass one hundred miles east of Tucson. Originally established in 1865 in the Military Plaza of Tucson, Camp Lowell was moved in 1873 to a site seven miles east on the Rillito River.
5. Bourke, *On the Border*, pp. 56-65. Born in Philadelphia in 1846, John Bourke served in the Civil War as an enlisted man in the Fifteenth Pennsylvania Cavalry. Graduating from the Military Academy in 1869, he came to Arizona a year later. Lt. Col. George Crook, upon assuming command of the Department of Arizona, appointed Bourke one of his aides.
6. Brodie, "A Soldier's Christmas in Old Tucson," *Los Angeles Herald Illustrated Magazine* (1902), copy in Scrapbook, 1899-1902, Box 3, George Smalley Family Papers (SFP), Arizona Historical Society (AHS), Tucson. Cited hereafter as SFP.
7. A native of Vermont, Anson Peacely Killen Safford came to Arizona from California. He served as governor from 1869 to 1877, the longest tenure of any territorial chief executive in Arizona. He is best noted for his efforts to promote mining, education, and solutions to the Indian problem. In his address to the Sixth Legislative Assembly in Tucson on January 11, 1871, Safford reiterated that hostile indians constituted the major problem facing Arizona. Wagoner, *Arizona Territory*, pp. 101-123; *Arizona Citizen*, December 24, 1870.
8. Camp Lowell and Camp Thomas Post Returns, December 31, 1870, January 30 and February 29, 1871; Robinson, (ed.), *Diaries of John Bourke*, vol. 1, p. 31.
9. Davisson, "Fort Apache," pp. 68-72. Established in 1864 at an unhealthy location on the north bank of the Gila River, one hundred miles south of Camp Thomas, Camp Goodwin was abandoned in 1871 because of malaria. Fort Wingate was located in 1860 near the friendly Zuñi Indian villages in northwest New Mexico.
10. Camp Thomas Post Return, January 31, 1877. Regulations set the strength of each cavalry troop at three officers and one hundred enlisted men. Infantry companies had three officers and as few as fifty enlisted men. On January 31, 1871, L and M Troops reported ninety-three and eighty-four assigned enlisted men, respectively. B Company recorded twenty-four enlisted men assigned. Of the 168 men physically on post, forty-six had been assigned special duty, seven reported sick and eleven were under arrest.
11. Altshuler, *Cavalry Yellow*, pp. 144, 156-157, 172-173.
12. Camp Apache Post Return, February 29, 1871. Camp Thomas was redesignated Camp Apache in February in honor of an earlier visit by Cochise, the well-known Chiricahua leader.
13 Davisson, "New Light on the Cibicue Fight," pp. 427-430. Esh-kel-dah-silah is spelled several ways. The version used here is preferred by Davisson.
14. Gilbert, "Chasing the Nimble Apache," *Winners of the West*, vol. 9, Octo-

ber 30, 1926; Summerhayes, *Vanished Arizona*, p. 91.
15. [Upham], "Incidents of Regular Army Life," p. 429. Born in Castine, Maine, in 1841, Frank Upham first came to Arizona in 1864 as a second lieutenant in the Seventh California Infantry. Commissioned in the First Cavalry after the Civil War, he took leave from Camp Thomas in October 1870, to be married. He returned with his bride on July 25, 1871.
16. ANJ, August 21, 1871, p. 830. Cpl. Henry J. Hyde enlisted in M Troop on August 23, 1869, in New York City.
17. Marion, *Notes of Travel*. Established in 1863, Fort Whipple was relocated a year later on a site one mile northeast of Prescott.
18. *Arizona Miner*, May 6, 1871.
19. *Ibid*. Colonel Stoneman and others believed that a group of Tucson merchants, for monetary reasons, actively conspired to maintain a strong military presence in Arizona by over-emphasizing the Indian threat. Existence of the "Tucson Ring" never has been proven or disproven. There is no doubt, however, that many Arizona businessmen relied heavily on lucrative military contracts such as freighting. See Bourke, *On the Border*, pp. 215-219.
20. *Arizona Miner*, May 13, 1871; *Arizona Citizen*, December 24, 1870.
21. *Arizona Miner*, January 7, 1871.
22. Camp Apache Post Return, February 29, 1871.
23. *Arizona Citizen*, March 11, 1871.
24. The story of the Camp Grant Massacre has been told many times with varying degrees of accuracy. For a dated but popular account see Schellie, *Vast Domain of Blood*.

Chapter 4

1. The decision to replace Colonel Stoneman with Lieutenant Colonel Crook actually had been made prior to the Camp Grant Massacre. See Altshuler, *Chains of Command*, pp. 195-196. There is little doubt that George Crook made an excellent commander. Born in Ohio in 1826, he graduated from the Military Academy in 1853, immediately thereafter seeing action in the Rogue River War in Oregon. He earned a superb reputation in the Civil War, rising to the rank of major general of U.S. volunteers. Crook reverted to rank of lieutenant colonel in 1866 and assumed command of the Department of Arizona on June 4, 1871.
2. Green to Assistant Adjutant General (AAG), Department of Arizona, May 16, 1871, Records of the Bureau of Indian Affairs (RBIA), reel 4. Microfilm copies in University of Arizona Library (UAL). Cited hereafter as Green's Report, May 16, 1871. Brodie's relief force included one infantryman, Pvt. William Shaw, who recalled thirty two years later that the Indians withdrew to the north of Camp Apache. Unidentified newspaper clipping, Folder 1, Biography—Brodie, Alexander O. (Governor) File, McClintock Papers, Phoenix Public Library (PPL). Cited hereafter as Shaw's Account.
3. Green's Report, May 16, 1871; Shaw's Account. Born in Maine, William D. Fuller graduated from the Military Academy in 1861 and saw much service as an artillery officer during the Civil War. Joining the Twenty-first Infantry in 1867, he arrived at Camp Apache to assume command of Company B on

March 20, 1871.
4. Green's Report, May 16, 1871. Established in 1864, Camp Goodwin was closed effective March 14, 1871.
5. Green to AAG, Department of Arizona, May 18, 1871, RBIA, reel 4. Cited hereafter as Green's Report, May 18, 1871.
6. Green's Reports, May 16 and 18, 1871.
7. *Arizona Citizen*, June 10, 1871.
8. Colyer to Columbus Delano, September 18, 1871, RBIA, reel 4. Cited hereafter as Colyer's Report, September 18, 1871.
9. Unidentified newspaper clipping, Scrapbook, 1899-1902, Box 3, SFP.
10. A native of Ohio, John Wasson published the first issue of the *Arizona Citizen* on October 15, 1870. Like many frontier editors he was opinionated and freely mixed factual reporting with editorializing.
11. *Arizona Citizen*, March 25, 1871. Although no John Thompson was stationed at Camp Apache, a private by that name was assigned to Fort Bowie.
12. *Ibid.*, April 1, 1871.
13. *Ibid.*, April 22, 1871.
14. Schmitt, (ed.), *General Crook*, pp. 164-165; Bourke, *On the Border*, p. 181.
15. Bourke, *On the Border*, p. 110; Schmitt, *General Crook*, pp. 165-166. Capt. Guy V. Henry enjoyed a long career. Born in Arkansas in 1839 and an 1861 graduate of the Military Academy, he became a colonel in the Union Army during the Civil War and a general in the Spanish-American War.
16. Schmitt, *General Crook*, pp. 167-168. In 1869 President Grant appointed a Permanent Board of Indian Commissioners to cooperate with the Secretary of the Interior to establish peace with Indians still considered hostile. Vincent Colyer of New York became Secretary of the Board. See Ogle, *Federal Control*, pp. 86-91.
17. Colyer's Report, September 18, 1871; ANJ, October 7, 1871, p. 120; Camp Apache Post Return, February 28, 1872.
18. Walsh, "Corydon E. Cooley," pp. 286-296. The legal status of Cooley's marriage is open to question, but apparently some kind of ceremony did take place.
19. Thrapp, *Apachería*, pp. 105-107. Born November 8, 1830, in Maine, Howard graduated from the Military Academy in 1854. He rose in rank to major general of volunteers during the Civil War, losing an arm at the Battle of Fair Oaks, Virginia. After the war, he headed the Freedmen's Bureau.
20. Dallas to Howard, September 8, 1873, RBIA, reel 8; Altshuler, *Cavalry Yellow*, p. 92. The story of Howard's indiscretions in dealing with Arizona Indians never has been told.
21. Ogle, *Federal Control*, p. 106.
22. Altshuler, *Cavalry Yellow*, p. 92; Dallas to AAG, Department of Arizona, June 6, 1872, Records of the United States Army Continental Commands (UUSACC), Post Letters, Fort Apache, Arizona, vol. 37. Cited hereafter as Fort Apache Post Letters.
23. *Arizona Citizen*, April 13, 1872; *Arizona Miner*, April 6, 1872.
24. Camp Apache Post Return, March 31, April 30, June 30, August 31,

1872. Because Dallas withheld filing charges against Hunt with the understanding that the captain would resign, the reason for Hunt's arrest is not a matter of record.
25. Altshuler, *Cavalry Yellow*, pp. 272-273.
26. Schmitt, *General Crook*, p. 176.

Chapter 5
1. Bourke, *On the Border*, pp. 176-182.
2. Altshuler, *Cavalry Yellow*, pp. 272-273.
3. Thrapp, *Apachería*, pp. 119-124. Located in 1864 sixty miles southwest of Prescott, Camp Date Creek was abandoned in 1877. Camp Verde, established in 1865 on the Verde River approximately forty miles north of Camp McDowell, played an important role in Crook's campaign.
4. Camp Apache Post Return, December 31, 1872.
5. Bourke, *On the Border*, p.178; Muster Roll of 2d. Lt. Alex O. Brodie's Detachment of Indian Scouts, Fort Apache, 2 December-31 December, 1872, Records of the Adjutant General's Office (RAGO).
6. Radbourne, *Mickey Free*, pp. 3-8; Sweeney, *Cochise*, pp. 142-165. A native of Kentucky, George Nicholas Bascom graduated from the Military Academy in 1858. He died at the battle of Valverde, New Mexico, in February, 1862. One of the early and important posts in southern Arizona, Fort Buchanan was laid out in 1856 on Sonoita Creek south of Tucson and abandoned in 1861.
7. Schmitt, *General Crook*, p. 180.
8. Brodie To Whom It May Concern, January 9, 1873, Post Records, 1866-1887, Fort McDowell, RAGO. In addition to Stratford's reduction, Corporal Branagan was downgraded to private. The fact that Stratford was not incarcerated or discharged suggests that he might well have acted in self-defense.
9. Camp Apache Post Return, January 31, 1873. In December 1872, the military moved Camp Grant from its original location at the confluence of Aravaipa Creek and San Pedro River to the west slope of Mount Graham, twenty-five miles north of Willcox. The second site became known as New Camp Grant.
10. *Ibid.*
11. Robinson, *Diaries of John Bourke*, vol. 1, pp. 64-65. 1st Lt. Jacob Almy, a native of Massachusetts and Civil War veteran, graduated from the Military Academy in 1867. He arrived at Camp Grant in February 1872.
12. Muster Roll, M Troop, First Cavalry, 28 February-30 April, 1873; Robinson, *Diaries of John Bourke*, vol. 1, pp. 64-71.
13. Muster Roll, Brodie's Detachment of Indian Scouts, 28 February-30 April, 1873; Bourke, *On the Border*, pp. 207-208. Maj. William H. Brown, a Maryland-born Union Civil War veteran, like Randall, seems to have retained his fighting edge after the war, but cut short his promising career by committing suicide in 1875. There is very little information available on "Mace" McCoy. Apparently, he came to Arizona from Oregon with Crook and returned to that territory after the campaign. Thrapp, *Apachería*, p. 119.
14. Robinson, *Diaries of John Bourke*, vol. 1, pp. 71-72. Albert Emmett Woodson, born in Kentucky in 1840, served in the First Washington Territorial

Infantry during the Civil War. He joined the Fifth Cavalry in 1872.
15. *Ibid.*; Thrapp, *Apachería*, pp. 123-134.
16. Regimental Return from Regular Army Regiments, 1833-1916, Fifth Cavalry, April 30, 1873, RAGO. Crook related the capture of the Indian woman quite differently: "One of our scouts, while prowling around and watching, caught a squaw, brought her into camp, and by intimidation made her tell where her people were . . . ." Schmitt, *General Crook*, p. 177.
17. Regimental Return, Fifth Cavalry, April 30, 1873.
18. Bourke, *On the Border*, pp. 208-209; Schmitt, *General Crook*, pp. 177-178.
19. Thrapp, "Where Was the Battle of Turret Mountain Fought?" pp. 105-119. Dr. Sam Palmer, a Phoenix dentist and avid artifact collector, whose hobby was locating Indian war battle sites, deserves credit for pinpointing the exact location of the fight on Turret Mountain. In October 1995, Palmer and R. W. Munson from the Camp Verde Historical State Park found seventy-two cartridge cases, .50-70 caliber, on the ridge below the Indian camp site and other objects indicating earlier presence of a ranchería. Palmer reported leaving the ammunition hulls in place, but they had been removed prior to the author visiting the site the following April. Interview with Dr. Sam Palmer, April 27, 1996, Phoenix. Unfortunately, without the cartridge cases in place, the exact position of Randall's skirmish line and point of contact between the soldiers and Indians cannot now be established. This illustrates the need and wisdom of current laws prohibiting removal of such artifacts from federal land.
20. This reconstruction of the battle is based on a personal survey of the battlefield and information contained in Muster Roll, A Troop, Fifth Cavalry, and Muster Roll, I Company, Twenty-third Infantry, both 28 Feburary-30 April, 1873; Regimental Return, Fifth Cavalry, March 31, 1873 and Camp Apache Post Return, April 30, 1873. None of these accounts mention the use of gunny sacks, or the necessity of soldiers crawling into an attack position, or Indians leaping to their death to avoid the soldiers.
21. The flat rock ledge upon which the Tontos camped offered little protection. Perhaps 300 yards long and fifty yards wide, the formation easily can be scaled at several points. Only at the extreme southeast end is it high enough to cause the death of someone jumping into the canyon below.
22. Muster Roll, A Troop, Fifth Cavalry, 28 February-30 April 1873. A few days after the battle, some participants claimed that forty-one Indians had been killed. *Arizona Miner*, April 12, 1873.
23. The Muster Rolls of A Troop and I Company both report that Hill's and Randall's fights occurred on March 22 and 24, respectively. The Camp Apache Post Return indicates March 25 and 27. These latter two dates also appear in other sources, such as *Chronological List of Actions, etc., With Indians*, pp. 53-54. It appears, however, that the *Chronological List* is based on the Camp Apache Post Return. Camp Verde Post Returns clearly reveal that both Randall's and Woodson's commands reached Camp Verde by March 27, confirming that the dates of March 22 and 24 for the two arrangements must be correct.
24. Captain Randall made a strong effort to see that 1st Sgt. James M. Hill, a twenty-eight-year-old native of Pennsylvania, received credit for his partici-

pation. The Camp Apache Post Return, April 30, 1873, which would have been prepared under Randall's supervision, gives Hill full credit for his role in the March 22 skirmish—although Randall reported the date incorrectly. Moreover, Randall included Hill with six others he recommended for a Medal of Honor for the fight on Turret Mountain. Hill, of course, was not present at that engagement, but Randall and Crook resolved that technicality by citing Hill for "gallantry and good conduct during the engagements near Turret Mountain, A.T., Mar. 25th and 27th [*sic*], 1873." Copy of Department of Arizona General Order Number 10 in *Arizona Miner*, April 12, 1873. See also Price, *Across the Continent*, p. 676.

25. Muster Roll, M Troop, First Cavalry, 28 February-30 April, 1873; Camp Verde Post Return, March 31 and April 30, 1873.

26. Bourke, *On the Border*, p. 212.

27. *Arizona Miner*, April 12, 1873.

28. Randall to Acting Assistant Adjutant General (AAAG), Department of Arizona, May 15, 1873, Fort Apache Post Letters, vol. 37.

29. *Ibid.* Neither Crook nor Bourke mentioned Delchay's capture. Thrapp, relying on newspaper accounts, erroneously compressed the two events into one, stating simply that Randall surrounded Delchay's group, opened fire, and the Indians capitulated. See Thrapp, *Apachería*, p. 142.

30. Randall to AAAG, Department of Arizona, May 15, 1873, Fort Apache Post Letters, vol. 37. The exact number of Delchay's band is not known. Randall failed to give a number in his report. James E. Roberts, Indian agent at Camp Apache, reported "about one hundred Indians, including men, women and children." Roberts to Herman Bendell, April 29, 1873, RBIA, reel 7.

31. An 1839 graduate of the Military Academy, Brig. Gen. Edward Canby served in both the Mexican War and Civil War, where, commanding troops in New Mexico, he repelled a Confederate invasion from Texas. Canby holds the distinction of being the only general officer in the Regular Army to be killed by Indians. See Utley, *Frontier Regulars*, p. 198. Following Captain Hunt's arrest and resignation in the summer of 1872, Lieutenant Harris took command of M Troop.

32. Randall to AAAG, Department of Arizona, April 30, May 15, 1873, Fort Apache Post Letters, vol. 37.

Chapter 6

1. Camp Apache Post Return, April 30, May 31, 1873.

2. Frazer, *Forts of the West*, p. 127; Fort Walla Walla Post Return, August 31, 1872.

3. Bennett, *Walla Walla*, p. 86.

4. Benicia Barracks Post Return, September 30, 1874.

5. Information on Benicia Barracks provided courtesy Harry Wassman; Benicia Barracks Post Return, September 30, 1874.

6. Heitman, *Historical Register*, vol. 1, p. 402.

7. Hein, *Memories of Long Ago*, p. 71.

8. DeLanie Interview; Elliott to AAG, Military Division of the Pacific, April 22, 1875, First Cavalry Letter Book, vol. 5, p. 407.

9. Freeman Notes.
10. Various documents in Brodie's Appointment, Commission, and Personnel Branch Document File, RAGO. Cited hereafter as Brodie's ACP File.
11. *Ibid.*; Fort Vancouver Post Return, March 31, 1876; Fort Walla Walla Post Return, March 31, 1876. Fort Vancouver was garrisoned in 1849 on the site of an abandoned Hudson's Bay Company fort across the Columbia River from Portland.
12. Elliott to AG, U.S. Army, July 29, 1876, First Cavalry Letter Book, vol. 6, p. 25.
13. *Walla Walla Union*, May 27, 1876. Information on the Reynolds family provided courtesy Lolita A. Clayton.
14. *Walla Walla Weekly Statesman*, June 3, 1876; Fort Colville Post Return, June 30, 1876.
15. *Walla Walla Weekly Statesman*, March 11, 1876.
16. Fort Colville Post Return, June 30, July 31, 1877.
17. Lawrence L. Dodd to the author; Brodie Genealogical Table in Watson, *Alexander Cowan*. The infant Brodie's first name and initial obviously came from her mother. Louisa may have been selected in honor of Brodie's aunt, Louisa Brodie.

Chapter 7

1. *Walla Walla Union*, June 30, 1877; Statement of Military Service, Brodie's ACP File. Fort Canby, an artillery post, was positioned in 1863 near the mouth of the Columbia River in Washington Territory.
2. Muster Roll, M Troop, First Cavalry, 1 May-30 June, 1877.
3. Utley, *Frontier Regulars*, pp. 296-298; McDermott, *Forlorn Hope*, pp.xiii-xv.
4. McDermott, *Forlorn Hope*, pp. xiii-xv. Established in 1862 on the Lapwai River near the agency of the Nez Perce Reservation, Fort Lapwai could be reached from Walla Walla as far as Lewiston by riverboat up the Columbia and Snake Rivers.
5. Fort Walla Walla Post Return, June 30, 1877. Born in Maine in 1829, Col. Cuvier Grover graduated from the Military Academy in 1850, rising to rank of brigadier general of volunteers during the Civil War. An infantry officer, he became colonel of the First Cavalry upon the death of Colonel Gillem in 1875.
6. McDermott, *Forlorn Hope*, pp. 47-54. David Perry had a reputation for being an excellent officer. Born in Connecticut in 1841, he had been commissioned a second lieutenant in the First Cavalry in 1862. After the Civil War, he campaigned against the Snake Indians in 1866, the Modocs in 1873, and the Nez Perce in 1877. He served with Brodie at Fort Walla Walla in 1873 and 1874.
7. Utley, *Frontier Regulars*, p. 301.
8. Josephy, *Nez Perce*, pp. 527-530.
9. Fort Walla Walla Post Return, July 3, 1877; Josephy, *Nez Perce*, pp. 546-559.
10. Howard's Field Order No. 31, July 18, 1877, in Letters, Telegrams and Field Orders Sent Relating to Chief Joseph and the *Nez Perce* Campaign,

vol. 1, RG 393, NA.
11. Josephy, *Nez Perce*, pp. 557-560.
12. *Ibid*., pp. 559-561. Born May 8, 1833, in Rhode Island, Frank Wheaton later resigned from the United States and Mexico Boundary Commission to accept an appointment as first lieutenant in the First Cavalry, subsequently serving in the Civil War. As lieutenant colonel of the Twenty-first Infantry, he fought with limited success against the Modocs. He took command of the Second Infantry in 1874.
13. Muster Roll, F Troop, First Cavalry, 30 June-31 August, 1877.
14. Fort Lapwai Post Return, July 31, 1877. Kate M. Louisa Brodie was buried in the Reynolds plot in the Walla Walla Masonic Cemetery.
15. *Ibid*., October 31, 1877.
16. Harris to AAG, Department of Columbia, September 23, 1877, Brodie's ACP File.
17. Fort Lapwai Post Return, September 30, 1877.
18. Lieutenant E. K. Webster to Post Adjutant, Fort Spokane, November 23, 1884, Folder: Fort Collville [*sic*], Washington Territory, Box 390, Office of the Quartermaster General (OQM).
19. Brodie to Watson, January 13, BFP. In this thirteen-page letter, Brodie failed to mention his marriage or death of his daughter. On other occasions, when pressed, Brodie stated that he resigned to follow civilian pursuits. His terse 1877 letter of resignation offers no explanation.
20. *Walla Walla Union*, September 8, 1877.

Chapter 8
1. Brodie to Watson, January 13, 1913, BFP.
2. Freeman Notes.
3. *Ibid.*
4. *St. Lawrence Plaindealer*, July 25, 1878.
5. Jeff Hokanson to the author.
6. Brodie to Watson, January 13, 1913, BFP.
7. Muster Roll, M Troop, Sixth Cavalry, 31 August-30 October, 1883. Located south of St. Louis, Jefferson Barracks was the cavalry recruiting depot. New enlistees normally stayed at the depot a few weeks to learn the basic fundamentals of soldering. Brodie, of course, because of prior service, left immediately to join his troop at Fort Bowie. A native of New Jersey and an 1865 graduate of the Military Academy, Rafferty came to Arizona from Texas with his troop in 1875.
8. Muster Roll, M Troop, Sixth Cavalry, 31 August-30 October, 1883.
9. *Ibid*.; Fort Bowie Post Return, November 30, 1883. Leopold Oscar Parker, a Missouri native, was born July 6, 1843. He served as a volunteer officer in the Union Army during the Civil War, receiving an appointment as a second lieutenant in the First Infantry in 1866.
10. Fort Bowie Post Return, January 31, 1884.
11. Muster Roll, M Troop, Sixth Cavalry, 31 December, 1883-29 February, 1884. Because a court-martial board never convened, the charges filed by Captain Parker against Brodie are not a matter of record.

12. Tuttle Interview.
13. Unidentified newspaper clipping, Tuttle Papers, Author's Files.

Chapter 9

1. Dill, "Terror on the Hassayampa," p. 290; *Arizona Weekly Journal-Miner*, March 14, July 18, 1888. The Hassayampa River rises in the Bradshaw Mountains nine miles south of Prescott and flows into the Gila River west of Phoenix. Details are not clear, but in addition to the two iron pipes, another opening, approximately three by five feet, existed in the bottom of the dam to channel water into wooden flumes for conveyance to the placer fields. This idea later was abandoned. Liggett Interview.
2. Dill, "Terror on the Hassayampa," p. 284-288. Pioneered in California, hydraulic placer mining involved the use of high-pressure hoses to wash gold-bearing sand into sluice boxes, where the metal could be recovered by gravity separation.
3. *Ibid.*, pp. 288-293.
4. Born in New York City October 24, 1834, Henry Springer Van Beuren was well-known in the Empire State. Upon his father's death in 1878 he and four siblings inherited an estate valued at $13,000,000. See Jones, "The Van Beuren Family," pp. 43, 48; *New York Times*, July 20, 1878; *Weekly Journal-Miner*, July 18, 1888.
5. Dill, "Terror on the Hassayampa," p. 294.
6. *Ibid.* A native of Ohio, John Emmett Anderson came to Prescott in 1876, following service in the United States Navy. His qualifications as an engineer are not known.
7. Brodie to Van Beuren, December 8, 1888, Van Beuren Family Papers (VBFP).
8. *Weekly Journal-Miner*, August 28, 1889.
9. Henry S. Van Beuren Diary, January 1-7, 1890, Sharlot Hall Museum. No additional information is available on James Redington.
10. *Ibid.*, February 17, 1890; Mary Hanlon to her mother, February 26, 1890, BFP.
11. Mary Hanlon to her mother, February 26, 1890, BFP.
12. Van Beuren Diary, February 19-23, 1890; *Arizona Daily Gazette*, February 25, 1890.
13. Dill, "Terror on the Hassayampa," pp. 297-298. A month and a half after the dam collapsed, Hunt died suddenly at his home in Walnut Grove, leaving a wife and two daughters. Van Beuren made the burial arrangements and delivered a short eulogy.
14. *Weekly Journal-Miner*, February 26, March 5, 1890. Strong feelings against Burke in Prescott caused authorities to take the man into protective custody. A charge of manslaughter was considered, but charges were not filed and Burke was released. Some accounts indicate that William Akard was a young cowboy, but he was not a victim of the flood, as some have suggested.
15. *Ibid.*, February 26, 1890.
16. William Owen "Buckey" O'Neill was an extremely popular and well-known miner, local politician, and newspaperman. Born in Ireland in 1860,

he arrived in Arizona nineteen years later. An inveterate gambler, O'Neill acquired the name "Buckey" (his spelling) as a result of his fondness for playing faro or "bucking the tiger" as it was called. He was elected sheriff in 1888. The exact number of deaths at Walnut Grove never has been determined. Possibly, it may have been as high as sixty.
17. Mary Hanlon to her mother, February 26, 1890, BFP.
18. *Ibid.*
19. *Ibid.*; DeLanie Interview.
20. Mary Hanlon to her mother, February 26, 1890, BFP.
21. *Prescott Weekly Courier*, March 20, 1890; *Daily Gazette*, March 21, 1890. The praise Mary Hanlon received for alleged heroism is difficult to understand. Mary's letter to her mother reveals clearly that for two days she did nothing more than huddle under her blanket at the survivor's camp above the river. By Mary's own admission, James Redington organized the rescue efforts, an action for which he never received credit.
22. *The Engineering and Mining Journal*, March 1, 1890; *Engineering News and American Railway Journal*, March 8, April 24, 1890.
23. Brodie to Van Beuren, April 12, 1891, VBFP.
24. *Arizona Republican*, February 21, 1890. A distinguished jurist, Joseph H. Kibbey, considered to be an authority on water rights, was born in Indiana in 1851. He came to Arizona in 1885, and soon became an associate justice of the Arizona Supreme Court.
25. Van Beuren to the Bond and Stock-Holders of the Walnut Grove Water Storage Company, April, 1891, VBFP.
26. Brodie to Van Beuren, July 7, 1890, VBFP. No additional information is available on Hall. Shortly after Brodie wrote this letter, Thomas H. Brown, Brodie's former assistant engineer at Walnut Grove, replaced Hall at the ranch.
27. *Weekly Journal-Miner*, June 4, November 25, 1891.
28. "A Narrative of the Hassayampa River Project in Arizona, 1882-1936," no date, no author, VBFP.
29. Mary Hanlon to Brodie, June 26, 1892, Brodie Papers, Arizona Historical Foundation, Hayden Library, Arizona State University (ASU). Cited hereafter as Brodie Papers, AHF.

Chapter 10

1. Brodie Interview; Korin L. Rosenkrams to the author; Jocelyne Rubinetti to the author.
2. Mary A. Hanlon to Brodie, May 14, 1890, author's files.
3 *Ibid.*
4. Van Beuren Diary, July 1, 8, 1890.
5. Mary A. Hanlon to Brodie, May 14, 1890, author's files.
6. General Index to Deeds, Book Two, 1890-97, pp. 44-45, Yavapai County Recorder's Office; *Prescott Weekly Courier*, July 21, 1899. Robert Brow and George Merwin were well-known in northern Arizona. Brow, born in 1857 to Swiss immigrants in Missouri, came to Prescott in 1883. Merwin, born in Iowa in 1842, prospected, mined, and farmed for many years in Walnut

Grove.
7. Deed Book Number 27, pp. 306-308, and Book Number 28, pp. 436-437, 528-529, Yavapai County Recorder's Office.
8. Information on the Arizona National Guard provided courtesy William D. Tackenburg.
9. Wagoner, *Arizona Territory*, pp. 295-297; *Weekly Journal-Miner*, May 25, 1892.
10. *Weekly Journal-Miner*, September 21, October 12, 1892; *Weekly Courier*, October 14, November 4, 1892.
11. Unidentified newspaper clipping, BFP.
12. *Weekly Journal-Miner*, November 8, 1893. Following the death of her first husband, Wilbur A. Bignall, Elizabeth married John F. Anderson, a merchant in Knoxville. Elizabeth raised three children from her first marriage: Robert, Clinton, and Helen Louisa.
13. *Ibid.*, September 18, 1894.
14. *Daily Journal-Miner*, September 18, 1894.
15. Brodie to Van Beuren, November 16, 1896, VBFP.
16. *Ibid.*, December 16, 1896.
17. Agreement, Brodie et al., December 8, 1894, Brodie Papers, AHF.
18. Brodie to Van Beuren, June 2, March 4, 1897, VBFP. Purchased by Phelps Dodge Corporation in 1935, the Jerome mines produced approximately $800,000,000 in gold, silver, and copper.
19. *Ibid.*, December 16, 1897.
20. *Weekly Journal-Miner*, March 4, April 1, 29, 1896.
21. *Ibid.*, July 29, 1896.

Chapter 11
1. Musicant, *Empire by Default*, pp. 78-104.
2. James McClintock, who was in a position to know, claimed that Buckey O'Neill conceived the plan to raise an Arizona cowboy regiment and asked Brodie to be the commander. See McClintock, *Arizona*, vol. 2, p. 513. All other contemporary accounts credit Brodie with originating the idea. Perhaps, McClintock merely wanted to secure for his dead friend a niche in Arizona folklore.
3. Herner, *Arizona Rough Riders*, pp. 16-17.
4. *Ibid.*, p. 12.
5. Born in Pennsylvania in 1840, Myron McCord later moved to Wisconsin, where he prospered in the lumber business. Elected to Congress in 1880, he became good friends with Representative William McKinley of Ohio.
6. Probably, an accidental internal explosion destroyed the *Maine*, but the exact cause of the blast still is being debated.
7. Brodie to the President, March 3, 10, 1898; McCord to the President, April 2, 1898, both in RAGO.
8. Herner, *Arizona Rough Riders*, pp. 21-22.
9. *Arizona Daily Star*, April 19, 1898. At this time, of course, Theodore Roosevelt had absolutely nothing to do with Brodie's efforts to form a regiment.
10. Cosmas, *Army for Empire*, pp. 85-94.

11. Herner, *Arizona Rough Riders*, pp. 23-24. Born in Ohio in 1836, Russell Alger served under Gen. George A. Custer in the Civil War, commanding the Fifth Michigan Cavalry.
12. Roosevelt, *Rough Riders*, pp. 6-7. Leonard Wood and Theodore Roosevelt made an unusual team to command a regiment. Wood, born in New Hampshire in 1860, entered the army in 1886 as a contract surgeon. Two years later, he won the Medal of Honor for campaigning after Geronimo in Mexico, although he did not actually receive the award until 1898. A native of New York, the thirty-nine-year-old Roosevelt, a rising star in the Republican Party and outspoken jingo in Washington, had been appointed assistant secretary of the navy in 1897.
13. Herner, *Arizona Rough Riders*, p. 8.
14. *Arizona Republican*, April 26, 1898.
15. Herner, *Arizona Rough Riders*, p. 27.
16. *Weekly Journal-Miner*, April 27, 1898; Brodie Interview.
17. *Weekly Courier*, April 29, 1898.
18. Hagedorn, *Leonard Wood*, vol. 1, p. 145.
19. *Weekly Courier*, April 29, 1898.
20. Herner, *Arizona Rough Riders*, pp. 28, 32.
21. *Ibid.*, pp. 34-35.
22. *Weekly Journal-Miner*, April 27, 1898; Muster Roll, M Troop, First Cavalry, 30 April-30 June, 1871; Muster-In Roll, A Troop, First United States Volunteer Cavalry, May 17, 1898, RAGO; Tuttle Interview.
23. Biographical data on George Taylor provided courtesy Pat Atchison.
24. Walker, *Boys of '98*, p. 92.
25. Herner, *Arizona Rough Riders*, pp. 36, 37, 55.
26. *Weekly Journal-Miner*, May 11, 1898.
27. McClintock, *Arizona*, vol. 2, p. 513.

Chapter 12
1. Herner, *Arizona Rough Riders*, pp.40-46.
2. Roosevelt, *Rough Riders*, pp. 9-12.
3. Herner, *Arizona Rough Riders*, pp. 45-46.
4. *San Antonio Daily Express*, May 8, 1898; Todd, "Letters of Robert Huston," pp. 5-7.
5. Todd, "Letters of Robert Huston," p. 7.
6. *San Antonio Daily Express*, May 11, 1898; Walker, *Boys of '98*, pp. 92-94. A native of Vermont, Henry B. Hersey came to New Mexico as an employee of the National Weather Service. In 1897, at age thirty-six, he became adjutant general of New Mexico. Unlike Brodie, he drew heavily on the National Guard to fill his quota of Rough Riders.
7. Herner, (ed.), *Grandest Sight*, p. 10.
8. Biographical material on David Goodrich provided courtesy B. F. Goodrich Company.
9. Herner, *Arizona Rough Riders*, pp.60-61. Wood's determination to arm his regiment with the modern, six-shot Krag carbine using smokeless powder proved to be critical, for it ensured that the Rough Riders would carry the

same weapon as the Regular Cavalry. Most Volunteer units drew obsolete, single-shot .45 caliber rifles charged with black powder.

10. Roosevelt to Wood, May 9, 1898; Flagler to Roosevelt, May 8, 1898, both in Folder 1, Box 26, Leonard Wood Papers.

11. Herner, *Arizona Rough Riders*, p. 59; Hagedorn, *Leonard Wood*, vol. 1, p. 148.

12. *San Antonio Daily Express*, May 2, 6, 1898.

13. Tuttle Interview.

14. Brodie to Watson, January 13, 1913, BFP.

15. Huston to his wife, May 10, 1898, Huston papers, Oklahoma Historical Society, Oklahoma City; Herner, *Grandest Sight*, pp. 60-61.

16. Tuttle Interview. Tuttle always suspected that his mother, who strongly opposed his enlistment, contacted someone at Whipple Barracks disclosing his actual age. Tuttle's father, however, who first had come to Arizona during the Civil War as an officer in the California Column, supported his son's decision to enlist. Tuttle's father knew Brodie well.

17. Herner, *Arizona Rough Riders*, p. 70.

18. Wood Diary, May 29, 1898, Wood Papers.

Chapter 13

1. Wood Diary, June 2, 1898. A native of Michigan, William Rufus Shafter sported an impressive Civil War record, winning the Medal of Honor for gallantry at the battle of Fair Oaks, Virginia. After the war, he served with distinction in the West. Late in April 1898, he became a major-general of Volunteers and directed to organize the Fifth Corps. Sixty-six years old, Shafter stood just under six feet and weighed over 300 pounds.

2. *Ibid.* Courteous and restrained in demeanor, white-bearded Brig. Gen. Joseph Wheeler was sixty-one years old, standing but five feet and two inches in height. He acquired the sobriquet "Fighting Joe" for his exploits as a Confederate cavalry officer during the Civil War. President McKinley requested that Wheeler accept command of Shafter's Cavalry Division to demonstrate that the divisive legacy of the Civil War had ended.

3. *Ibid.*, June 3, 1898; *Morning Tribune*, May 28, June 4, 1898.

4. Azoy, *Charge*, pp. 33-35.

5. Altshuler, *Cavalry Yellow*, pp. 383-384.

6. Regimental Returns from Regular Army Regiments, First and Second Cavalry, June 30, 1898.

7. Herner, *Grandest Sight*, p. 18.

8. Roosevelt never admitted that political considerations influenced Wood's decisions regarding which troops to take to Cuba. See Roosevelt, *Rough Riders*, pp. 55-57.

9. Of Scottish ancestry, Walter Mitchell was born in 1854 in Halifax. In 1896, he and his brother established the firm of W. and C. H. Mitchell, which exported fish and lumber to the West Indies.

10. Huston to his wife, June 17, 1898, Huston Papers.

11. Roosevelt, *Rough Riders*, pp. 57-60; Herner, *Arizona Rough Riders*, pp. 83-85.

12. Brodie to Mary, June 18, 1898, BFP.
13. Musicant, *Empire by Default*, pp. 357-362.
14. Herner, *Arizona Rough Riders*, pp. 93-94.
15. *Ibid.*, p. 95.
16. Musicant, *Empire by Default*, pp. 368-370. Born March 7, 1843, in Ohio, Henry Lawton served with distinction in the Civil War. In 1883, as a captain, he commanded a well-known expedition into Mexico in pursuit of Geronimo, Surgeon Leonard Wood accompanied him.
17. *Ibid.*, pp. 375-377.
18. *Ibid.*, pp. 378-379.
19. Herner, *Arizona Rough Riders*, pp. 100-103.
20. Undated, unidentified partial manuscript filed with Wood Diary, Wood Papers.
21. Herner, *Arizona Rough Riders*, pp. 103-104.
22. *Ibid.*, pp. 104-106.
23. *Ibid.*, pp. 109-112.
24. *Ibid.*, pp. 111-112; Lawrence Huston to Vianna Huston, July 1898, Huston Papers. Total Rough Rider casualties at Las Guasimas amounted to eight killed and thirty-four wounded.
25. Herner, *Arizona Rough Riders*, pp. 113-114; Marshall, *Story of the Rough Riders*, pp. 103-136. A native of New York, Thomas W. Hall graduated from the Military Academy in 1887. Assigned to the Tenth Cavalry, he resigned his commission two years later. Even today, an occasional writer, ignoring the preponderance of evidence, attempts to revive the tired myth that the Rough Riders walked into an ambush at Las Guasimas. Some, obviously harboring a personal anti-Roosevelt bias, even hint darkly that Roosevelt instigated some kind of conspiracy to "cover-up" the Las Guasimas fight.
26. Brodie to Mary, June 28, 1898, BFP. Censorship and lack of communication facilities rendered it difficult for soldiers to contact friends and relatives from Cuba. Brodie and others prevailed upon military attaches and foreign observers to send messages on their behalf. Still others found newspaper correspondents willing to use their outlets for personal messages. The "Catherine" mentioned by Brodie was George Taylor's first wife. Apparently, Taylor assumed that Mary remained in contact with friends in Prescott, who would convey Taylor's message to Catherine.
27. Musicant, *Empire by Default*, pp. 410, 415-419.
28. The story still circulates in Arizona that O'Neill was shot shortly after remarking that "the Spanish bullet has never been molded that will kill Buckey O'Neill." Undoubtedly, this is just another legend, but it probably will never die. See Herner, *Arizona Rough Riders*, pp. 158-159.
29. Roosevelt, *Rough Riders*, p. 210.
30. Lawrence Huston to Captain Huston, August 17, 1898, Huston Papers; Roosevelt to Elihu Root, August 11, 1899, Morison, *Letters*, vol. 2, p. 1059. A native of South Carolina, Micah John Jenkins, following his graduation from West Point in 1879, served in the Fourth Cavalry until he resigned in 1886.
31. Brodie to Van Beuren, November 16, 1896, VBFP.
32. Herner, *Arizona Rough Riders*, p. 209.

Chapter 14

1. *Weekly Courier*, September 23, 1898.
2. *Ibid.*; Goff, *Arizona Officials*, vol. 5, pp. 170-171.
3. *Weekly Journal-Miner*, September 28, 1898. Born in Iowa, George Christy interrupted his education in the Harvard law school to accept a commission in the First Arizona Volunteer Infantry commanded by former governor Myron H. McCord. The regiment never saw combat.
4. *Ibid.*
5. Goff, *Arizona Officials*, vol. 3, pp. 160-162.
6. *Arizona Republican*, October 15, 1898. A close friend and associate of Governor Murphy, George Vickers was born in London in 1852. Twenty years later he received a "Doctor in Medicine" degree from Starling Medical College in Columbus, Ohio. Relocating to Arizona, he found employment in the Congress Mine as company physician. Frank Murphy was his employer. Vickers was appointed auditor by Governor McCord in 1897. George Herbert Smalley, born June 17, 1872, in Wisconsin, moved to Arizona in 1896 for health reasons. He found employment in 1898 as a reporter for the *Arizona Republican*.
7. Kittell, "Administration of Alexander Brodie," pp. 25-26; Smalley, *Adventures in Arizona*, pp. 82-84.
8. *Arizona Republican*, October 5, 1898.
9. *Ibid.*, October 22, 25, 1898; *Weekly Courier*, October 21, 1898.
10. Kittell, "Administration of Alexander Brodie," pp. 26-27; *Arizona Republican*, November 7, 1898.
11. Tuttle Interview; Brodie to Roosevelt, January 17, 1901, Series I, reel 8, Roosevelt Papers LC. Microfilm copies in UAL used.
12. *Weekly Courier*, September 23, October 23, November 18, 1898.

Chapter 15

1. Various Documents, Brodie's ACP File.
2. Brodie to McKinley, December 26, 1898, *Ibid.*
3. Roosevelt to Brodie, March 28, 1899, Series 2, reel 319, Roosevelt Papers.
4. Fraser and Chalmers to Brodie, November 23, 1898, VBFP.
5. *Las Vegas Daily Optic*, May 11, 1899.
6. Brodie to Van Beuren, June 4, 1899, VBFP.
7. Unidentified newspaper clipping, Rough Riders Reunion Folder, McClintock Papers.
8. *Weekly Journal-Miner*, July 19, 1899.
9. Unidentified newspaper clipping, Miscellaneous Mines, Folder 2, Sharlot Hall Museum.
10. Brodie to Van Beuren, January 7, June 10, 1899, January 12, 1900, VBFP.
11. *Ibid.*, January 12, 15, 1900.
12. *Ibid.* January 12, February 9, 1900.
13. *Ibid.*, March 15, 1900. In addition to his California mining ventures, Thomas E. Farish had an interest in politics, at one time serving in the California legislature. He also made an effort in 1893 to be appointed governor of Arizona. Appointed the first Arizona state historian in 1913, Farish is best

known for authoring an eight volume *History of Arizona.*
14. *Ibid.*, January 11, March 1, 1901.
15. Merwin to Wittmann, December 26, 1909, VBFP. Henry S. Van Beuren died at age seventy-two on November 29, 1906, leaving his Arizona property to his daughter and her second husband.
16. Lindren, *Ore Deposits*, pp. 182-187.
17. Brodie to Van Beuren, January 12, 1900, VBFP.
18. Brodie to Roosevelt, April 15, 1900, Series I, reel 5, Roosevelt Papers.
19. *Ibid.*, January 17, 1901, Series I, reel 8. Born in 1857 in Iowa, Charles Henry Akers moved to Arizona at age twenty-three. President McKinley appointed him secretary in 1897. Brodie's condemnation of Akers is puzzling, as the secretary does not appear to have been a staunch supporter of Murphy. Quite possibly, Brodie misjudged the man.
20. *Ibid.*, April 21, 1901, Series I, reel 13.
21. Brodie to Smalley, February 6, 1901, Folder F, Box 1, SFP.
22. Goff, *Arizona Officials*, vol. 4, pp. 60-62; Brodie to McClintock, April 21, June 3, 1901, Folder 1, Brodie Biographic File, McClintock Papers. Thomas Collier Platt was born in 1933. Entering politics at an early age, he slowly built a powerful political machine which virtually left him the undisputed "boss" of New York Republican politics. In 1898, Platt supported Roosevelt for governor, believing him to be the only Republican with enough influence to carry the state. Two years later, however, feeling that the headstrong Roosevelt could not be controlled and now anxious to get him out of New York, Platt led the movement to draft Roosevelt for the vice presidency. Obviously, Stoddard boasted an extremely powerful ally in Tom Platt.

Chapter 16
1. *Arizona Citizen*, October 19, 1901; Ives to William Muldoon, January 28, 1902, Ives Personal Letterbook, vol. 4, Eugene S. Ives Papers, Special Collections, UAL. Born in Washington, DC, in 1858, Eugene Semmes Ives practiced law in New York, where he served six years in the legislature. He moved to Arizona in 1895. Although Ives took the high road in condemning Murphy and Vickers, he had a skeleton of sorts hanging in his own closet. Representing Yuma County in the Arizona Legislature, Ives actually resided in Tucson, Pima County, where he maintained a law office. He had several investments in Yuma County, however.
2. Wagoner, *Arizona Territory*, pp. 355-356; Ives to William Christy, December 19, 1901, Smith and Ives Letterbook, vol. 1, Ives Papers.
3. Ives to Christy, December 19, 1901, Smith and Ives Letterbook, vol. 1, Ives Papers.
4. *Arizona Citizen*, October 21, 1901.
5. Brodie to Smalley, December 29, 1901, January 2, 1902, Folder 9, Box 1, SFP.
6. Brodie to McClintock, January 19, 1902, Folder 2, Brodie's Biographical File, McClintock Papers.
7. Harbaugh, *Power and Responsibility*, pp. 321-322; *Arizona Citizen*, January 22, 1902.

8. Stoddard to A. L. Smith, March 7, 1902, Stoddard Letterbook, Personal Correspondence, Isaac Taft Stoddard Papers, AHS.
9. Stoddard to Brodie, January 23, February 11, March 14, 1902, *Ibid.*
10. Smalley, *Adventures in Arizona*, pp. 110-111.
11. *Arizona Citizen*, April 26, 28, 1902.
12. McClintock to Brodie, May 6, 1902, Folder 2, Brodie's Biographical File, McClintock Papers.
13. Brodie to McClintock, June 14, 20, 1902, *Ibid.*
14. Brodie to Smalley, May 11, June 17, 1902, Folder 1, Box 1, SFP.
15. *Arizona Republican*, July 2, 1902.

Chapter 17

1. Sims Ely to Brodie, July 1, 1902, Letters of Governor Brodie, Letterbook, No. 1, Arizona State Department of Library and Archives (ASDLA). Cited hereafter as Governor Brodie's Letterbook No. 1.
2. Kittle, "Administration of Alexander Brodie," pp. 37-40.
3. Smalley to his father, September 29, 1907, Folder 7, Box 1, SFP.
4. Smalley to his wife, July 1, 1902, Folder 5, Box 1, *Ibid.*
5. Goff, *Arizona Officials*, vol. 1, pp. 134-137; *Arizona Republican*, July 31, 1902.
6. Goff, *Arizona Officials*, vol. 5, pp. 182-183.
7. O'Neal, *Arizona Rangers*, pp. 2-4, 23-24.
8. Rynning, *Gun Notches*, p. 203; Ball, United States Marshalls, p. 217.
9. Feess, *Roosevelt's Arizona Boys*, pp. 63-68.
10. *Ibid.* The reason for Roosevelt's friendship with Daniels never has been explained, but for years a rumor circulated in southern Arizona that the relationship originated during the fighting in Cuba. The story goes that Daniels suffered from a painful back condition, which made it difficult for him to kneel or lie down. Consequently, when attacking under fire at San Juan, he remained upright, firing exclusively from a standing position. Roosevelt, interpreting Daniels's actions as a sign of bravery, held the private in high regard thereafter.
11. McClintock, *History of Arizona*, vol. 2, p. 352.
12. Kittle, "Administration of Alexander Brodie," pp. 40-41, 58-61.
13. *Arizona Bulletin*, September 19, 1902.
14. *Ibid*, October 10, 1902; O'Neal, *Arizona Rangers*, p. 38.
15. Brodie to Rynning, October 13, 1902, Governor Brodie's Letterbook No. 1; *Arizona Bulletin*, October 24, 31, 1902.
16. Brodie to George R. Green, July 15, 1902, and Brodie to John E. Wilson, January 9, 1904, Governor Brodie's Letterbook No. 1 and 2.
17. Kittle, "Administration of Alexander Brodie," pp. 46-48. A native of Illinois, Robert Emmett Morrison came to Arizona in 1884.
18. *Prescott Weekly Courier*, September 19, 1902.
19. *Phoenix Enterprise*, September 18, 1902.
20. *Ibid.*
21. Brodie to Andrew Kimball, February 19, 1903, Governor Brodie's Letterbook No. 1.

22. *Report of the Governor of Arizona to the Secretary of the Interior for the Year ended June 30, 1902*. Cited hereafter as *Governor's Report*, 1902.
23. *Ibid.*
24. Braeman, "Albert J. Beveridge," pp. 313-315. Mark Smith, one of Arizona's most highly regarded Democrat politicians, was born in Kentucky in 1851. He came to Arizona thirty years later and opened a law office in Tombstone. Always a strong advocate of statehood, Smith was elected delegate to Congress eight times. In 1912, he became one of the two Senators selected to represent the new State of Arizona. Albert J. Beveridge, born in Ohio in 1862, won election to the Senate from Indiana in 1898. Beveridge strongly opposed the use of silver to support the nation's currency, which possibly explains his determination to block statehood for Arizona.
25. *Ibid.*, pp. 316-317.
26. *Arizona Republican*, November 17, 18, 1902.
27. *Ibid.*, November 20, 1902.
28. Kittell, "Administration of Alexander Brodie," p. 58; William Staunton, "Memoirs of William Field Staunton II," unpublished manuscript, p. 130, Box 1, William Field Staunton Papers, Special Collections, UAL.
29. Brodie to Smalley, October 11, 1905, Folder 6, Box 1, SFP.
30. Brodie to Roosevelt, November 15, 1902, Governor Brodie's Letterbook No. 1.
31. *Arizona Republican*, December 2, 10, 12, 17, 1902.
32. Reid Interview.
33. Cleere Interview. One albeit unlikely rumor suggests that the father of Pearl's child was Billy Stiles, a former Arizona Ranger turned bank robber.

Chapter 18

1. Kittle, "Administration of Alexander Brodie," p. 65.
2. *Message of Governor Alexander O. Brodie to the Twenty Second Legislative Assembly of Arizona, 1903*, pp. 6-11, 16.
3. *Ibid.*, p. 12.
4. *Ibid.*, pp. 6-8.
5 *Arizona Republican*, March 4, 1903.
6. *Arizona Daily Star*, September 6, 1902; *Phoenix Enterprise*, January 20, 1903.
7. *Arizona Republican*, January 20, 1903.
8. Stoddard to Brodie, January 19, 1903, Secretary of the Territory Records, Folder 8, Box 37, RG 6, ASDLA.
9. *Arizona Republican*, January 28, 1903; *Arizona Citizen*, February 19, 1903; *Phoenix Enterprise*, March 10, 1903.
10. *Journals of the Twenty-Second Legislature*, p. 62. A native of South Carolina, Lawrence Cowan moved to Mohave County in 1882, where he engaged in mining, ranching, and politics. He relocated to Tucson in 1898 after serving as Mohave County recorder.
11. *Ibid.*, p. 339.
12. Unidentified newspaper clipping in Governor Brodie's Scrapbook, BFP. An iron worker by profession, Gus Williams moved from his birthplace in Alabama to Clifton in 1899. He served one term in the House.

13. *Journals of the Twenty-Second Legislature*, p. 329; Unidentified newspaper clipping, Governor Brodie's Scrapbook, BFP.
14. *Arizona Republican*, March 4, 13, 1903. There is no explanation for the House voting on the Cowan Bill prior to receiving the report of the special committee. Possibly, members already knew that the report would not favor Stoddard, who had admitted to the committee that he had ordered the fee books destroyed.
15. *Arizona Republican*, March 13, 1903; Rochester Ford to Stoddard, February 18, 1903, Folder: I.T. Stoddard Miscellaneous Personal Papers, Isaac Taft Stoddard Papers, UAL.
16. *Arizona Citizen*, February 24, 1903. Henry F. Ashurst enjoyed a long and rewarding career in Arizona politics. Elected to the Senate after statehood in 1912, he served in that capacity until 1940. Always quotable, colorful, and unpredictable, Ashurst died in 1962.
17. *Arizona Republican*, March 17, 1903.
18. *Journals of the Twenty-Second Legislature*, pp. 186, 381. An employee of the Railway Express Agency, Roemer moved to Benson, Arizona, from California in 1895. In the legislature, he acquired the reputation of being a skilled politician.
19. O'Neal, *Arizona Rangers*, pp. 24-32.
20. *Ibid.*, pp. 40-43.
21. *Journals of the Twenty-Second Legislature*, pp. 186-187, 380-381. See also O'Neal, *Arizona Rangers*, pp. 163-166.
22. Brodie to Cameron, November 28, 1902, Governor Brodie's Letterbook No. 1. A native of Pennsylvania, Colin Cameron came to Arizona in 1882 at age thirty-three. Purchasing the San Rafael de la Zanja land grant east of Nogales, Cameron probably became the first man in Arizona to stock his ranch with registered Herefords.
23. DeLanie Interview. Contrary to current folklore and even some reservations expressed when Brodie became governor, the Rough Riders never dominated the Rangers. Of the 107 men who served as Rangers, only seven had been Rough Riders, and most of them served only a short time.
24 *Journals of the Twenty-Second Legislature*, pp. 174, 303. A native of New Mexico, Carlos Tafolla became the fifth man to enlist in the Rangers and the only one to die in the line of duty.
25. *Arizona Republican*, February 12, 1903; *Phoenix Enterprise*, January 20, 1903. Born in Vicksburg, Mississippi, in 1852, Morrison moved to Arizona at age twenty-two and entered the mining business near Jerome. He served one term in the legislature.
26. Brodie to Kimball, February 19, 1903, Governor Brodie's Letterbook No. 1. Born in Salt Lake in 1859, Alexander Kimball became president of the St. Joseph stake at Thatcher in 1898. Brodie had great confidence in Kimball's integrity and judgment.
27. *Journals of the Twenty-Second Legislature*, pp. 171, 305.
28. Brodie to the House of Representatives, Arizona Legislature, March 19, 1903, Governor Brodie's Letterbook No. 1.
29. *Arizona Republican*, March 20, 1903.

30. *Arizona Daily Star*, March 20, 1903.
31. *Arizona Bulletin*, March 27, 1903.
32. *Journals of the Twenty-Second Legislature*, p. 60.
33. *Arizona Bulletin*, February 13, 1903.
34. *Acts, Resolutions and Memorials of the Twenty-Second Legislature*, p. 167.
35. Martin, *Lamp in the Desert*, pp. 77-80; Kittle, "Administration of Alexander Brodie," pp. 82-83. The third president of the university, Millard Mayhew Parker, came to Arizona from California, where he served as vice president of Throop Polytechnic Institute, a forerunner of the California Institute of Technology. Frank Adams had been a principal in a New York high school and had taught in a West Point preparation school prior to arriving in Tucson.
36. *Arizona Star*, June 5, 7, 20, 1903; *Arizona Citizen*, June 19, 20, 1903.
37. Martin, *Lamp in the Desert*, pp. 80-82; *Arizona Republican*, September 17, 1903.
38. *Arizona Gazette*, February 5, 1903.
39. *Journals of the Twenty-Second Legislature*, p. 63; *Arizona Gazette*, March 3, 1903.
40. *Journals of the Twenty-Second Legislature*, pp. 383-384.
41. Brodie to Dillingham, August 14, 1903, Governor Brodie's Letterbook No. 1; *Arizona Gazette*, February 9, 1903.
42. *Arizona Gazette*, March 19, 1903. A native of Pennsylvania, Burdette Packard came to Arizona in 1880, settling first in Tombstone. Engaged at various times in mining, cattle ranching, and banking, he and his partner, the legendary William C. Greene of Cananea, at one time owned over 200,000 acres in Arizona and Sonora south of Douglas. Upon his death in 1935, Packard's estate was valued in excess of $100,000.
43. Campbell, "Republican Politics," pp. 177-178. Born in Fort Whipple in 1878, Thomas E. Campbell entered politics at an early age in Jerome. Selected a Republican delegate to the territorial party convention in 1902, Campbell traveled to Phoenix with the Yavapai County delegation on Frank Murphy's private railroad car. In Phoenix, he dutifully cast his ballot for Robert E. Morrison, the Murphy-backed candidate for delegate to Congress, but soon thereafter shifted his loyalty to Brodie. In 1916, Campbell defeated Democrat George W. P. Hunt for governor, only to see his victory overturned by the Arizona Supreme Court, which ruled that Hunt had won by forty-three votes.

Chapter 19

1. Brands, *T. R.*, pp. 449-471; Unidentified newspaper clipping, Governor Brodie's Scrapbook, BFP.
2. Unidentified newspaper clipping, Governor Brodie's Scrapbook, BFP. Born in California in 1858, Utting enlisted in McClintock's B Troop on April 30, 1898, recording his occupation as cowboy.
3. Smalley to his father, August 1, 1903, Folder 5, Box 1, SFP.
4. Unidentified newspaper clipping, Governor Brodie's Scrapbook, BFP.
5. *Ibid.*
6. *Ibid.*

7. Smalley to his father, August 1, 1903, Folder 5, Box 1, SFP. Brodie held William Loeb in high regard. A thirty-seven-year-old native of Albany, Loeb had been chosen private secretary by Vice President Roosevelt, who had been impressed with Loeb's skill as a stenographer.
8. Unidentified newspaper clipping, Governor Brodie's Scrapbook, BFP.
9. Brodie to Secretary of the Interior, March 21, 1903, Appointment Papers, Arizona Territory, Department of the Interior, RG 48, NA, reel 1, microfilm copy in AHF.
10. *Phoenix Enterprise*, May 25, 26, 1903.
11. *Governor's Report*, 1902, pp. 42-43; Herner, *Arizona Rough Riders*, pp. 170-171.
12. *Arizona Silver Belt*, June 4, 1903.
13. Wagoner, *Arizona Territory*, pp. 387-389; Mellinger, *Race and Labor*, pp. 43-54.
14. Stoddard to the President, June 9, 1903; Stoddard to Brodie, June 9, 1903, both in Acting Governor's Letterbook, Isaac Taft Stoddard Papers, AHS.
15. Stoddard to Brodie, June 12, 1903, *Ibid.*
16. *Arizona Star*, June 28, 1903; Brodie to Roosevelt, July 25, 1903, Series I, reel 35, Roosevelt Papers; Smalley to his father, June 20, 1903, Folder 5, Box 4, SFP. H. W. Brand stated that a special guard protected Roosevelt on his swing through Montana in fear that miners, upset with his ordering federal troops to Morenci, possibly could retaliate. But the timing is wrong. Roosevelt had returned to Washington from his Western trip before the Morenci strike occurred. See Brand, *T. R.*, pp. 474-475.
17. Tinker to Roosevelt, June 9, 1903, Charge Files, Records of the Secretary of the Interior, RG 48, NA. Cited hereafter as Stoddard Charge Files. The Maricopa County Republican Press Association appears to have been a relatively obscure organization formed to promote Republican Arizona newspapers. Little is known of John Tinker. Born in Arizona in 1870 and a printer by profession, he moved to Winslow shortly after his quarrel with Stoddard.
18. *Arizona Republican*, June 25, 1903. A native of New York, Stoddard's father-in-law, Judge Celora Martin, served on the New York Court of Appeals from 1895 to 1904. He remained for many years an active force in New York Republican politics.
19. Brodie to William Loeb, July 11, 1903, Series I, reel 34, Roosevelt Papers.
20. Hitchcock to Roosevelt, October 29, 1903, Stoddard Charge Files. Brodie's September 25 report to Hitchcock has not surfaced, but the secretary summarized Brodie's findings in his own report. An Alabama native, Hitchcock first had been appointed Secretary of the Interior by McKinley.
21. Stoddard to Hitchcock, October 19, 1903, with enclosures, *Ibid.* A native of New York, the fifty-year-old Ainsworth arrived in Phoenix in 1888. Appointed attorney general ten years later by Governor Murphy, he resigned effective the same day Brodie became governor. His legal justification of Stoddard's disregard of the law requiring fee books is vague, lengthy, and packed with legal jargon. Arizona Attorney General Edmund Wells and the United States Attorney General disagreed with Ainsworth's interpretation.
22. *Ibid.*; Hitchcock to Roosevelt, October 29, 1903, *Ibid.*

23. Stoddard to Hitchcock, October 19, 1903, *Ibid.*
24. James C. Thompson and J. C. Adams Sworn Testimony, *Ibid.*
25. Brodie to McKinley, February 16, 1897, *Ibid.*
26. James Douglas, September 2, A. F. Kent, August 26, W. J. Martin, September 12, James Colquhoun, August 25, and Cleveland H. Dodge, November 5, 1903, to the President, all in *Ibid.* Born in New York in 1860, Dodge became vice president and director of the Phelps Dodge Company in 1884, replacing his older brother who died. No stranger to the Southwest, Dodge frequently visited the company holdings in Arizona and Sonora.
27. *Arizona Republican*, October 13, 1903.
28. Hitchcock to Roosevelt, October 29, 1903, Stoddard Charge Files.
29. Smalley to his father, December 13, 1903, Folder 5, Box 4, SFP.
30. Brodie to Roosevelt, October 27, 1903, Stoddard Charge Files.
31. E. F. Garrison to Roosevelt, June 23, 1903, *Ibid.* There is no additional information available on Garrison.
32. Smalley to his father, December 13, 1903, Folder 5, Box 4, SFP.
33. Wagoner, *Arizona Territory*, pp. 423-430.
34. Smith, *Magnificent Experiment*, pp. 39-48.
35. Typescript copies of Joseph Alexander's undated speeches in Folder 68, Box 5, Alexander Family Collection, AHS, Tempe.
36. Zarbin, *Roosevelt Dam*, pp. 63-64. Born in Missouri in 1854, Weedin came to Tombstone in 1880, moving the following year to Florence, where he edited a newspaper and later won election to the legislature as a Democrat. A harsh critic of the Arizona Rangers, in 1909 he introduced a bill calling for their disbandment.
37. *Arizona Republican*, November 19, 1903.

Chapter 20

1. Born in Lisbon, Ohio, in 1837, Mark Hanna built a formidable party machine in his home state, serving as chairman of the Republican National Committee from 1896 to 1904 and, during the same period, a senator from Ohio. An influential advisor to President McKinley, Hanna did not like Roosevelt, once remarking in 1900 when Roosevelt was selected to be McKinley's running mate: "Don't any of you realize there's only one life between that madman and the Presidency"? See Brand, T. R., p. 397.
2. *Arizona Republican*, February 2, 1904.
3. *Phoenix Enterprise*, January 26, 1904.
4. *Arizona Republican*, February 2, 3, 1904. Hanna died in Washington of typhoid on February 15, 1904.
5. *Phoenix Enterprise*, January 12, 1904.
6. *Tucson Citizen*, March 7, 1904. Bernard S. Rodey, an Irish-born politician, came to New Mexico in 1881 as secretary to the general manager of the Atlantic and Pacific Railway. Elected delegate to Congress in 1900, he championed separate statehood until 1904. His motivation in changing his position is not known. See Larson, *Quest for Statehood*, pp. 226-235.
7. *Arizona Republican*, March 9, 1904.
8. *Ibid.*

9. Smalley to his father, March 23, 1904, Folder 6, Box 1, SFP.
10. McCormick, *Realignment to Reform*, p. 172.
11. *Ibid.*, pp. 172-173; Roosevelt to Platt, March 2, 1904, Morison, *Letters*, vol. 4, p. 742. Benjamin Odell, a rising star in the New York Republican Party, was born in Newburgh, New York, in 1854. He enthusiastically supported Thomas Platt's successful 1898 effort to secure Roosevelt's nomination for New York governor. Two years later, Platt selected Odell to replace Governor Roosevelt, who had been tapped for the vice presidency.
12. A sixty-four-year-old native of Boone County, New York, Col. George Washington Dunn served in the Civil War and became chairman of the New York Republican Party in 1900. He should not be confused with Maj. George Morton Dunn of the Rough Riders.
13. Platt to Stoddard, March 3, 1904, Folder: I. T. Stoddard Miscellaneous Personal Papers, Stoddard Papers, UAL.
14. Brodie to Roosevelt, March 9, 1904, Series I, reel 42, Roosevelt Papers. There is no additional information available on Garrett H. Ryan.
15. Roosevelt to Brodie, March 9, 1904, Series I, reel 333, Roosevelt Papers.
16 *Phoenix Enterprise*, March 12, 1904; Brodie to Roosevelt, March 14, 1904, Series I, reel 42, Roosevelt Papers.
17. Brodie to Roosevelt, March 14, 1904, Series I, reel 42, Roosevelt Papers. Unsaid was Brodie's obvious position that it had taken him nearly two years to get rid of Stoddard, and he would not willingly accept one of the former secretary's friends as a replacement.
18. Brodie to Roosevelt, March 9, 1904, *Ibid.*
19. Smalley to his father, March 5, 1904, Folder 6, Box 1, SFP.
20. *Arizona Republican*, April 29, 1904; Brodie to Watson, January 13, 1913, BFP; Weir, "Menzies, Sir William." William Menzies's father, Allan Menzies, married Helen Cowan, a sister of Brodie's grandfather, Joseph Brodie.
21. *Arizona Republican*, April 29, 1904; O'Neal, *Arizona Rangers*, pp. 53-54. For his participation in the escape attempt, Loustaunau had ten additional years added to his sentence at Yuma, but two years later died of syphilis. A native of Pennsylvania, Griffith served as United States marshal for Arizona, 1897-1901. Shortly after becoming governor, Brodie appointed him superintendent of the Yuma prison. Little is known of George Wilder, a longtime resident of Yuma actively involved in mining and law enforcement.
22. *Phoenix Enterprise*, May 16, 1904.
23. *Arizona Gazette*, June 23, 1904.
24. Telegram, Brodie et al. to Roosevelt, June 23, 1904, vol. I, Series C, Roosevelt papers.
25. Smalley, *Adventures in Arizona*, p. 112; *The Cosmopolitan*, vol. xxxii, No. 6, October, 1904, copy in SFP. The Colorado River, or Yuma Project, approved by the Interior Department that summer, authorized construction of a weir-type diversion dam ten feet above the river's low water level at Laguna, sixteen miles north of Yuma. Government studies indicated that such a dam would provide sufficient water in Arizona and California to irrigate 107,000 acres.
26. *Arizona Gazette*, July 26, 28, 1904; *Arizona Republican*, July 28, 1904.

Joseph Gurney Cannon, born in North Carolina in 1836, later moved with his parents to Illinois. A Republican, he first was elected to Congress in 1872, serving as Speaker of the House from 1903-1911. Cannon often clashed with Roosevelt.

27. Report of the Governor, 1904.

28. *Phoenix Gazette*, October 13, 1904; *Arizona Journal-Miner*, September 21, 1904.

29. *Arizona Republican*, September 18, 1904.

30. Brophy, *Foundlings on the Frontier*, pp. 8-11, 27-71.

31. Kittel, "Administration of Governor Brodie," pp. 117-119.

32. Brodie to Loeb, November 9, 1904, Series I, reel 34, Roosevelt Papers.

33. Brophy, *Foundlings on the Frontier*, pp. 84-90.

34. *Arizona Republican*, November 10, December 17, 1904.

35. *Arizona Daily Star*, November 18, December 31, 1904; P. J. Smalley to George Smalley, August 18, 1904, Folder 6, Box 1, SFP.

36. *Governor's Message to the Twenty-Third Legislature*.

37. *Arizona Republican*, January 21, 1905.

38. *Ibid.*; Redfield Proctor to Brodie, January 17, 1905, Brodie's ACP File. Maj. Edward S. Fowler, a New York native, served in the Spanish-American War as a Volunteer paymaster. As did many Volunteer officers, Fowler subsequently attempted to secure an appointment in the Regular Army. Born in Vermont in 1831, Redfield Proctor served in the Union Army during the Civil War and as Secretary of War, 1889-1891. Later elected to the U.S. Senate, he served on the Committee of Military Affairs.

39. *Arizona Republican*, February 11, 1905; Kent to Roosevelt, January 26, 1905, Series I, reel 52, Roosevelt Papers.

40. Brodie to Roosevelt, January 26, 1905, Series I, reel 52, Roosevelt Papers.

41. *Ibid.* Brodie never shared Roosevelt's confidence in Edward Kent, concerned that the judge remained too friendly with the Murphy brothers.

42 *Ibid.*

43. Roosevelt to Brodie, February 3, 1905, Series II, reel 337, Roosevelt Papers.

44. Wagoner, *Arizona Territory*, pp. 420-421.

45. *Arizona Republican*, February 15, 1905.

46. *Ibid.*, February 18, 1905. Brodie later sold his interest in the Crown Point mine to Henry Van Beuren, but records of that transaction have not been located.

47. Unidentified newspaper clippings, Governor Brodie's Scrapbook, BFP.

Chapter 21

1. Brodie to Roosevelt, December 26, 1904, Series I, reel 51, Roosevelt Papers.

2. Roosevelt to Brodie, December 31, 1904, Series II, reel 36, *Ibid.* The Arizona delegation included Brodie, James McClintock, Joseph L. B. Alexander, Charles E. Mills, and Ben Daniels.

3. Brodie to Roosevelt, December 26, 1904, Series I, reel 51, *Ibid.*

4. Roosevelt, *Rough Riders*, p. 13; Miller, *Isabella Greenway*, pp. 13-14; Fer-

guson to his mother, July 15, 1898, folder 2976, Box 211, John and Isabella Greenway Papers, AHS.

5. Linn, *The Philippine War*, pp. 198-225. Born March 22, 1869, in Cavite, Emilio Aguinaldo became the primary leader of the revolt first against Spain and later against the United States. His capture in 1901 ended organized resistance, but sporadic fighting continued for several years.

6. *Ibid.*

7. Brodie to Smalley, June 16, 1905, Folder 9, Box 1, SFP.

8. Duffy, *Taft*, pp. 107-144; *Annual Report of the War Department, 1905*, vol. III, p. 261.

9. Duffy, *Taft*, pp. 148-149.

10. Brodie to Smalley, October 11, 1905, Folder 6, Box 1, SFP.

11. *Ibid.*; Brodie's Individual Service Report, June 30, 1907, Brodie's ACP File.

12. Brodie to Loeb, December 3, 1907, Series I, reel 61, Roosevelt Papers.

13. *Ibid.*

14. Brodie to Sandy, January 13, June 7, 1906, BFP.

15. Wood to the War Department, February 2, 1907, Brodie's ACP File

16. Brodie's Individual Service Report, June 28, 1908, *Ibid.*

17. *War Department Annual Report, 1908*, vol. III, pp. 113, 115.

18. Reports of Physical Examination and Riding or Walking Test, 1907-1912, Brodie's ACP File; Brodie Interview.

19. Known in some circles as the "Boy Orator of the Platte," William Jennings Bryan of Nebraska secured the Democratic nomination for president in 1896, 1900, and 1908. He lost the election each time. Bryan strongly advocated the free and unlimited coinage of silver, a concept popular in Arizona which Brodie had once embraced.

20. Brodie to Roosevelt, February 8, 1909, Series I, reel 8, Roosevelt Papers.

21. *St. Paul Pioneer Press*, September 5, 6, 7, 1910.

22. Unidentified newspaper clipping, Governor Brodie's Scrapbook, BFP.

23. Harbaugh, *Power and Responsibility*, pp. 383-385.

24. Brodie to Roosevelt, April 12, 1912, Series I, reel 136, and November 9, 1912, reel 157, Roosevelt Papers. Born in Virginia in 1856, Thomas Woodrow Wilson served as president of Princeton University from 1902 until 1910, when he became governor of New Jersey.

25. A.B. Campbell to Yndia Moore, August 18, 1962, Folder 2, Series I, Campbell Family Papers, AHS.

26. Steve L. Nure to the author.

27. Brodie Interview

28 Brodie to the AG of the Army, May 7, 13, Brodie's ACP File; Brodie to Smalley, May 12, 1914, Folder 9, Box 1, SFP.

29. Brodie Interview.

30. Brodie to Smalley, May 12, 1914, March 25, 1915, Folder 9, Box 1, SFP.

31. Brodie to Smalley, March 25, 1915, *Ibid.* Born in Missouri, John Joseph Pershing graduated from the Military Academy in 1886, subsequently serving with the Sixth Cavalry in New Mexico and Arizona. Later he fought in Cuba and still later in the Philippines. Brodie knew Pershing casually.

32. Roosevelt to Brodie, February 9, 1917, Series I, reel 221, Roosevelt Papers; Brand, T. R., pp. 776-783.
33. Brodie to the AG of the Army, March 20, 1917, Brodie's ACP File.
34. Governor Hunt to Mary Brodie, May 11, 1918, BFP. Born in Missouri in 1859, George Wiley Paul Hunt served seven terms in the Arizona legislature and the same number as elected governor after Arizona became a state in 1912.
35. Tuttle Interview.

Afterword

1. In addition to the funds provided by Henry Van Beuren, Brodie invested some of his personal money developing Crown Point, as well as lesser amounts provided by his wife.
2. Concluding that Brodie did not provide detailed reports based on documents contained in the Van Beuren Papers may be misleading. The collection contains numerous letters between Brodie and Van Beuren discussing Crown Point, but there are no formal mine or mill reports. It is possible, of course, that formal accountings at one time existed, but subsequently have been purged from the collection. But, in that event, why are not such reports referenced in the existing correspondence? Exactly how much underground work Brodie accomplished at Crown Point and the value of gold actually recovered undoubtedly will never be known.
3. Lamar, "Carpetbaggers Full of Dreams," pp. 192-195, 198-105.

Appendix: Biographical Reference

Alexander, Joseph L. B. An attorney by profession, the former Rough Rider Captain of C Troop received an appointment as United States Attorney for Arizona in 1905 by President Roosevelt. Originally a Democrat, Alexander became the Arizona Progressive Party's unsuccessful nominee for attorney general in 1914. He died in San Francisco in 1931.

Bomus, Peter S. After serving three years with Brodie at Camp Apache, Bomus relocated with his troop to Washington Territory, where he participated in the Bannock campaign in 1878. Following his retirement in 1907, Lieutenant Colonel Bomus helped organize the Boy Scouts of America. He died in 1916.

Brodie, Alexander O. ("Sandy"). Rejecting his father's advice that he follow a military career, Sandy instead became a successful commercial artist. In 1949, upon losing his vision to the extent that he no longer could practice his profession, he became curator of art at the Museum of Art in Flagstaff, Arizona. He died six years later, leaving a widow, Mary Donovan Brodie, a daughter, Mary Helen Brodie, and two sons, Alexander Oswald and David Bonsall Brodie.

Brodie, Mary Louise Hanlon. Although Mary complained of poor health for many years, she lived to be ninety-three, dying in 1957 at her home on Long Island. In her later years, obviously relishing her role as the family matriarch, she thoroughly enjoyed entertaining her grandchildren with stories of her experiences on the Arizona frontier. Her habit of keeping her husband's old .45 caliber service revolver loaded and suspended in a holster from her bedpost lent credibility to her recollections. Mary also reversed her earlier rejection of alcohol, habitually insisting on a dram of scotch each evening before retiring.

Brow, Robert. Extremely popular in Yavapai County, Brodie's friend and one-time partner in the Crown Point mine suffered a serious economic setback when the Walnut Grove flood washed away his saloon located near the lower dam. Brow's safe, reputedly containing between five and ten thousand dollars, never has been recovered. Following the flood, Brow moved to Prescott and operated the Palace Saloon on Whiskey Row until his death in 1909.

Delchay. Contrary to the promise made to Captain Randall upon his surrender in the Tonto Basin, Delchay soon bolted the reservation, but late in 1873 he died at the hands of Apaches loyal to Colonel Crook. Exact circumstances surrounding his death are not known.

Green, John. Brodie's commander at Camp Apache enjoyed a long military career. First enlisting in 1846, he retired in 1889 as a lieutenant colonel. Green received the Medal of Honor for gallantry in the Modoc War and also participated in the Nez Perce uprising.

Huston, Robert Bell. Commander of D Troop of the Rough Riders, Huston later received a captain's commission in the Forty Seventh Volunteer Infantry. Assigned with his regiment to the Philippines, he died there in 1900 of disease.

McClintock, James Harvey. Disappointed in not having been appointed secretary of Arizona Territory, when Roosevelt became president, the former commander of B Troop instead served for a time as Phoenix postmaster. He also commanded the Arizona National Guard during the labor disputes at Clifton and Morenci. In Arizona today, McClintock is best remembered for authoring a three-volume history of Arizona. He died in 1934.

Merwin, George. Following his disassociation with the Crown Point mine, Merwin continued to involve himself in farming and mining in Yavapai County. At one point he joined the gold rush to Alaska, but thoroughly disillusioned with the Klondike goldfields, he soon returned to Prescott, where he died in 1920.

Murphy, Nathan Oakes. Following his resignation as governor in 1902, Murphy's influence faded rapidly, although he continued to champion separate statehood whenever and wherever the opportunity arose to do so. Traveling extensively with a new wife, Murphy died unexpectedly while vacationing in Coronado, California, in 1908.

Randall, George Morton. Transferred from Camp Apache in 1874, Randall at one time served as General Crook's aide in the Division of the Missouri. Later, he served in Cuba and in the Philippines. Promoted to major general in 1905, he retired the following year and died in Denver in 1918.

Smalley, George Herbert. Before leaving for Washington to rejoin the army in 1905, Governor Brodie arranged to have President Roosevelt appoint Smalley clerk of a district court in Globe. After several years in that position, Smalley reentered the newspaper business in California. He soon returned to Arizona, holding a number of minor government positions and doing freelance writing until his death in 1961 in Tucson.

Stoddard, Isaac Taft. Following his resignation as secretary of Arizona Territory, Stoddard stepped away from public life, but he continued to prosper in the private sector. His extensive mine holdings near the town of Stoddard in Yavapai County flourished, and a corporation he founded to provide assistance to companies hoping to incorporate in Arizona proved extremely successful. Stoddard died of apoplexy at his Phoenix home in 1914.

Wood, Leonard. In part because of his friendship with President Roosevelt, Wood rose rapidly in the military hierarchy. After serving as military governor of Santiago and later of Cuba, he won promotion to brigadier general in 1901. Upon returning from assignment to the Philippines he became Chief of Staff. In 1920, seven years before his death, he became an unsuccessful candidate for the Republican nomination for president.

Bibliography

Archival Material

Arizona Historical Foundation. Arizona State University Library, Tempe.
  Alexander O. Brodie papers.

Arizona Historical Society, Tempe.
  Alexander Family Collection, 1882-1953.

Arizona Historical Society, Tucson.
  Alexander O. Brodie Papers.
  Campbell Family Papers.
  George Smalley Family Papers.
  Isaac Taft Stoddard Papers.
  John and Isabella Greenway Papers.

Arizona State Department of Library and Archives.
  Letterbooks of Governor Brodie (two).
  Secretary of the Territory Records, RG. 6.

Library of Congress.
  Leonard Wood Papers.
  Theodore Roosevelt Papers. Microfilm copies in University of Arizona Library, Tucson.

National Archives.
  Record Group 48: Department of the Interior.
    Appointment Papers, Arizona Territory, 1857-1907, Governors A-E, 1877-1907. Microfilm copies in Arizona Historical Foundation, Arizona State University Library, Tempe.
    Charge Files, Isaac Taft Stoddard File.

  Record Group 75: Office of the Bureau of Indian Affairs.
    Letters Received by the Office of Indian Affairs, Arizona Superintendency, 1863-1880. Microfilm copies in University of Arizona Library, Tucson

  Record Group 92: Office of the Quartermaster General.
    Consolidated Correspondence File, Fort Spokane, Washington Territory, 1794-1915, Fort Collville [sic], Washington Territory.

  Record Group 94: Records of the Adjutant General's Office.
    Commission and Personnel Branch Document File: Alexander O. Brodie.
    Post Records (various).
    Post Returns (various camps and forts).
    Regimental Returns from Regular Regiments, 1836-1916 (various).
    Unit Muster Rolls (various).

Record Group 391: Records of U.S. Regular Army Mobile Units, 1st Cavalry (and 1st Dragoons).
  Letters Sent 1832-1916, vol. 5.

Record Group 393: Records of the United States Army Continental Commands.
Letters, Telegrams and Field Orders Sent Relating to Chief Joseph and the Nez Perce Campaign, April-July 1877.
Post Letters, Fort Apache, Arizona, vol. 37.

Oklahoma Historical Society, Oklahoma City.
Robert Bell Huston Papers.

Personal Collections.
Alexander O. Brodie Papers. Author's Files.
Alexander O. Brodie Papers. In the possession of Pat DeLanie, Phoenix.
Arthur L. Tuttle Papers. Author's Files.
Henry S. Van Beuren Papers. In the possession of Joseph Wittmann, Somers, New York. Copies in Author's Files.

Phoenix Public Library.
James H. McClintock Papers.

Sharlot Hall Museum, Prescott, Arizona.
Henry S. Van Beuren Diary, 1890.
Miscellaneous Mines Records.

University of Arizona Library, Special Collections, Tucson, Arizona.
Eugene S. Ives Papers.
Isaac Taft Stoddard Papers.
William Field Staunton Papers.

Yavapai County Recorder's Office, Prescott.
Deed Books, Numbers 27 and 28.
General Index to Deeds, Book 2, 1890-97.

Articles

Braeman, John. "Albert J. Beveridge and Statehood for the Southwest, 1902-1912." *Arizona and the West*, 10 (Winter 1968): 313-342.

Brodie, Alexander O. "Reclaiming the Arid Southwest." *Cosmopolitan*, 37 (October 1904): 715-722.

Campbell, Allen. "Republican Politics in Democratic Arizona: Tom Campbell's Career." *Arizona and the West*, 23 (Summer 1981): 313-342.

Davisson, Lori. "Fort Apache, Arizona Territory: 1870-1922." *The Smoke Signal*, Tucson Corral of the Westerners, 33 (Spring 1977): 62-67.

———. "New Light on the Cibicue Fight: Untangling Apache Identities." *The Journal of Arizona History*, 20 (Winter 1979): 427-430.

Dill, David B., Jr. "Terror on the Hassayampa: The Walnut Grove Dam Disaster of 1890." *The Journal of Arizona History*, 28 (Autumn 1987): 283-306.

Gilbert, W. J. "Chasing the Nimble and Elusive Apaches." *Winners of the West*, (October 30, 1926).

Jones, William. "The Van Beuren Family of New York and New Jersey." *The New York Genealogical and Biographic Record*, 63 (1932): 23-51.

Lamar, Howard R. "Carpetbaggers Full of Dreams: A Functional View of the Arizona Pioneer Politician." *Arizona and the West*, 7 (Autumn 1965): 192-195, 198-205.

Manley, Atwood. "The Little-Known Alexander Macomb." *The Quarterly*, St. Lawrence County Historical Association, 4 (January 1959): 1-8.

Thrapp, Dan L. "Where Was the Battle of Turret Mountain Fought?" In Ray Brandes, editor, *Troopers West: Military and Indian Affairs on the American Frontier*, 105-119. San Diego: Frontier Heritage Press, 1970.

Todd, Joe L. "'Softened as into a Dream': The Letters of Robert B. Huston, Oklahoma Rough Rider." *The Chronicles of Oklahoma*, Oklahoma Historical Society, 76 (Spring 1998): 4-19.

Upham, Frank K. "Incidents of Regular Army Life in Time of Peace." *Overland Monthly*, 5 (April 1885): 423-429.

Walsh, Michael E. "Corydon E. Cooley—Pioneer in Two Worlds." *The Journal of Arizona History*, 20 (Autumn 1979): 285-296.

Weir, Ronald B. "Menzies, Sir William John (1834-1905), Lawyer and Financier." *Oxford Dictionary of National Biography*. Oxford: Oxford University Press, 2004-2006.

Books

Altshuler, Constance Wynn. *Cavalry Yellow and Infantry Blue: Army Officers in Arizona between 1851 and 1886*. Tucson: Arizona Historical Society, 1991.

———. *Chains of Command: Arizona and the Army 1856-1875*. Tucson: Arizona Historical Society, 1987.

Ambrose, Stephen B. *Duty, Honor, Country: A History of West Point*. Baltimore: Johns Hopkins Press, 1966.

Azoy, A. C. M. *Charge: The Story of the Battle of San Juan Hill*. New York: David McKay Company, Inc., 1961.

Ball, Larry D. *The United States Marshals of New Mexico and Arizona Territories, 1846-1912*. Albuquerque: University of New Mexico Press, 1978.

Bennett, Robert A. *Walla Walla: A Portrait of a Western Town, 1804-1899*. Walla Walla, WA: Pioneer Press, 1980.

Bourke, John Gregory. *On the Border With Crook*. Reprint. Chicago: Rio Grande Press, 1962.

Brandes, Ray. *Frontier Military Posts of Arizona*. Globe, AZ: Dale Stewart King, 1960.

Brands, H. W. *T. R.: The Last Romantic*. New York: Basic Books, Perseus Book Company, 1997.

Brophy, A. Blake. *Foundlings on the Frontier: Racial and Religious Conflict in Arizona Territory, 1904-1905*. Tucson: University of Arizona Press, 1972.

Cosmas, Graham A. *An Army for Empire: The United States Army in the Spanish-American War*. Reprint. Shippensburg, PA: White Mane Publishing Company, 1994.

Cullum, George W. *Biographical Register of the Officers and Graduates of the U.S. Military Academy at West Point*. 9 vols. Cambridge, MA: Riverside Press, 1901.

Duffy, Herbert S. *William Howard Taft*. New York: Minton, Batch and Company, 1930.

Durant, Samuel W. and Henry B. Pierce. *History of St. Lawrence County, New York, with Illustrations and Biographical Sketches of Some of Its Prominent Men and Pioneers*. Philadelphia: L. H. Everts and Company, 1878.

Feess, Marty L. *Theodore Roosevelt's Arizona Boys: Cowboys and Politics in the Old West*. Lincoln: Writers Club Press, 2001.

Frazer, Robert W. *Forts of the West*. Norman: University of Oklahoma Press, 1965.

Freeman, LaVerne, et al., eds. *Edwards on the Oswegotchie 1812-1976*. N.P.

Goff, John S. *Arizona Territorial Officials*. 6 vols. Cave Creek, AZ: Black Mountain Press, 1975-1996.

Hagedorn, Herman. *Leonard Wood: A Biography*. 2 vols. New York: Harper and Brothers, 1931.

Harbaugh, William Henry. *Power and Responsibility: The Life and Times of Theodore Roosevelt*. New York: Farrar, Straus and Cudahy, 1961.

Hein, Otto L. *Memories of Long Ago: By an Old Army Officer, Lieut-Colonel O. L. Hein, U.S. Army, Retired*. New York: Putnam's Sons, 1925.

Herner, Charles. *The Arizona Rough Riders*. Tucson: University of Arizona Press, 1970.

———, ed. *It Was the Grandest Sight I Ever Saw: Experiences of a Rough Rider as Recorded in the Letters of Lieutenant John Campbell Greenway*. Tucson: Arizona Historical Society, 2001.

Josephy, Alvin M., Jr. *The Nez Perce Indians and the Opening of the Northwest*. Reprint. New York: Houghton Mifflin Company, 1965.

Larson, Robert W. *New Mexico's Quest for Statehood*. Albuquerque: University of New Mexico Press, 1968.

Linn, Brian McAllister. *The Philippine War 1899-1902*. Lawrence, KS: University of Kansas Press, 2000.

Maclean, Fitzoy. *Highlanders: A History of the Highland Clans*. London: David Campbell, Ltd., 1995.

Marion, J. H. *Notes of Travel Through the Territory of Arizona: Being an Account of the Trip Made by General George Stoneman and Others in the Autumn of 1870*. Edited by Donald M. Powell. Tucson: University of Arizona Press, 1965.

Marshall, Edward. *The Story of the Rough Riders, 1st U.S. Volunteer Cavalry: The Regiment in Camp and on the Battlefield*. New York: G. W. Dillingham Company, 1899.

Martin, Douglas D. *The Lamp in the Desert: The Story of the University of Arizona*. Tucson: University of Arizona Press, 1960.

McClintock, James H. *Arizona: Prehistoric, Aboriginal, Pioneer and Modern.* 3 vols. Chicago: S. J. Clark Company, 1916.

McCormick, Richard L. *From Realignment to Reform: Political Change in New York State, 1893-1910.* Ithaca, NY: Cornell University Press, 1981.

Mellinger, Philip J. *Race and Labor in Western Copper: The Fight for Equality, 1896-1918.* Tucson: University of Arizona Press, 1995.

Miller, Kristie. *Isabella Greenway: An Enterprising Woman.* Tucson: University of Arizona Press, 2004.

Morison, Elting E., John M. Blum, and John J. Buckley, eds. *The Letters of Theodore Roosevelt.* 8 vols. Cambridge, MA: Harvard University Press, 1951.

Murphy, Richard C., and Lawrence J. Mannion. *The History of the Friendly Sons of Saint Patrick in the City of New York.* New York: J. C. Dillon Company, 1962.

Musicant, Ivan. *Empire by Default: The Spanish-American War and the Dawn of the American Century.* New York: Henry Holt and Company, 1998.

Ogle, Ralph Hedrick. *Federal Control of the Western Apaches, 1848-1886.* Reprint. Albuquerque: University of New Mexico Press, 1970.

O'Neal, Bill. *The Arizona Rangers.* Austin, TX: Eakins Press, 1987.

Price, George F. *Across the Continent with the Fifth Cavalry.* New York: D. Van Nostrand, Publisher, 1883.

Radbourne, Allen. *Mickey Free: Apache Captive, Interpreter, and Indian Scout.* Tucson: Arizona Historical Society, 2005.

Robinson, Charles M., III, ed. *The Diaries of John Gregory Bourke.* 2 vols. Denton, TX: University of North Texas Press, 2003.

Roosevelt, Theodore. *The Rough Riders.* Reprint. New York: Da Capro Press, 1970.

Rynning, Thomas H. *Gun Notches: A Saga of Frontier Lawman Captain Thomas H. Rynning as Told to Al Cohn and Joe Chisholm.* Reprint. San Diego: Frontier Heritage Press, 1971.

Schellie, Don. *Vast Domain of Blood: The Story of the Camp Grant Massacre.* Los Angeles: Westerlore Press, 1968.

Schmitt, Martin F., ed. *General George Crook: His Autobiography.* Reprint. Norman: University of Oklahoma Press, 1968.

Smalley, George H. *My Adventures in Arizona: Leaves from a Reporter's Notebook.* Edited by Yndia Smalley Moore. Tucson: Arizona Pioneers' Historical Society, 1966.

Smith, Karen L. *The Magnificent Experiment: Building the Salt River Reclamation Project, 1890-1917.* Tucson: University of Arizona Press, 1986.

Summerhayes, Martha. *Vanished Arizona: Recollections of the Army Life of a New England Woman.* Reprint. Lincoln: University of Nebraska Press, 1979.

Sweeney, Edwin R. *Cochise: Chiricahua Apache Chief.* Norman: University of Oklahoma Press, 1991.

Thrapp, Dan L. *The Conquest of Apachería.* Norman: University of Oklahoma Press, 1967.

Wagoner, Jay J. *Arizona Territory, 1863-1912: A Political History.* Tucson: University of Arizona Press, 1970.

Walker, Dale L. *The Boys of '98: Theodore Roosevelt and the Rough Riders*. New York: Tom Doherty Associates, 1998.

Watson, Charles Brodie Boog. *Alexander Cowan of Morey House and Valleyfield: His Kinfolk and Connections*. Perth, Scotland: privately printed, 1915.

Utley, Robert M. *Frontier Regulars: The United States Army and the Indian Wars, 1866-1891*. Reprint. Lincoln: University of Nebraska Press, 1984.

Zarbin, Earl A. *Roosevelt Dam: A History to 1911*. Phoenix: The Salt River Project, 1994.

Federal and Territorial Government Publications

Army and Navy Journal. November 26, 1870, August 21, 1871, October 7, 1871.

Acts, Resolution, and Memorials of the Twenty-Second Legislature Assembly of the Territory of Arizona. Session Began on the Nineteenth Day of January A.D. 1903. Phoenix: Press of the Arizona Republican, 1903.

Chronological List of Actions, etc. With Indians From January 1, 1866 to January, 1891. Washington: Adjutant General's Office, 1891.

Governor's Message to the Twenty-third Legislature Assembly of the Territory of Arizona. Tucson: The Citizen Printing and Publishing Company, 1904.

Heitman, Francis B. *Historical Register and Dictionary of the United States Army, From its Organization, September 29, 1789 to March 2, 1903*. 2 vols. Washington: Government Printing Office, 1903.

Journals of the Twenty-second Legislative Assembly of the Territory of Arizona, Session Began on the Nineteenth Day of January, A.D., 1903. Phoenix: Press of the Arizona Republican, 1903.

Lindgren, Waldemar. *Ore Deposits of the Jerome and Bradshaw Mountains Quadrangle, Arizona*. U.S. Geological Survey Bulletin 782. Washington: Government Printing Office, 1926.

McDermott, John Dishon. *Forlorn Hope: A Study of the Battle of White Bird Canyon, Idaho, and the Beginning of the Nez Perce Indian War*. Washington: Office of Archaeology and Historic Preservation, National Park Service, 1968.

Messages of Governor Alexander O. Brodie to the Twenty-second and Twenty-third Legislative Assemblies of Arizona. Tucson: The Citizen Printing and Publishing Company, 1903, 1905.

Regulations for the U.S. Military Academy at West Point, New York. New York: Baldwin and Jones, Printers, 1866.

Report of the Governor of Arizona to the Secretary of the Interior for the Year Ended, June 30, 1902. Washington: Government Printing Office, 1902.

Report of the Governor of Arizona to the Secretary of the Interior for the Year Ended June 30, 1903. Washington: Government Printing Office, 1903.

Report of the Governor of Arizona to the Secretary of the Interior for the Year Ended June 30, 1904. Washington: Government Printing Office, 1904.

Report of the Secretary of the Interior for the Fiscal Year Ended June 30, 1902. Washington: Government Printing Office, 1902.

United States Military Academy, Register of Officers and Cadets, 1870. Washington: Government Printing Office, 1870.
War Department Annual Reports (1904-1912). Washington: Government Printing Office, 1904-1912.

Periodicals and Newspapers

Arizona Journal-Miner
Arizona Weekly Journal-Miner
Globe Arizona Silver Belt.
Las Vegas (New Mexico) Daily Optic.
New York Engineering and Mining Journal.
New York Engineering News and American Railway Journal.
New York Times.
Ogdensburg (New York) St. Lawrence Plaindealer.
Phoenix Arizona Daily Gazette.
Phoenix Enterprise.
Phoenix Arizona Republican.
Prescott Arizona Miner.
Prescott Courier (Weekly and Daily).
Prescott Journal- Miner.
San Antonio Daily Express.
San Diego Union.
Solomonville Arizona Bulletin.
Tampa Morning Tribune.
Tucson Arizona Citizen.
Tucson Arizona Star (Weekly and Daily).
Walla Walla (Washington) Statesman.
Walla Walla (Washington) Union.

Personal Communications

Letters to Author

Atchison, Pat, Yavapai County Cemetery Association. 27 July 1998.
B. F. Goodrich Company. 15 September 1998.
Blackdon, Dr. Stephanie, Brodie Castle, Scotland. 2 April 1997.
Clayton, Lolita R., Walla Walla Genealogical Association. 26 May 1999.
Dill, David B., Jr. 2 August 1997.
Dodd, Lawrence L., Whitman College Archives. 25 March 1998.
Freeman, LaVerne H. 11 October 1997.
Hokanson, Jeff, Greenwood County Historical Society. 18 April 1997.
Nure, Steve L., Golden Gate National Cemetery. 14 October 1999.
Rosenkrans, Korin L., Joint Free Library of Morristown. 19 July 2000.
Rubinetti, Jocelyne, Drew University. 22 August 2000.
Wassmann, Harey, Benicia Historical Museum. 3 June 1999.

Interviews with Author

Brodie, David Bonsall. Yuma, AZ, 7 December 1999.
Cleere, Jan. Tucson, AZ, 22 August 2005.
DeLanie, Mary. Flagstaff, AZ, 26 June 1963.
Liggett, James, Professor Emeritus, Cornell University. Tucson, AZ, 1 September 2007.
Palmer, Dr. Sam. Phoenix, AZ, 27 April 1996.
Reid, Chris, Florence Historical Society. Tucson, AZ, 21 December 2004.
Tackenburg, William D., Arizona Historical Society. Tucson, AZ, 2004.
Tuttle, Arthur L. Tucson, AZ, 20-23 February 1963.

Unpublished Manuscripts and Thesis

Kittell, Larry Waite. "The Administration of Alexander O. Brodie: Arizona Territorial Governor, 1902-1905." Master's thesis, University of Arizona, 1973.
"A Narrative of the Hassayampa River Project in Arizona, 1882-1936." Van Beuren Family Papers, Somers, NY.
Staunton, William Field, II. "The First Fifty Years, 1860-1910." William Staunton Papers. Special Collections, University of Arizona Library, Tucson.

Index

Author of *The Arizona Rough Riders*, Charles H. Herner is a native of Arizona who received two degrees in US History from the University of Arizona. He taught history at Canyon del Oro High School in Tucson from 1963 until his retirement in 1990, and reached the rank of colonel before his retirement from the United States Army Reserve. He now lives in Tucson with his wife Joan.